Charles Merivale

Catilina

For use in schools by Charles Merivale

Charles Merivale

Catilina
For use in schools by Charles Merivale

ISBN/EAN: 9783337282165

Printed in Europe, USA, Canada, Australia, Japan

Cover: Foto ©Paul-Georg Meister /pixelio.de

More available books at **www.hansebooks.com**

CAII SALLUSTII CRISPI

CATILINA.

FOR USE IN SCHOOLS.

BY

CHARLES MERIVALE, D.D.
DEAN OF ELY.

London:
MACMILLAN AND CO.
AND NEW YORK.
1888

FASTI CONSULARES.

A.U. 631—691.
B.C. 123—63.

A.U. 631.	Q. Cæcilius Metellus, *postea* Balearicus.
B.C. 123.	T. Quinctius Flamininus.
A.U. 632.	Cn. Domitius Ahenobarbus.
B.C. 122.	C. Fannius Strabo.
A.U. 633.	L. Opimius.
B.C. 121.	Q. Fabius Maximus.
A.U. 634.	P. Manilius.
B.C. 120.	C. Papirius Carbo.
A.U. 635.	L. Cæcilius Metellus, *postea* Dalmaticus.
B.C. 119.	L. Aurelius Cotta.
A.U. 636.	M. Porcius Cato.
B.C. 118.	Q. Marcius Rex.
A.U. 637.	L. Cæcilius Metellus Diadematus.
B.C. 117.	Q. Mucius Scævola.
A.U. 638.	C. Licinius Geta.
B.C. 116.	Q. Fabius Maximus Eburnus.
A.U. 639.	M. Æmilius Scaurus.
B.C. 115.	M. Cæcilius Metellus.
A.U. 640.	M. Acilius Balbus.
B.C. 114.	C. Porcius Cato.
A.U. 641.	C. Cæcilius Metellus Caprarius.
B.C. 113.	Cn. Papirius Carbo.
A.U. 642.	M. Livius Drusus.
B.C. 112.	L. Calpurnius Piso Cæsoninus.

b

FASTI CONSULARES.

A.U. 643.	P. Cornelius Scipio Nasica.
B.C. 111.	L. Calpurnius Bestia.
A.U. 644.	M. Minucius Rufus.
B.C. 110.	Sp. Postumius Albinus.
A.U. 645.	Q. Cæcilius Metellus, *postea* Numidicus.
B.C. 109.	M. Junius Silanus.
A.U. 646.	Ser. Sulpicius Galba.
B.C. 108.	L. Hortensius (M. Aurelius Scaurus *suffect.*)
A.U. 647.	L. Cassius Longinus.
B.C. 107.	C. Marius.
A.U. 648.	C. Atilius Serranus.
B.C. 106.	Q. Servilius Cæpio.
A.U. 649.	P. Rutilius Rufus.
B.C. 105.	Cn. Mallius Maximus.
A.U. 650.	C. Marius II.
B.C. 104.	C. Flavius Fimbria.
A.U. 651.	C. Marius III.
B.C. 103.	L. Aurelius Orestes.
A.U. 652.	C. Marius IV.
B.C. 102.	Q. Lutatius Catulus.
A.U. 653.	C. Marius V.
B.C. 101.	M'. Aquilius.
A.U. 654.	C. Marius VI.
B.C. 100.	L. Valerius Flaccus.
A.U. 655.	M. Antonius.
B.C. 99.	A. Postumius Albinus.
A.U. 656.	Q. Cæcilius Metellus Nepos.
B.C. 98.	T. Didius.
A.U. 657.	Cn. Cornelius Lentulus.
B.C. 97.	P. Licinius Crassus.
A.U. 658.	Cn. Domitius Ahenobarbus.
B.C. 96.	C. Cassius Longinus.
A.U. 659.	L. Licinius Crassus.
B.C. 95.	Q. Mucius Scævola.

FASTI CONSULARES.

A.U. 660.	C. Cælius Caldus.
B.C. 94.	L. Domitius Ahenobarbus.
A.U. 661.	C. Valerius Flaccus.
B.C. 93.	M. Herennius.
A.U. 662.	C. Claudius Pulcher.
B.C. 92.	M. Perperna.
A.U. 663.	L. Marcius Philippus.
B.C. 91.	Sex. Julius Cæsar.
A.U. 664.	L. Julius Cæsar.
B.C. 90.	P. Rutilius Lupus.
A.U. 665.	Cn. Pompeius Strabo.
B.C. 89.	L. Porcius Cato.
A.U. 666.	L. Cornelius Sulla.
B.C. 88.	Q. Pompeius Rufus.
A.U. 667.	Cn. Octavius.
B.C. 87.	L. Cornelius Cinna.
A.U. 668.	L. Cornelius Cinna II.
B.C. 86.	C. Marius VII. (L. Valerius Flaccus I i. *suffect.*)
A.U. 669	L. Cornelius Cinna III.
B.C. 85.	Cn. Papirius Carbo.
A.U. 670.	Cn. Papirius Carbo II.
B.C. 84.	L. Cornelius Cinna IV.
A.U. 671.	L. Cornelius Scipio Asiaticus.
B.C. 83.	C. Norbanus Balbus.
A.U. 672.	C. Marius, C. f.
B.C. 82.	Cn. Papirius Carbo III.
	L. Cornelius Sulla, Dictator.
A.U. 673.	M. Tullius Decula.
B.C. 81.	Cn. Cornelius Dolabella.
	L. Cornelius Sulla, Dictator.
A.U. 674.	L. Cornelius Sulla II.
B.C. 80.	Q. Cæcilius Metellus Pius.
A.U. 675.	P. Servilius Vatia.
B.C. 79.	Ap. Claudius Pulcher.

FASTI CONSULARES.

A.U. 676.	M. Æmilius Lepidus.	
B.C. 78.	Q. Lutatius Catulus.	
A.U. 677.	D. Junius Brutus.	
B.C. 77.	Mam. Æmilius Lepidus.	
A.U. 678.	Cn. Octavius.	
B.C. 76.	C. Scribonius Curio.	
A.U. 679.	L. Octavius.	
B.C. 75.	C. Aurelius Cotta.	
A.U. 680.	L. Licinius Lucullus.	
B.C. 74.	M. Aurelius Cotta.	
A.U. 681.	M. Terentius Varro.	
B.C. 73.	C. Cassius Varus.	
A.U. 682.	L. Gellius Publicola.	
B.C. 72.	Cn. Cornelius Lentulus Clodianus.	
A.U. 683.	P. Cornelius Lentulus Sura.	
B.C. 71.	Cn. Aufidius Orestes.	
A.U. 684.	Cn. Pompeius Magnus.	
B.C. 70.	M. Licinius Crassus Dives.	
A.U. 685.	Q. Hortensius.	
B.C. 69.	Q. Cæcilius Metellus, *postea* Creticus.	
A.U. 686.	L. Cæcilius Metellus.	
B.C. 68.	Q. Marcius Rex.	
A.U. 687.	C. Calpurnius Piso.	
B.C. 67.	M'. Acilius Glabrio.	
A.U. 688.	M'. Æmilius Lepidus.	
B.C. 66.	Q. Volcatius Tullus.	
A.U. 689.	L. Aurelius Cotta.	
B.C. 65.	L. Manlius Torquatus.	
A.U. 690.	L. Julius Cæsar.	
B.C. 64.	C. Marcius Figulus.	
A.U. 691.	M. Tullius Cicero.	
B.C. 63	C. Antonius.	

INTRODUCTION.

CAIUS SALLUSTIUS CRISPUS was born at Amiternum, in the country of the Sabines, A.U. 668, B.C. 86, being nine years younger than Cato, fourteen younger than Cæsar, and twenty younger than Cicero. His family was Plebeian. We do not hear that any of the name obtained public distinction before the historian himself, who became Quæstor about the year B.C. 59, and tribune of the Plebs in 52. Little dependence can be placed on the *Declamatio in Sallustium*, a piece which is founded perhaps on the invective against him by Lenæus, a freedman of Pompeius; but according to the constant tradition of Roman antiquity, Sallust was, as there asserted, a dissipated man and a profligate politician, who attached himself to the popular party, and sought the offices of the state in succession, in order to finish his career with the enjoyment of a lucrative province, and the means of accumulating a large fortune. He was an active promoter of the prosecution of Milo for the murder of Clodius, B.C. 52, and thus perhaps ingratiated himself with the most factions of the parties in the city. The share he took in this business may have been partly owing to the chastisement he is said to have received from Milo, for the seduction of his wife. (Varro, quoted by Gellius, xvii. 18.) In the year 50, at a moment when the spirits of the senatorial party were unusually elated, Censors were appointed, the first after a long interval, and the list of the senate was purged of many of the opposite faction upon the plea of scandalous life, or other personal disqualifications. Among the sufferers was Sallust, and his intrigue with Milo's wife has been alleged as the cause assigned. It is hardly probable however that such a cause could have been put forth at a time when profligacy was so common among the ranks of the nobility, still less that it could have been the real motive for his expulsion. Hereupon, it is affirmed, Sallust repaired to Cæsar's quarters in Gaul, and enrolled himself at once among his warmest partizans. Such is the statement of the author of the *Declamatio*, which however is not in itself of much value. On the contrary, Cicero speaks at a later period of Cæsar pardoning a Sallustius: *etiam Sallustio ignovit:* (*ad Att.* xi. 20), as a captured or converted opponent; and we know of no other Sallustius to whom he is likely to refer. But from this event we may, at all events, more confidently date the bitter hostility to the Roman oligarchy which Sallust displays throughout his writings.

The disgrace he had undergone did not prevent Sallust from succeeding, under Cæsar's supremacy, to the high office of prætor, which he acquired in the year 47, the next after the battle of Pharsalia. This appointment restored him to a place in the Senate. He was employed in the following year in Cæsar's campaign in Africa, against the remnant of the senatorial party under Scipio and Cato. Upon its successful termination, he was left there as governor of the province of Numidia, which, upon the death of its king Juba, was incorporated with the possessions of the republic. It does not appear that he continued in this post beyond the usual term of one year; yet, in that short time, he contrived to amass the vast treasures for which he became afterwards notorious. His countrymen were shocked at the alleged profligacy of his conduct, especially, as we are told, after the vehement indignation he had expressed in his writings against the corruption and extortion of the Roman nobles. See Dion's *Roman History*, xliii. 9. καὶ τοὺς Νομάδας λαβὼν ἔς τε τὸ ὑπήκοον ἐπήγαγε, καὶ τῷ Σαλουστίῳ, λόγῳ μὲν, ἄρχειν, ἔργῳ δὲ, ἄγειν τε καὶ φέρειν ἐπέτρεψε. ἀμέλει καὶ ἐδωροδόκησε πολλὰ καὶ ἥρπασεν· ὥστε καὶ κατηγορηθῆναι αἰσχύνην αἰσχίστην ὀφλῆσαι, ὅτι τοιαῦτα συγγράμματα συγγράψας, καὶ πολλὰ καὶ πικρὰ περὶ τῶν ἐκκαρπουμένων τινὰς εἰπών, οὐκ ἐμιμή-σατο τῷ ἔργῳ τοὺς λόγους. Sallust was even menaced with an impeachment for the spoliation of his province; but it does not appear that he was brought to trial. He returned to Rome and formed the magnificent gardens, known by his name, on the

Pincian hill, which became eventually the property of the Emperors, and were a favourite resort of Augustus, Vespasian, Nerva, and other sovereign rulers. The story that he married Terentia, whom Cicero had divorced, is devoid of probability. Sallust lived from henceforth in luxurious retirement, having attained wealth and ease, the main objects of his ambition. He died B.C. 34, three years before the battle of Actium.

Some of the worst reflections upon Sallust's character are derived, as we have seen, from the *Declamatio in Sallustium*, the authenticity of which is at least doubtful. He had spoken disparagingly of Pompeius, calling him a man, *oris probi*, (some read, *improbi*) *animo inverecundo*, and Lenæus, Pompey's freedman, had attacked him furiously in consequence, describing him, among other things, as *nebulonem vita scriptisque monstrosum*, with which he coupled a charge of ignorance, affectation, and plagiarism. He is said to have been defended by Asconius Pedianus, who wrote a life of him, in the time of Augustus: but the unfavourable view of his character prevailed. Porcius Latro, a grammarian of the reign of Claudius, repeated the charges against him, and we have seen that Dion believed and propagated one, at least, of the gravest of them. We can only say that Dion, as is well known, generally inclines to the worst view of every man's character. Impressed with this concurrence of authorities, critics have commonly supposed

INTRODUCTION.

that the Sallustius, whose profligacy is noticed in the second satire of Horace's first book, is no other than the historian; for which however there is no further ground than the identity of name. Sallust left no descendants of his own, but he had a brother by whom the name was perpetuated; and the Crispus Sallustius to whom Horace addressed the second ode of his second book was the historian's grandnephew. The allusion there made to the wealth of Libya is the more appropriate, considering their relationship, and the probability that the person addressed inherited the fortune which had been accumulated in that country.

> Latius regnes avidum domando
> Spiritum, quam si Libyam remotis
> Gadibus jungas, et uterque Pœnus,
>   Serviat uni.

The extant works of Sallust are two historical pieces, on the conspiracy of Catilina, and the war with Jugurtha. He is believed to have written also a contemporary history of Rome, beginning with the insurrection of Lepidus, B.C. 78, and continued in five books to the year 66. This may have been intended as a continuation of the work of Sisenna on the civil wars of Sulla. See Vell. ii. 9. It has perished with the exception of a few considerable extracts from the speeches it contained, and a large number of detached sentences, collected from a variety of writers, and evincing the great and long-continued popularity of the work. Two extant epistles or harangues addressed to Julius Cæsar, and entitled *Epistolæ de republica ordinanda,* have also been ascribed to Sallust, but their authenticity is very questionable.

The *Catilina,* or *Bellum Catilinarium,* is a history of the conspiracy of Catilina, B.C. 63. It contains in itself no distinct evidence of the date of its composition. Those who affirm on the authority of St Jerome (*in Jovin.* i. p. 52) that the author married Terentia, presume that subsequently to his marriage he would not have alluded to the disgrace of Terentia's sister, the Vestal Virgin whom Catilina was accused of seducing (see *Catil.* ch. 15). But as both the date and fact of the marriage are quite uncertain, such a presumption can be of little force for determining the period of this composition. Others again contend that Sallust would not have invented a speech for Cæsar (*Catil.* ch. 51), instead of giving the genuine oration, during Cæsar's actual lifetime, and therefore argue that the work must have been written as late as B.C. 44, the year of Cæsar's death. There can be no force, however, in this argument to those who know the indifference of Sallust, and of the ancients in general, to the authenticity of such rhetorical exercises as the harangues with which they studied to adorn their narratives. On the other hand, we have to set Dion's remarks about the inconsistency observed at the time between Sallust's conduct in his province, and the sentiments declared in his writings. Now the *Jugurtha* was certainly written after his provincial administration, in B.C. 46; and we can hardly doubt therefore that Dion refers to the reflexions on the nobility at the beginning of the *Catilina*, which accordingly must have been written at an earlier period. That the *Jugurtha* was written after B.C. 46, may be safely inferred from the author's reference to the Punic books of king Hiempsal, which he consulted for it, or rather which had been explained to him (see *Jugurtha*, ch. 17), indicating clearly that he was himself on the spot at the time.

The *Catilina* and *Jugurtha* are what are denominated in modern times Monographies; *i. e.* narratives of a detached series of connected events; nor is it unlikely that the fragments of Sallust's *Histories* belong, in fact, to similar treatises on the war of Lepidus, the war of Spartacus, and possibly the wars of Sulla and Marius. Altogether, these works would have formed a pretty complete history of Roman affairs between the years B.C. 117 and 62. The events belonging to the earlier portion of this series had already been related by Roman writers. Sisenna had composed an account of the wars of Marius and Sulla; personal memoirs had been written by Rutilius Rufus, consul, B.C. 105, by Æmilius Scaurus, by Sulla himself, and by Lucullus. Of Sisenna's work at least the testimony both of Cicero and Sallust leaves us little to regret; and it does not appear that the ancients themselves made much use of those of the distinguished statesmen mentioned above. Sallust therefore is the first Roman historian whose account of these times became generally accepted by his own countrymen as authoritative. He owes this distinction probably quite as much to the charm of his style, as to any presumed authenticity in his narration. Indeed he seems to have been the first of the Roman writers who made style a matter of primary importance. The idea however that he took Thucydides for his model, rests upon the occurrence of a few philosophical reflexions, which seem to be directly imitated from the Greek writer. In the mere form of Sallust's expressions it would be difficult to point out any such resemblances to his supposed master. Seneca speaks correctly of his *amputatæ sententiæ et verba ante expectatum cadentia*. The charge against him of affecting archaic words was made by his own contemporaries. Lenæus, above spoken of, calls him *priscorum Catonisque verborum ineruditissimum furem*. Another writer, Ateius the grammarian, was supposed to have assisted the historian by collecting antique words for him to interweave with his own language.

I cannot however distinguish any such character in Sallust's extant writings. In the *Catilina* and *Jugurtha* there is not, I believe, a single word used which is not also of frequent occurrence in contemporary and later writers. It is probable indeed that he clung to the old orthography of many words at a time when great innovations in that respect were taking place, and even affected to recur to modes of spelling which were becoming obsolete. Some of the best MSS. continue to present antique forms of many words, and these we may suppose have been faithfully transmitted to us from the original exemplars. But even these fluctuate in their orthography, and in an edition intended for the use of youthful students it seems best to abide by the standard of the best age of Latin literature. Accordingly, in this edition, the nom. and acc. plural of nouns of the third declension are always written with *es*, not *is:* the termination of the superlative with *imus*, not *umus: verto* and its derivatives are spelt with *e*, not *o:* the abl. and dat. plural of the relative pronoun appears as *queis*, not *quis:* the gerundial form is written with *endo*, not *undo;* and so on in some other cases. Possibly the principle may be thought to be violated in the retention of the older form *adtineo* for *attineo*, &c.: and also in writing *lubido*, *Sulla*, and perhaps some other words according to the more ancient orthography. The genitives *Senati*, *tumulti*, *fide*, *die*, the dat. *usu*, &c. are retained as belonging not to Sallust's orthography, but to his grammar.

The prevalent notion of the great brevity of Sallust's style, is derived perhaps from the description of Seneca above cited. It has had the effect of inducing the older commentators, and especially Cortius, whose authority was considered paramount for many generations, to reject as insititious, in innumerable places, the occurrence of the verb substantive after the partic. passive, and to expunge all repetitions of words which seemed superfluous to the sense of a passage, in spite of the concurrent testimony of the MSS. For instance, in one place (*Catil.* 51) the word *lex* occurs three times in one sentence: *Tum lex Porcia aliæque leges paratæ sunt quibus legibus*, etc. But the fact is, that unless we are to suppose that his MSS., many of them very excellent ones, have been corrupted by officious transcribers beyond all others, Sallust is in some respects a writer more than usually redundant. Such in fact is generally the character of authors who write before the maturity of their language: and we may be sure that the affectation of cutting up sentences by the suppression of words which logically belong to them would be the vice of a later age, and foreign to the spirit of an ancient writer, especially of one who rather studied to copy a still remoter antiquity. We may conclude then that the *amputatæ sententiæ* referred to by Seneca, are the author's peculiar turns of thought, which are studiously abrupt and antithetical; the *verba ante expectatum cadentia* are certain harsh and jerking cadences in the composition, which are evidently prepared with a view to striking effects.

The text of the present edition is formed with due deference to the authority of the MSS. and of the citations of ancient writers. Several of the most disputed passages are quoted by the old Roman grammarians, and their reading of them is of course entitled to careful consideration.

The text given by Gerlach in his last edition, Berlin, 1852, very nearly corresponds, at last, after much fluctuation of opinion, with that of Kritz, Leipsic, 1828—1834, and, with the exceptions indicated above adopted for the convenience of the young reader, I shall be found to agree, I believe, in almost every case either with one or the other of these eminent critics. In two or three places I have ventured to omit a gross expression; a course which for my own part I could wish to see more extensively adopted in an age when the reading of Latin is becoming almost as common among women of polished education as in the good old times of Jane Grey and Elizabeth.

The annotations here offered to the student have been principally drawn from the variorum notes of Havercamp's edition, from Gerlach, and from Kritz. Much novelty of illustration is hardly to be expected upon a subject which has been so repeatedly treated, and most of the editors have done little more in this respect than copy from one another. The edition of Kritz however, which is mainly devoted to an examination of the author's grammatical constructions, is distinguished by great originality of research. I have appended his name only to a few of the notes; but my obligation to his learning and acumen are manifold throughout. Some use has also been made of the recent edition by Dietsch, which has only reached me while these sheets were printing.

In the commencement of the *Catilina* Sallust describes in general terms the profligacy of his contemporaries, and particularly of the class of candidates for public office and distinction. The character of the arch conspirator which he proceeds to draw is represented as a natural development of the licentiousness of the times, and the conspiracy itself appears to be the legitimate fruit of the general abandonment of principles, and prostration of public and private virtues. But in order fully to understand it, we must supply a serious omission on the historian's part, and give some account of the state of parties at Rome at the moment of this frightful explosion. The civil wars of Marius and Sulla had been a contest between the mass of the citizens marshalled by a few ambitious nobles, and headed by a fortunate soldier, and the ruling class of senators and patricians, who maintained with tenacity the exclusive privileges assured to them by an obsolete constitution. Their families had been ennobled by public office, and enriched by public service, and they strove to keep to themselves the exclusive enjoyment of these advantages. This class however had suffered a severe defeat in the admission of the Italians to the Roman franchise, which, after a sanguinary war, though successful in the field, they had been constrained eventually to concede. Marius at the head of the popular party had humbled them by the successive acquisition of no less than seven consulships. They had invoked the aid of their military champion Sulla. A bloody civil war had ensued, with alternate success, and massacres had been perpetrated on both sides. Marius had died, and Sulla had ultimately established the ascendancy of the nobles or optimates, and in his dictatorship had imposed upon the nation a series of enactments called from his name *leges Corneliæ*, for curtailing the prerogatives of the inferior orders, and confirming the supremacy of the senate as the ruling body of the state. The office of tribune particularly, the old constitutional safeguard of the Plebs, he had shorn of its principal functions, and he had excluded the knights from presiding along with the senate on the bench of justice. After three years' possession of the dictatorship, which had been decreed to him in perpetuity, Sulla abdicated his extraordinary functions, and retired into privacy. Immediately M. Æmilius Lepidus, a factious noble, had raised an insurrection, with the promise of restoring the popular rights, Catulus, his colleague in the consulship, had taken up arms at the bidding of the senate and optimates, and had succeeded in putting him down. But the senatorial party was never free from the machinations of discontented or ambitious men of its own order, who sought to raise themselves to preeminence by intriguing with the popular faction. M. Licinius Crassus, and Cn. Pompeius, who had recently obtained the surname of Magnus, becoming consuls, B.C. 80, rescinded some of Sulla's measures, and conciliated in some degree the favour of the depressed Marians. When however Pompeius was called away from Rome to combat Mithridates the king of Pontus, the senate was persuaded to concede to him powers of unprecedented extent, the command namely of all the eastern provinces of the empire, for the sake of getting rid of him at the centre of affairs. During his absence rumours were rife of a fearful plot against the commonwealth, in which several men of high family and personal distinction were supposed to be concerned. The danger was believed to be pressing, and to combat it, the senate consented to the election to the consulship of a *new man*, M. Tullius Cicero, influenced partly by its reliance on his talents and activity, but partly, it may be believed, with a view to employ him as its instrument for the bold but hazardous *coup d'état* which it meditated.

The parties into which the Roman people were at this time divided were four : 1. The Senatorial, above described as the ruling class, comprising the greater number of the highest nobility, numbering perhaps an hundred or more great families, and constituting an oligarchy, powerful from its wealth, its long experience of office, and its almost hereditary command of the national armies. Among its leaders were Catulus, Lucullus, Sulpicius, Silanus, Scribonius, Hortensius ; and it had recently enlisted as its champions both Cicero and Cato : 2. The popular or Marian party, of whom Cæsar, a connexion both of Marius and of Cinna, was now the chief, the strength of which lay in the numerous families which had been proscribed and excluded from office by Sulla,—in the favour of the lower classes of the city, and of a large portion of the knights, who were anxious to recover the privileges they had been deprived of, and to acquire more,—in the goodwill of the Italian communities, which had obtained the Roman franchise through the efforts of the leaders of this party at an earlier period,—and generally in the support of the provincials, who look forward to similar enfranchisement through the liberal policy which it continued to advocate : 3. The moderate aristocracy, who sought to mediate between these parties ; some, as Cicero at an earlier period, with a view to strengthen the existing constitution by reforming it, others, as Pompeius and Crassus, in order to make themselves independent of the control of a jealous oligarchy : 4. The discontented and turbulent class, mostly military adventurers, who had been raised to importance in the civil wars, and had lost their consideration upon the re-establishment of peaceful government. Rejected by the ruling oligarchy, they attached to themselves the men of broken fortunes of every order of the state, especially the veterans whom Sulla had planted on confiscated lands throughout Italy, and who had squandered their ill-gotten plunder, and were ready to embark upon any new enterprise to recruit their fortunes. Of this military faction Catilina was the most conspicuous chief. He had been himself one of Sulla's officers, and is said to have made himself notorious even in his youth for rapacity and cruelty. He had killed with his own hand his brother-in-law Q. Cæcilius; he had tortured and slain Marius Gratidianus, a friend and fellow-townsman of Cicero; he is said moreover to have murdered his own brother; nor does Sallust fail to mention other crimes of peculiar atrocity as generally ascribed to him.

Although we learn the story of Catilina's wickedness chiefly from the mouth of his enemies, the popularity he enjoyed among a large class of licentious and dissolute young nobles may serve rather to confirm than to invalidate it. Rome was thronged with men of this character, who shrank from no atrocity in the prospect of plunder or advancement, and were ready to lend all their influence to a leader, however justly infamous, whose abilities might promote their selfish ends. A deeper shade of suspicion, however, has been thrown upon the genuineness of the colours with which Cicero and Sallust have painted the arch conspirator, from the fact of his having been a candidate for the consulship, and therefore we must suppose not altogether unacceptable to a much larger number of honourable citizens. Is it possible, we ask ourselves, that a man generally suspected of aiming at an abolition of debts no less than the subversion of institutions, could have hoped for a preponderance of suffrages among the citizens of any regulated community? In the face however of the concurrent testimony of all our authorities, we cannot doubt the general correctness of the charges against Catilina. Could they have been fairly questioned, we must suppose that Sallust, as a bitter enemy of his adversaries, would not have failed to suggest some extenuation of them. On the whole Sallust's history seems to be written with remarkable fairness. His character of his patron Cæsar exhibits no party bias, and his respect for Cato, the most determined of his opponents, is strongly felt and boldly expressed. He is accused of undervaluing Cicero's merit. It is difficult at least to fasten upon him any charge of overtly disparaging that statesman; though, were we to take Cicero's own account of the affair, or indeed those of some other writers, we should doubtless be disposed to rate the consul's importance at this time much higher than Sallust himself would allow us to understand. This is a point which must always be open to difference of opinion. It is not unreasonable, however, to believe that Cicero's influence has been generally overrated. The nobles had been long aware of the imminence of such an outbreak as that of Catilina: they were secretly well pleased at the opportunity it would give them to take up a bold attitude, and strike a blow, which, while it crushed the military faction, would inspire terror into both the Marians and the moderates. They were glad to use Cicero, as an able and popular man, but one who, as a *new man*, could be easily disowned and discarded if unsuccessful, as their instrument in this measure. Accordingly they helped to raise him to the consulship at the critical moment, to the surprise of all the world, and even of himself, such an elevation having never before been accorded to one of his rank, except to the great military champion Marius. As soon as their object was attained and the outbreak crushed, the nobles suffered Cicero to drop. When Pompeius returned from Asia, and encouraged the impeachment with which Clodius threatened him, for his stretch of the consular prerogative, they drew back from his defence, and he fell without an arm held forth to save him. It then appeared how totally devoid he was of personal influence or substantial power in the state. From that time, though suffered to return from his exile, his part in public affairs was only secondary, and became indeed daily more trivial. During the civil wars of Cæsar and Pompeius he was neglected, his counsel disregarded, and himself almost driven contemptuously from the camp of the oligarchs. Cæsar condescended to solicit his countenance, but received his refusal with the coldest indifference. The conspirators against Cæsar did not care to consult him, and after they had struck their blow were but little elated by his tardy adhesion. It was not till the liberators, Brutus, Cassius, and the rest, had quitted Rome for the East, till Antonius had taken up arms in the north of Italy, till Octavius had repaired to his legions to watch him, till even the consuls Hirtius and Pansa had marched forth from the city, that Cicero became at last the first man in the senate and the forum. For the few months, indeed, next ensuing he continued to take the lead in the domestic affairs of the republic; his influence within that sphere became really effective; he enacted a great part, and crowned his long political life with a glorious ἀριστεία. It is no reflection upon the wisdom and integrity of Cicero's public conduct to point out the inferiority of the position he was allowed to hold among his contemporaries; on the contrary, it may serve to display more fully the contrast between his honourable character and the selfish corruption of his times, that neither his talents nor his genuine patriotism availed to place him on the eminence from whence he could save the state from its conflicting factions. It is due however to Sallust to shew that the secondary place he assigns him is not really below the truth, nor to be ascribed to any unworthy jealousy on the part of the historian.

The *Jugurtha*, it must be admitted, is a work of far less interest than the *Catilina*. Farther removed himself from the period to which it refers, and with no personal knowledge of the events and characters it brings before us, Sallust in the second of his histories enters into an unequal rivalry with his earlier achievement. Nevertheless there is much life and expression in his portraiture of the times at Rome; the ambition of the nobles and the growing corruption of the people, as there represented, prepare us for the crisis of the civil wars which was soon about to be developed. The early career of Marius and Sulla, their selfish ambition and personal antagonism, serve as a preface to the records of slaughter and proscription with which their names were to become conspicuously blended. Jugurtha himself, the crafty Numidian, bold and active, with inexhaustible resources and devoid of scruples, combining the subtilty of the Carthaginian with the ferocity of the Moor, is interesting not only on his own account, but as a type of the African character, such as it was afterwards exemplified in Tacfarinas, and recently in Abd-el-kader. The struggle of the serpent and the eagle, so favourite a subject with poets and painters, has been delineated by no historian more vividly than by Sallust.

In the present revised edition the readings of Kritz's text (Lips. 1828) have been generally adopted, and his system of punctuation followed. The notes have been carefully corrected, and some addition made to them. It will be observed that many idiomatic passages from the poets have been introduced, to assist the understanding of the text, but partly also to show how much the style of Sallust approaches to that of poetry, and still more from the idea that youthful readers will take more interest in verse than in prose illustrations, and better retain what they learn from them.

Ely, 1882.   C. M.

C. SALLUSTII CRISPI
CATILINA.

I. Omnes homines qui sese student praestare ceteris animalibus summa ope niti decet ne vitam silentio transeant, veluti pecora, quae natura prona atque ventri obedientia finxit. Sed nostra omnis vis in animo et corpore sita est; animi imperio, corporis servitio magis utimur; alterum nobis cum dis, alterum cum belluis commune est. Quo mihi rectius videtur ingenii quam virium opibus gloriam quaerere; et, quoniam vita ipsa qua fruimur brevis est, memoriam nostri quam maxime longam efficere. Nam divitiarum et formae gloria fluxa atque fragilis est; virtus clara aeternaque habetur. Sed diu magnum inter mortales certamen fuit, vine corporis an virtute animi res militaris magis procederet. Nam et prius quam incipias consulto, et, ubi consulueris, mature facto opus est. Ita utrumque per se indigens alterum alterius auxilio eget.

II. Igitur initio reges (nam in terris nomen imperii id primum fuit) diversi pars ingenium, alii corpus exercebant: etiam tum vita hominum sine cupiditate agitabatur; sua cuique satis placebant. Postea vero quam in Asia Cyrus, in Graecia Lacedaemonii et

Athenienses coepere urbes atque nationes subigere, lubidinem dominandi caussam belli habere, maximam gloriam in maximo imperio putare; tum demum periculo atque negotiis compertum est in bello plurimum ingenium posse. Quodsi regum atque imperatorum animi virtus in pace ita uti in bello valeret, aequabilius atque constantius sese res humanae haberent; neque aliud alio ferri, neque mutari ac misceri omnia cerneres. Nam imperium facile his artibus retinetur quibus initio partum est. Verum ubi pro labore desidia, pro continentia et aequitate lubido atque superbia invasere, fortuna simul cum moribus immutatur. Ita imperium semper ad optimum quemque a minus bono transfertur. Quae homines arant, navigant, aedificant, virtuti omnia parent. Sed multi mortales, dediti ventri atque somno, indocti incultique vitam sicuti peregrinantes transegere; quibus profecto contra naturam corpus voluptati, anima oneri fuit. Eorum ego vitam mortemque juxta aestimo, quoniam de utraque siletur. Verum enim vero is demum mihi vivere atque frui anima videtur qui, aliquo negotio intentus, praeclari facinoris aut artis bonae famam quaerit. Sed in magna copia rerum aliud alii natura iter ostendit.

III. Pulchrum est bene facere reipublicae; etiam bene dicere haud absurdum est. Vel pace vel bello clarum fieri licet; et qui fecere, et qui facta aliorum scripsere, multi laudantur. Ac mihi quidem, tametsi haudquaquam par gloria sequatur scriptorem et auctorem rerum, tamen in primis arduum videtur res gestas scribere; primum quod facta dictis sunt exaequanda; dehinc quia plerique, quae delicta reprehenderis, malevolentia et invidia dicta putant; ubi de magna virtute et gloria bonorum memores, quae sibi quisque facilia factu putat, aequo animo accipit; supra ea, veluti ficta, pro falsis ducit. Sed ego adolescentulus initio, sicuti plerique, studio ad rempublicam latus sum; ibique mihi adversa multa fuere. Nam pro pudore, pro abstinentia, pro virtute, audacia, largitio, avaritia vigebant. Quae tametsi animus aspernabatur, insolens malarum artium, tamen inter tanta vitia imbecilla aetas ambitione corrupta tenebatur; ac me, cum ab reliquorum malis moribus dissentirem, nihilo minus honoris cupido eadem, qua ceteros, fama atque invidia vexabat.

IV. Igitur, ubi animus ex multis miseriis atque periculis requievit, et mihi reliquam aetatem a republica procul habendam decrevi, non fuit consilium socordia atque desidia bonum otium conterere, neque vero agrum colendo aut venando, servilibus officiis, intentum aetatem agere; sed a quo incepto studio me ambitio mala detinuerat, eodem regressus statui res gestas populi Romani carptim, ut quaeque memoria digna videbantur, perscribere; eo magis, quod mihi a spe, metu, partibus reipublicae animus liber erat. Igitur de Catilinae conjuratione, quam verissime potero, paucis absolvam: nam id facinus in primis ego memorabile existimo sceleris atque periculi novitate. De cujus hominis moribus pauca prius explananda sunt quam initium narrandi faciam.

V. Lucius Catilina nobili genere natus, fuit magna vi et animi et corporis, sed ingenio malo pravoque. Huic ab adolescentia bella intestina, caedes, rapinae, discordia civilis grata fuere; ibique juventutem suam exercuit. Corpus patiens inediae, vigiliae, algoris, supra quam cuiquam credibile est; animus audax, subdolus, varius, cujus rei libet simulator ac dissimulator; alieni appetens, sui profusus; ardens in cupiditatibus; satis eloquentiae, sapientiae parum. Vastus animus immoderata, incredibilia, nimis alta semper cupiebat. Hunc post dominationem Lucii Sullae lubido maxima invaserat reipublicae capiendae, neque id quibus modis assequeretur, dum sibi regnum pararet, quidquam pensi habebat. Agitabatur magis magisque in dies animus ferox inopia rei familiaris et conscientia scelerum; quae utraque his artibus auxerat quas supra memoravi. Incitabant praeterea corrupti civitatis mores, quos pessima ac diversa inter se mala, luxuria atque avaritia, vexabant. Res ipsa hortari videtur, quoniam de moribus civitatis tempus admonuit, supra repetere, ac paucis instituta majorum domi militiaeque, quomodo rempublicam habuerint, quantamque reliquerint, ut paullatim immutata ex pulcherrima pessima ac flagitiosissima facta sit, disserere.

VI. Urbem Romam, sicuti ego accepi, condidere atque habuere initio Trojani, qui Aenea duce profugi sedibus incertis vagabantur; cumque his Aborigines, genus hominum agreste, sine legibus, sine imperio, liberum atque solutum. Hi postquam in una moenia convenere, dispari genere, dissimili lingua, alius alio more viventes, incredibile memoratu est quam facile coaluerint. Sed postquam res eorum civibus, moribus, agris aucta, satis prospera, satisque pollens videbatur, sicuti pleraque mortalium habentur, invidia ex opulentia orta est. Igitur reges populique finitimi bello tentare; pauci ex amicis auxilio esse; nam ceteri, metu perculsi, a periculis aberant. At Romani domi militiaeque intenti festinare, parare, alius alium hortari; hostibus obviam ire; libertatem, patriam, parentesque armis tegere : post, ubi pericula virtute propulerant, sociis atque amicis auxilia portabant; magisque dandis quam accipiendis beneficiis amicitias parabant. Imperium legitimum, nomen imperii regium habebant; delecti, quibus corpus annis infirmum, ingenium sapientia validum, reipublicae consultabant; hi, vel aetate vel curae similitudine PATRES appellabantur. Post, ubi regium imperium, quod initio conservandae libertatis atque augendae reipublicae fuerat, in superbiam dominationemque convertit, immutato more, annua imperia, binosque imperatores sibi fecere : eo modo minime posse putabant per licentiam insolescere animum humanum.

VII. Sed ea tempestate coepere se quisque extollere, magisque ingenium in promptu habere. Nam regibus boni, quam mali, suspectiores sunt, semperque his aliena virtus formidolosa est. Sed civitas incredibile memoratu est adepta libertate quantum brevi creverit; tanta cupido gloriae incesserat. Jam primum juventus, simulac belli patiens erat, in castris per laboris usum militiam discebat: magisque in decoris armis et militaribus equis, quam in scortis atque conviviis, lubidinem habebant. Igitur talibus viris non labos insolitus, non locus ullus asper aut arduus erat, non armatus hostis formidolosus : virtus omnia domuerat. Sed gloriae maximum certamen inter ipsos erat : sic se quisque hostem ferire, murum ascendere, conspici dum tale facinus faceret, properabat; eas divitias, eam bonam famam magnamque nobilitatem putabant; laudis avidi, pecuniae liberales erant; gloriam ingentem, divitias honestas volebant. Memorare possem quibus in locis maximas hostium copias populus Romanus parva manu fuderit, quas urbes natura munitas pugnando ceperit, ni ea res longius ab incepto traheret.

VIII. Sed profecto Fortuna in omni re dominatur; ea res cunctas ex lubidine magis quam ex vero celebrat obscuratque. Atheniensium res gestae, sicuti ego aestimo, satis amplae magnificaeque fuere; verum aliquanto minores tamen quam fama feruntur. Sed, quia provenere ibi scriptorum magna ingenia, per terrarum orbem Atheniensium facta pro maximis celebrantur. Ita eorum qui ea fecere virtus tanta habetur, quantum verbis eam potuere extollere praeclara ingenia. At populo Romano nunquam ea copia fuit, quia prudentissimus quisque negotiosus maxime erat; ingenium nemo sine corpore exercebat; optimus quisque facere, quam dicere; sua ab aliis benefacta laudari quam ipse aliorum narrare malebat.

IX. Igitur domi militiaeque boni mores colebantur; concordia maxima, minima avaritia erat; jus bonumque apud eos non legibus magis quam natura valebat. Jurgia, discordias, simultates cum hostibus exercebant; cives cum civibus de virtute certabant; in suppliciis deorum magnifici, domi parci, in amicis fideles erant. Duabus his artibus, audacia in bello, ubi pax evenerat aequitate, seque remque publicam curabant. Quarum rerum ego maxima documenta haec habeo, quod saepius vindicatum est in eos, qui contra imperium in hostem pugnaverant, quique tardius revocati bello excesserant, quam qui signa relinquere aut pulsi loco cedere ausi erant; in pace vero, quod beneficiis quam metu imperium agitabant, et accepta injuria ignoscere quam persequi malebant.

X. Sed ubi labore atque justitia respublica crevit, reges magni bello domiti, nationes ferae et populi ingentes vi subacti, Carthago, aemula imperii Romani, ab stirpe interiit, cuncta maria terraeque patebant, saevire Fortuna, ac miscere omnia, coepit. Qui labores, pericula, dubias atque asperas res facile toleraverant, iis otium, divitiae, optandae aliis, oneri miseriaeque fuere. Igitur primo pecuniae, deinde imperii cupido crevit; ea quasi materies omnium malorum fuere. Namque avaritia fidem, probitatem, ceterasque artes bonas subvertit; pro his superbiam, crudelitatem, deos negligere, omnia venalia habere, edocuit; ambitio multos mortales falsos fieri subegit; aliud clausum in pectore, aliud in lingua promptum habere; amicitias inimicitiasque non ex re sed ex commodo aestimare; magisque vultum quam ingenium bonum habere. Haec primo paullatim crescere, interdum vindicari: post, ubi contagio quasi pestilentia invasit, civitas immutata; imperium ex justissimo atque optimo crudele intolerandumque factum.

XI. Sed primo magis ambitio, quam avaritia, animos hominum exercebat; quod tamen vitium propius virtutem erat. Nam gloriam, honorem, imperium bonus et ignavus aeque sibi exoptant; sed ille vera via nititur, huic quia bonae artes desunt, dolis atque fallaciis contendit. Avaritia pecuniae studium habet, quam nemo sapiens concupivit; ea quasi venenis malis imbuta corpus animumque virilem effeminat:

semper infinita, insatiabilis est, neque copia neque inopia minuitur. Sed postquam L. Sulla, armis recepta republica, ex bonis initiis malos eventus habuit, rapere omnes, trahere, domum alius, alius agros cupere, neque modum neque modestiam victores habere, foeda crudeliaque in civibus facinora facere. Huc accedebat, quod L. Sulla exercitum, quem in Asia ductaverat, quo sibi fidum faceret, contra morem majorum luxuriose nimisque liberaliter habuerat; loca amoena, voluptaria facile in otio feroces militum animos molliverant. Ibi primum insuevit exercitus populi Romani amare, potare; signa, tabulas pictas, vasa caelata mirari; ea privatim ac publice rapere; delubra spoliare; sacra profanaque omnia polluere. Igitur hi milites, postquam victoriam adepti sunt, nihil reliqui victis fecere. Quippe secundae res sapientium animos fatigant; ne illi corruptis moribus victoriae temperarent.

XII. Postquam divitiae honori esse coepere, et eas gloria, imperium, potentia sequebatur, hebescere virtus, paupertas probro haberi, innocentia pro malevolentia duci coepit. Igitur ex divitiis juventutem luxuria atque avaritia cum superbia invasere; rapere, consumere; sua parvi pendere, aliena cupere; pudorem, pudicitiam, divina atque humana promiscua, nihil pensi neque moderati habere. Operae pretium est, quum domos atque villas cognoveris in urbium modum exaedificatas, visere templa deorum, quae nostri majores, religiosissimi mortales, fecere. Verum illi delubra deorum pietate, domos suas gloria decorabant; neque victis quidquam praeter injuriae licentiam eripiebant. At hi contra, ignavissimi homines, per summum scelus omnia ea sociis adimere, quae fortissimi viri victores hostibus reliquerant; proinde quasi injuriam facere id demum esset imperio uti.

XIII. Nam quid ea memorem, quae nisi his qui videre nemini credibilia sunt, a privatis compluribus subversos montes, maria constructa esse: quibus mihi videntur ludibrio fuisse divitiae; quippe quas honeste habere licebat abuti per turpitudinem properabant. Sed lubido ganeae, ceterique cultus, non minor incesserat:...vescendi caussa terra marique omnia exquirere; dormire prius quam somni cupido esset; non famem aut sitim, neque frigus neque lassitudinem opperiri, sed ea omnia luxu antecapere. Haec juventutem, ubi familiares opes defecerant, ad facinora incendebant. Animus imbutus malis artibus haud facile lubidinibus carebat; eo profusius omnibus modis quaestui atque sumptui deditus erat.

XIV. In tanta tamque corrupta civitate Catilina, id quod factu facillimum erat, omnium flagitiorum atque facinorum circum se, tanquam stipatorum, catervas habebat. Nam quicumque impudicus, adulter, ganeo,...bona patria laceraverat, quique alienum aes grande conflaverat, quo flagitium aut facinus redimeret, praeterea, omnes undique parricidae, sacrilegi, convicti judiciis, aut pro factis judicium timentes; ad hoc, quos manus atque lingua perjurio aut sanguine civili alebat; postremo, omnes quos flagitium, egestas, conscius animus exagitabat; ii Catilinae proximi familiaresque erant. Quod si quis etiam a culpa vacuus in amicitiam ejus inciderat, quotidiano usu atque illecebris facile par similisque ceteris efficiebatur. Sed maxime adolescentium familiaritates adpetebat; eorum animi, molles et aetate fluxi, dolis haud difficulter capiebantur. Nam uti cujusque studium ex aetate flagrabat, aliis scorta praebere, aliis canes atque equos mercari; postremo, neque sumptui, neque modestiae suae parcere, dum illos obnoxios fidosque sibi faceret....

XV. Jam primum adolescens Catilina multa nefanda stupra fecerat, cum virgine nobili, cum sacerdote Vestae, alia hujuscemodi contra jus fasque. Postremo, captus amore Aureliae Orestillae, cujus, praeter formam, nihil unquam bonus laudavit, quod ea nubere illi dubitabat, timens privignum adulta aetate, pro certo creditur, necato filio, vacuam domum scelestis nuptiis fecisse. Quae quidem res mihi in primis videtur caussa fuisse facinoris maturandi. Namque animus impurus, dis hominibusque infestus, neque vigiliis, neque quietibus sedari poterat; ita conscientia mentem excitam vastabat. Igitur colos exsanguis, foedi oculi, citus modo, modo tardus incessus; prorsus in facie vultuque vecordia inerat.

XVI. Sed juventutem, quam, ut supra diximus, illexerat, multis modis mala facinora edocebat. Ex illis testes signatoresque falsos commodare; fidem, fortunas, pericula vilia habere; post, ubi eorum famam atque pudorem attriverat, majora alia imperabat: si caussa peccandi in praesens minus suppetebat, nihilo minus insontes, sicuti sontes, circumvenire, jugulare: scilicet, ne per otium torpescerent manus aut animus, gratuito potius malus atque crudelis erat. His amicis sociisque confisus Catilina, simul quod aes alienum per omnes terras ingens erat, et quod plerique Sullani milites, largius suo usi, rapinarum et victoriae veteris memores, civile bellum exoptabant, opprimendae reipublicae consilium cepit. In Italia nullus exercitus; Cn. Pompeius in extremis terris bellum gerebat; ipsi consulatum petenti magna spes; senatus nihil sane intentus; tutae tranquillaeque res omnes; sed ea prorsus opportuna Catilinae.

XVII. Igitur circiter Kalendas Junias, L. Caesare et C. Figulo consulibus, primo singulos adpellare; hortari alios, alios tentare; opes suas, imparatam rempublicam, magna praemia conjurationis docere. Ubi satis explorata sunt, quae voluit, in unum omnes convocat, quibus maxima necessitudo et plurimum audaciae inerat. Eo convenere senatorii ordinis P. Lentulus Sura, P. Autronius, L. Cassius Longinus, C. Cethegus, P. et Servius Sullae, Servii filii, L. Vargunteius, Q. Annius, M. Porcius Lacca, L. Bestia, Q. Curius: praeterea ex equestri ordine M. Fulvius Nobilior, L. Statilius, P. Gabinius Capito, C. Cornelius: ad hoc multi ex coloniis et municipiis, domi nobiles. Erant praeterea complures paullo occultius consilii hujusce participes nobiles, quos magis dominationis spes hortabatur quam inopia aut alia necessitudo. Ceterum juventus pleraque, sed maxime nobilium, Catilinae inceptis favebat; quibus in otio vel magnifice, vel molliter vivere copia erat, incerta pro certis, bellum, quam pacem, malebant. Fuere item ea tempestate, qui crederent M. Licinium Crassum non ignarum ejus consilii fuisse; quia Cn. Pompeius, invisus ipsi, magnum exercitum ductabat, cujusvis opes voluisse contra illius potentiam crescere; simul confisum, si conjuratio valuisset, facile apud illos principem se fore.

XVIII. Sed antea item conjuravere pauci contra rempublicam, in quibus Catilina fuit; de qua quam verissime potero dicam. L. Tullo M' Lepido consulibus P. Autronius et P. Sulla, legibus ambitus interrogati, poenas dederant. Post paullo Catilina, pecuniarum repetundarum reus, prohibitus erat consulatum petere, quod intra legitimos dies profiteri nequiverat. Erat eodem tempore Cn. Piso, adolescens nobilis, summae audaciae, egens, factiosus, quem ad perturbandam rempublicam inopia atque mali mores stimulabant. Cum hoc Catilina et Autronius circa Nonas Decembres, consilio communicato parabant in Capitolio Kalendis Januariis L. Cottam et L. Torquatum consules interficere; ipsi, fascibus correptis Pisonem cum exercitu ad obtinendas duas Hispanias mittere. Ea re cognita, rursus in Nonas Februarias consilium caedis transtulerant. Jam tum non consulibus modo, sed plurisque senatoribus perniciem machinabantur. Quod ni Catilina maturasset pro curia signum sociis dare, eo die post conditam urbem Romanam pessimum facinus patratum foret. Quia nondum frequentes armati convenerant ea res consilium diremit.

XIX. Postea Piso in citeriorem Hispaniam quaestor pro praetore missus est, adnitente Crasso, quod eum infestum inimicum Cn. Pompeio cognoverat. Neque tamen senatus provinciam invitus dederat; quippe foedum hominem a republica procul esse volebat; simul, quia boni complures praesidium in eo putabant; et jam tum potentia Cn. Pompeii formidolosa erat. Sed is Piso in provincia ab equitibus Hispanis, quos in exercitu ductabat, iter faciens occisus est. Sunt qui ita dicunt, imperia ejus injusta, superba, crudelia barbaros nequivisse pati; alii autem equites illos, Cn. Pompeii veteres fidosque clientes, voluntate ejus Pisonem aggressos; nunquam Hispanos praeterea tale facinus fecisse, sed imperia saeva multa antea perpessos. Nos eam rem in medio relinquemus. De superiore conjuratione satis dictum.

XX. Catilina ubi eos, quos paullo ante memoravi, convenisse videt, tametsi cum singulis multa saepe egerat, tamen in rem fore credens universos appellare et cohortari, in abditam partem aedium secedit; atque ibi, omnibus arbitris procul amotis, orationem hujuscemodi habuit. "Ni virtus fidesque vestra spectata mihi forent, nequidquam opportuna res cecidisset; spes magna, dominatio, in manibus frustra fuissent; neque ego per ignaviam aut vana ingenia incerta pro certis captarem. Sed quia multis et magnis tempestatibus vos cognovi fortes fidosque mihi, eo animus ausus est maximum atque pulcherrimum facinus incipere; simul quia vobis eadem quae mihi bona malaque intellexi, nam idem velle atque idem nolle, ea demum firma amicitia est. Sed ego quae mente agitavi, omnes jam antea diversi audistis. Ceterum mihi in dies magis animus accenditur, quum considero, quae condicio vitae futura sit, nisi nosmet ipsi vindicamus in libertatem. Nam, postquam respublica in paucorum potentium jus atque dicionem concessit, semper illis reges tetrarchae vectigales esse; populi, nationes stipendia pendere; ceteri omnes, strenui, boni, nobiles atque ignobiles, vulgus fuimus sine gratia, sine auctoritate, iis obnoxii, quibus si respublica valeret formidini essemus. Itaque omnis gratia, potentia, honos, divitiae apud illos sunt, aut ubi illi volunt; nobis reliquere pericula, repulsas, judicia, egestatem. Quae quousque tandem patiemini, fortissimi viri? Nonne emori per virtutem praestat, quam vitam miseram atque inhonestam, ubi alienae superbiae ludibrio fueris, per dedecus amittere? Verum enim vero, pro deum atque hominum fidem! victoria in manu nobis est; viget aetas, animus valet; contra illis, annis atque divitiis, omnia consenuerunt. Tantum modo incepto opus est; cetera res expediet. Etenim quis mortalium, cui virile ingenium inest, tolerare potest illis divitias superare, quas profundant in exstruendo mari et montibus coaequandis, nobis rem familiarem etiam ad necessaria deesse? illos binas, aut amplius, domos continuare; nobis larem familiarem nusquam ullum esse? Quum tabulas, signa, toreumata emunt, nova diruunt, alia aedificant, postremo omnibus modis pecuniam trahunt, vexant, tamen summa lubidine divitias vincere nequeunt. At nobis est domi inopia, foris aes alienum; mala res, spes multo asperior: denique, quid reliqui habemus, praeter miseram animam? Quin igitur expergiscimini? En illa, illa quam saepe optastis, libertas, praeterea divitiae, decus, gloria in oculis sita sunt! fortuna omnia victoribus praemia posuit. Res, tempus, pericula, egestas, belli spolia magnifica, magis quam oratio hortentur. Vel imperatore vel milite me utimini: neque animus neque corpus a vobis aberit. Haec ipsa, ut spero, vobiscum una consul agam; nisi forte animus fallit, et vos servire magis quam imperare parati estis."

XXI. Postquam accepere ea homines, quibus

mala abunde omnia erant, sed neque res, neque spes bona ulla, tametsi illis quieta movere magna merces videbatur, tamen postulare plerique, uti proponeret quae condicio belli foret; quae praemia armis peterent; quid ubique opis aut spei haberent. Tum Catilina polliceri tabulas novas, proscriptionem locupletium, magistratus, sacerdotia, rapinas, alia omnia quae bellum atque lubido victorum fert. Praeterea esse in Hispania citeriore Pisonem, in Mauretania cum exercitu P. Sittium Nucerinum, consilii sui participes; petere consulatum C. Antonium, quem sibi collegam fore speraret, hominem et familiarem, et omnibus necessitudinibus circumventum: cum eo se consulem initium agendi facturum. Ad hoc maledictis increpat omnes bonos; suorum unumquemque nominans laudare: admonebat alium egestatis, alium cupiditatis suae, complures periculi aut ignominiae, multos victoriae Sullanae, quibus ea praedae fuerat. Postquam omnium animos alacres videt, cohortatus ut petitionem suam curae haberent, conventum dimisit.

XXII. Fuere ea tempestate qui dicerent, Catilinam, oratione habita, cum ad jusjurandum populares sceleris sui adigeret, humani corporis sanguinem, vino permixtum, in pateris circumtulisse; inde quum post exsecrationem omnes degustavissent, sicut in solemnibus sacris fieri consuevit, aperuisse consilium suum, atque eo dictitare fecisse, quo inter se fidi magis forent alius alii tanti facinoris conscii. Nonnulli ficta et haec et multa praeterea existimabant ab his, qui Ciceronis invidiam, quae postea orta est, leniri credebant atrocitate sceleris eorum, qui poenas dederant. Nobis ea res pro magnitudine parum comperta est.

XXIII. Sed in ea conjuratione fuit Q. Curius, natus haud obscuro loco, flagitiis atque facinoribus coopertus; quem censores senatu probri gratia moverant. Huic homini non minor vanitas quam audacia; neque reticere quae audierat, neque suamet ipse scelera occultare; prorsus neque dicere neque facere quidquam pensi habebat. Erat ei cum Fulvia, muliere nobili, vetus consuetudo; cui cum minus gratus esset, quia inopia minus largiri poterat, repente glorians maria montesque polliceri coepit; minari interdum ferro, nisi obnoxia foret; postremo ferocius agitare quam solitus erat. At Fulvia, insolentiae Curii caussa cognita, tale periculum reipublicae haud occultum habuit; sed, sublato auctore de Catilinae conjuratione, quae quoque modo audierat, compluribus narravit. Ea res in primis studia hominum accendit ad consulatum mandandum M. Tullio Ciceroni. Namque antea pleraque nobilitas invidia aestuabat, et quasi pollui consulatum credebant, si cum, quamvis egregius, homo novus adeptus foret. Sed ubi periculum advenit, invidia atque superbia post fuere.

XXIV. Igitur comitiis habitis consules declarantur M. Tullius et C. Antonius; quod factum primo populares conjurationis concusserat. Neque tamen Catilinae furor minuebatur; sed in dies plura agitare; arma per Italiam locis opportunis parare; pecuniam sua aut amicorum fide sumptam mutuam Faesulas ad Manlium quemdam portare, qui postea princeps fuit belli faciendi. Ea tempestate plurimos cujusque generis homines adscivisse dicitur; mulieres etiam aliquot, quae primo ingentes sumptus stupro corporis toleraverant; post, ubi aetas tantummodo quaestui neque luxuriae modum fecerat, aes alienum grande conflaverant. Per eas se Catilina credebat posse servitia urbana sollicitare, urbem incendere, viros earum vel adjungere sibi vel interficere.

XXV. Sed in his erat Sempronia, quae multa saepe virilis audaciae facinora commiserat. Haec mulier genere atque forma, praeterea viro atque liberis satis fortunata fuit; litteris Graecis atque Latinis docta; psallere, saltare elegantius, quam necesse est probae; multa alia, quae instrumenta luxuriae sunt. Sed ei cariora semper omnia quam decus atque pudicitia fuit; pecuniae an famae minus parceret, haud facile discerneres; lubidine sic accensa ut saepius peteret viros quam peteretur. Sed ea saepe antehac fidem prodiderat, creditum abjuraverat, caedis conscia fuerat, luxuria atque inopia praeceps abierat. Verum ingenium ejus haud absurdum: posse versus facere, jocum movere, sermone uti vel modesto, vel molli, vel procaci: prorsus multae facetiae multusque lepos inerat.

XXVI. His rebus comparatis, Catilina nihilo minus in proximum annum consulatum petebat, sperans, si designatus foret, facile se ex voluntate Antonio usurum. Neque interea quietus erat, sed omnibus modis insidias parabat Ciceroni. Neque illi tamen ad cavendum dolus aut astutiae deerant. Namque, a principio consulatus sui, multa pollicendo per Fulviam, effecerat ut Q. Curius, de quo paullo ante memoravi, consilia Catilinae sibi proderet. Ad hoc, collegam suum Antonium pactione provinciae perpulerat, ne contra rempublicam sentiret; circum se praesidia amicorum atque clientium occulte habebat.

Postquam dies comitiorum venit, et Catilinae neque petitio, neque insidiae quas consuli in campo fecerat, prospere cessere, constituit bellum facere et extrema omnia experiri, quoniam quae occulte tentaverat, aspera foedaque evenerant.

XXVII. Igitur C. Manlium Faesulas atque in eam partem Etruriae, Septimium quemdam Camertem in agrum Picenum, C. Julium in Apuliam dimisit; praeterea alium alio, quem ubique opportunum sibi fore credebat. Interea Romae multa simul moliri; consuli insidias tendere, parare incendia, opportuna loca armatis hominibus obsidere; ipse cum telo esse, item alios jubere; hortari uti semper intenti paratique essent; dies noctesque festinare, vigilare, neque insomniis neque labore fatigari. Postremo, ubi multa agitanti nihil procedit, rursus intempesta nocte conjurationis principes convocat per M. Porcium Laecam; ibique, multa de ignavia eorum questus, docet "se Manlium praemisisse ad eam multitudinem quam ad capienda arma paraverat; item alios in alia loca opportuna, qui initium belli facerent; seque ad exercitum proficisci cupere, si prius Ciceronem oppressisset; cum suis consiliis multum obficere."

XXVIII. Igitur, perterritis ac dubitantibus ceteris, C. Cornelius, eques Romanus, operam suam pollicitus, et cum eo L. Vargunteius, senator, constituere ea nocte paullo post cum armatis hominibus, sicuti salutatum, introire ad Ciceronem, ac de improviso domi suae imparatum confodere. Curius ubi intelligit quantum periculi consuli impendeat, propere per Fulviam dolum qui parabatur enunciat. Ita illi janua prohibiti tantum facinus frustra susceperant.

Interea Manlius in Etruria plebem sollicitare, egestate simul ac dolore injuriae novarum rerum cupidam, quod Sullae dominatione agros bonaque omnia amiserat; praeterea latrones cujusque generis, quorum in ea regione magna copia erat; nonnullos ex Sullanis colonis, quibus lubido atque luxuria ex magnis rapinis nihil reliqui fecerant.

XXIX. Ea quum Ciceroni nunciarentur, ancipiti malo permotus, quod neque urbem ab insidiis privato consilio longius tueri poterat, neque exercitus Manlii quantus, aut quo consilio foret, satis compertum habebat, rem ad senatum refert, jam antea vulgi rumoribus exagitatam. Itaque, quod plerumque in atroci negotio solet, senatus decrevit DARENT OPERAM CONSULES NE QUID RESPUBLICA DETRIMENTI CAPERET. Ea potestas per senatum, more Romano, magistratui maxima permittitur; exercitum parare, bellum gerere, coercere omnibus modis socios atque cives; domi militiaeque imperium atque judicium summum habere: aliter, sine populi jussu, nullius earum rerum consuli jus est.

XXX. Post paucos dies L. Saenius senator in senatu litteras recitavit, quas Faesulis adlatas sibi dicebat; in quibus scriptum erat, C. Manlium arma cepisse, cum magna multitudine, ante diem VI. Kalendas Novembres. Simul, id quod in tali re solet, alii portenta atque prodigia nunciabant; alii conventus fieri, arma portari, Capuae atque in Apulia servile bellum moveri. Igitur senati decreto Q. Marcius Rex Faesulas, Q. Metellus Creticus in Apuliam circumque ea loca missi: hi utrique ad urbem imperatores erant, impediti ne triumpharent calumniā paucorum, quibus omnia honesta atque inhonesta vendere mos erat. Sed praetores Q. Pompeius Rufus Capuam, Q. Metellus Celer in agrum Picenum; hisque permissum, "uti pro tempore atque periculo exercitum compararent." Ad hoc, "si quis indicavisset de conjuratione, quae contra rem publicam facta erat, praemium servo libertatem et sestertia centum; libero impunitatem ejus rei, et sestertia ducenta;" itemque decrevere, "uti gladiatoriae familiae Capuam et in cetera municipia distribuerentur pro cujusque opibus; Romae per totam urbem vigiliae haberentur, iisque minores magistratus praeessent."

XXXI. Quibus rebus permota civitas, atque immutata urbis facies erat; ex summa laetitia atque lascivia, quae diuturna quies pepererat, repente omnes tristitia invasit; festinare, trepidare; neque loco, nec homini cuiquam satis credere; neque bellum gerere neque pacem habere; suo quisque metu pericula metiri. Ad hoc mulieres, quibus reipublicae magnitudine belli timor insolitus incesserat, afflictare sese; manus supplices ad caelum tendere; miserari parvos liberos; rogitare; omnia pavere; superbia atque deliciis omissis, sibi patriaeque diffidere. At Catilinae crudelis animus eadem illa movebat, tametsi praesidia parabantur, et ipse lege Plautia interrogatus erat ab L. Paullo. Postremo dissimulandi caussa et ut sui expurgandi, sicuti jurgio lacessitus foret, in senatum venit. Tum M. Tullius consul, sive praesentiam ejus timens, seu ira commotus, orationem habuit luculentam atque utilem reipublicae, quam postea scriptam edidit. Sed ubi ille assedit, Catilina, ut erat paratus ad dissimulanda omnia, demisso vultu, voce supplici postulare, "Patres conscripti ne quid de se temere crederent; ea familia ortum, ita ab adolescentia vitam instituisse, ut omnia bona in spe haberet: ne existimarent, sibi patricio homini, cujus ipsius atque majorum plurima beneficia in plebem Romanam essent, perdita republica opus esse, cum eam servaret M. Tullius, inquilinus civis urbis Romae." Ad hoc maledicta alia cum adderet, obstrepere omnes, hostem atque parricidam vocare. Tum ille furibundus: "Quoniam quidem circumventus," inquit, "ab inimicis praeceps agor, incendium meum ruina restinguam."

XXXII. Dein se ex curia domum proripuit: ibi multa secum ipse volvens, quod neque insidiae consuli procedebant, et ab incendio intelligebat urbem vigiliis munitam, optimum factum credens exercitum augere, ac prius quam legiones scriberentur antecapere quae bello usui forent, nocte intempesta cum paucis in Manliana castra profectus est. Sed Cethego atque Lentulo, ceterisque quorum cognoverat promptam audaciam, mandat, quibus rebus possent, opes factionis confirment, insidias consuli maturent, caedem, incendia, aliaque belli facinora parent; sese prope diem cum magno exercitu ad urbem accessurum. Dum haec Romae geruntur, C. Manlius ex suo numero legatos ad Marcium Regem mittit, cum mandatis hujuscemodi:

XXXIII. "Deos hominesque testamur, imperator, nos arma neque contra patriam cepisse, neque quo periculum aliis faceremus, sed uti corpora nostra ab injuria tuta forent; qui miseri, egentes, violentia atque crudelitate feneratorum plerique patriae, sed omnes fama atque fortunis expertes sumus: neque cuiquam nostrum licuit more majorum lege uti, neque amisso patrimonio liberum corpus habere; tanta saevitia feneratorum atque praetoris fuit. Saepe majores vestrum, miseriti plebis Romanae, decretis suis inopiae opitulati sunt; ac novissime memoria nostra, propter magnitudinem aeris alieni, volentibus omnibus bonis argentum aere solutum est. Saepe ipsa plebes aut dominandi studio permota, aut superbia magistratuum, armata a patribus secessit. At nos non imperium neque divitias petimus, quarum rerum caussa bella atque certamina omnia inter mortales sunt, sed libertatem, quam nemo bonus nisi cum anima simul amittit. Te atque senatum obtestamur, consulatis miseris civibus; legis praesidium, quod iniquitas praetoris eripuit, restituatis; neve eam nobis necessitudinem imponatis, ut quaeramus quonam modo ulti maxime sanguinem nostrum pereamus."

XXXIV. Ad haec Q. Marcius: "Si quid ab senatu petere vellent ab armis discedant, Romam supplices proficiscantur; ea mansuetudine atque misericordia senatum populumque Romanum semper fuisse, ut nemo unquam ab eo frustra auxilium petiverit." At Catilina ex itinere plerisque consularibus, praeterea optimo cuique litteras mittit: "Se falsis criminibus circumventum, quoniam factioni inimicorum resistere nequiverit, fortunae cedere, Massiliam in exilium proficisci; non quo sibi tanti sceleris conscius esset, sed uti respublica quieta foret, neve ex sua contentione seditio oriretur." Ab his longe diversas litteras Q. Catulus in senatu recitavit, quas sibi nomine Catilinae redditas dicebat: earum exemplum infra scriptum:

XXXV. "L. Catilina Q. Catulo: Egregia tua fides, re cognita, gratam in magnis periculis fiduciam commendationi meae tribuit. Quamobrem defensionem in novo consilio non statui parare; satisfactionem ex nulla conscientia de culpa proponere decrevi, quam, me dius fidius, veram licet cognoscas. Injuriis contumeliisque concitatus, quod fructu laboris industriaeque meae privatus statum dignitatis non obtinebam, publicam miserorum caussam pro mea consuetudine suscepi; non quin aes alienum meis nominibus ex possessionibus solvere possem, cum et alienis nominibus liberalitas Orestillae suis filiaeque copiis persolveret, sed quod non dignos homines honore honestatos videbam, meque falsa suspicione alienatum sentiebam. Hoc nomine satis honestas pro meo casu spes reliquae dignitatis conservandae sum secutus. Plura quum scribere vellem, nunciatum est vim mihi parari. Nunc Orestillam commendo, tuaeque fidei trado: eam ab injuria defendas, per liberos tuos rogatus. Haveto."

XXXVI. Sed ipse, paucos dies commoratus apud C. Flaminium in agro Arretino, dum vicinitatem antea sollicitatam armis exornat, cum fascibus atque aliis imperii insignibus in castra ad Manlium contendit. Haec ubi Romae comperta sunt, senatus Catilinam et Manlium hostes judicat; ceterae multitudini diem statuit, ante quam sine fraude liceret ab armis discedere, praeter rerum capitalium condemnatis. Praeterea decernit, uti consules delectum habeant; Antonius cum exercitu Catilinam persequi maturet; Cicero urbi praesidio sit. Ea tempestate mihi imperium populi Romani multo maxime miserabile visum; cui quum ad occasum ab ortu solis omnia domita armis paterent, domi otium atque divitiae, quae prima mortales putant, adfluerent, fuere tamen cives qui seque remque publicam obstinatis animis perditum irent. Namque duobus senati decretis ex tanta multitudine neque praemio inductus conjurationem patefecerat, neque ex castris Catilinae quisquam omnium discesserat; tanta vis morbi, uti tabes, plerosque civium animos invaserat.

XXXVII. Neque solum illis alieua mens erat qui conscii conjurationis fuerant; sed omnino cuncta plebes, novarum rerum studio, Catilinae incepta probabat. Id adeo more suo videbatur facere. Nam semper in civitate quibus opes nullae sunt bonis invident, malos extollunt; vetera odere, nova exoptant; odio suarum rerum mutari omnia student; turba atque seditionibus sine cura aluntur, quoniam egestas facile habetur sine damno. Sed urbana plebes, ea vero praeceps ierat multis de caussis. Primum omnium, qui ubique probro atque petulantia maxime praestabant; item alii per dedecora patrimoniis amissis; postremo omnes quos flagitium aut facinus domo expulerat; hi Romam, sicuti in sentinam, confluxerant. Deinde multi memores Sullanae victoriae, quod ex gregariis militibus alios senatores videbant, alios ita divites uti regio victu atque cultu aetatem agerent, sibi quisque, si in armis forent, ex victoria talia sperabant. Praeterea, juventus quae in agris manuum mercede inopiam toleraverat, privatis atque publicis largitionibus excita, urbanum otium ingrato labori praetulerat; eos atque alios omnes malum publicum alebat. Quo minus mirandum est homines egentes, malis moribus, maxima spe, reipublicae juxta ac sibi consuluisse. Praeterea quorum victoria Sullae parentes proscripti, bona erepta, jus libertatis imminutum erat, haud sane alio animo belli eventum exspectabant. Ad hoc, quicumque aliarum atque senati partium erant, conturbari rempublicam quam minus valere ipsi malebant. Id adeo malum multos post annos in civitatem reverterat.

XXXVIII. Nam postquam Cn. Pompeio et M. Crasso consulibus, tribunicia potestas restituta est, homines adolescentes, summam potestatem nacti, quibus aetas animusque ferox erat, coepere senatum criminando plebem exagitare, dein largiendo atque pollicitando magis incendere ; ita ipsi clari potentesque fieri. Contra eos summa ope nitebatur pleraque nobilitas, senati specie pro sua magnitudine. Namque, uti paucis absolvam, per illa tempora quicumque rempublicam agitavere, honestis nominibus, alii, sicuti populi jura defenderent, pars, quo senati auctoritas maxima foret, bonum publicum simulantes, pro sua quisque potentia certabant : neque modestia, neque modus contentionis erat : utrique victoriam crudeliter excercebant.

XXXIX. Sed postquam Cn. Pompeius ad bellum maritimum atque Mithridaticum missus est, plebis opes imminutae, paucorum potentia crevit. Hi magistratus, provincias, aliaque omnia tenere ; ipsi innoxii, florentes, sine metu aetatem agere ; ceteros judiciis terrere, quo plebem in magistratu placidius tractarent. Sed ubi primum dubiis rebus novandi spes oblata est, vetus certamen animos eorum arrexit. Quodsi primo proelio Catilina superior aut aequa manu discessisset, profecto magna clades atque calamitas rempublicam oppressisset; neque illis, qui victoriam adepti forent, diutius ea uti licuisset, quin defessis et exsanguibus qui plus posset imperium atque libertatem extorqueret. Fuere tamen extra conjurationem complures, qui ad Catilinam initio profecti sunt; in his A. Fulvius, senatoris filius, quem retractum ex itinere parens necari jussit. Iisdem temporibus Romae Lentulus, sicuti Catilina praeceperat, quoscumque moribus aut fortuna novis rebus idoneos credebat, aut per se, aut per alios sollicitabat; neque solum cives, sed cujusque modi genus hominum, quod modo bello usui foret.

XL. Igitur P. Umbreno cuidam negotium dat, uti legatos Allobrogum requirat, eosque, si possit, impellat ad societatem belli; existimans, publice privatimque aere alieno oppressos, praeterea quod natura gens Gallica bellicosa esset, facile eos ad tale consilium adduci posse. Umbrenus, quod in Gallia negotiatus erat, plerisque principibus civitatium notus erat, atque eos noverat; itaque sine mora, ubi primum legatos in foro conspexit, percunctatus pauca de statu civitatis et quasi dolens ejus casum requirere coepit, "quem exitum tantis malis sperarent?" Postquam illos videt "queri de avaritia magistratuum, accusare senatum, quod in eo auxilii nihil esset; miseriis suis remedium mortem exspectare:" "At ego," inquit, "vobis, si modo viri esse vultis, rationem ostendam qua tanta ista mala effugiatis." Haec ubi dixit, Allobroges in maximam spem adducti Umbrenum orare, uti sui misereretur; nihil tam asperum neque tam difficile esse, quod non cupidissime facturi essent, dum ea res civitatem aere alieno liberaret. Ille eos in domum

D. Bruti perducit, quod foro propinqua erat, neque aliena consilii propter Semproniam; nam tum Brutus ab Roma aberat. Praeterea Gabinium accersit, quo major auctoritas sermoni inesset: eo praesente conjurationem aperit; nominat socios, praeterea multos cujusque generis innoxios, quo legatis animus amplior esset; deinde eos pollicitos operam suam domum dimittit.

XLI. Sed Allobroges diu in incerto habuere, quidnam consilii caperent. In altera parte erat aes alienum, studium belli, magna merces in spe victoriae; at in altera majores opes, tuta consilia, pro incerta spe certa praemia. Haec illis volventibus tandem vicit fortuna reipublicae. Itaque Q. Fabio Sangae, cujus patrocinio civitas plurimum utebatur, rem omnem, uti cognoverant, aperiunt. Cicero, per Sangam consilio cognito, legatis praecepit, ut studium conjurationis vehementer simulent, ceteros adeant, bene polliceantur, dentque operam uti eos quam maxime manifestos habeant.

XLII. Iisdem fere temporibus in Gallia Citeriore atque Ulteriore, item in agro Piceno, Bruttio, Apulia motus erat. Namque illi, quos antea Catilina dimiserat, inconsulte ac veluti per dementiam cuncta simul agebant; nocturnis consiliis, armorum atque telorum portationibus, festinando, agitando omnia plus timoris quam periculi effecerant. Ex eo numero complures Q. Metellus Celer praetor ex senati consulto, caussa cognita, in vincula conjecerat; item in Ulteriore Gallia C. Murena, qui ei provinciae legatus praeerat.

XLIII. At Romae Lentulus cum ceteris, qui

principes conjurationis erant, paratis, ut videbantur, magnis copiis, constituerant uti, quum Catilina in agrum Faesulanum cum exercitu venisset, L. Bestia tribunus plebis concione habita quereretur de actionibus Ciceronis, bellique gravissimi invidiam optimo consuli imponeret; eo signo proxima nocte cetera multitudo conjurationis suum quisque negotium exsequeretur. Sed ea divisa hoc modo dicebantur; Statilius et Gabinius uti cum magna manu duodecim simul opportuna loca urbis incenderent, quo tumultu facilior aditus ad consulem ceterosque, quibus insidiae parabantur, fieret; Cethegus Ciceronis januam obsideret, cum vi adgrederetur, alius autem alium; sed filii familiarum, quorum ex nobilitate maxima pars, parentes interficerent; simul, caede et incendio perculsis omnibus, ad Catilinam erumperent. Inter haec parata atque decreta Cethegus semper querebatur de ignavia sociorum; illos dubitando, et dies prolatando, magnas opportunitates corrumpere; facto, non consulto, in tali periculo opus esse; seque, si pauci adjuvarent, languentibus aliis, impetum in curiam facturum. Natura ferox, vehemens, manu promptus erat; maximum bonum in celeritate putabat.

XLIV. Sed Allobroges, ex praecepto Ciceronis, per Gabinium ceteros conveniunt; ab Lentulo, Cethego, Statilio, item Cassio, postulant jusjurandum, quod signatum ad cives perferant; aliter haud facile eos ad tantum negotium impelli posse. Ceteri nihil suspicantes dant: Cassius semet eo brevi venturum pollicetur, ac paullo ante legatos ex urbe proficiscitur. Lentulus cum his T. Volturcium quemdam, Crotoniensem, mittit, uti Allobroges prius quam domum pergerent cum Catilina, data et accepta fide, societatem confirmarent. Ipse Volturcio litteras ad Catilinam dat, quarum exemplum infra scriptum est : " Quis sim, ex eo quem ad te misi cognosces. Fac cogites in quanta calamitate sis, et memineris te virum esse; consideres, quid tuae rationes postulent; auxilium petas ab omnibus, etiam ab infimis." Ad hoc mandata verbis dat: "quum ab senatu hostis judicatus sit, quo consilio servitia repudiet? in urbe parata esse quae jusserit; ne cunctetur ipse propius accedere."

XLV. His rebus ita actis, constituta nocte qua proficiscerentur, Cicero per legatos cuncta edoctus L. Valerio Flacco et C. Pomptinio praetoribus imperat, uti in ponte Mulvio per insidias Allobrogum comitatus deprehendant; rem omnem aperit, cujus gratia mittebantur; cetera, uti facto opus sit, ita agant, permittit. Illi, homines militares, sine tumultu praesidiis collocatis, sicuti praeceptum erat, occulte pontem obsidunt. Postquam ad id loci legati cum Volturcio venere, et simul utrimque clamor exortus est, Galli, cito cognito consilio, sine mora praetoribus se tradunt. Volturcius primo, cohortatus ceteros, gladio se a multitudine defendit; deinde ubi a legatis desertus est, multa prius de salute sua Pomptinium obtestatus, quod ei notus erat, postremo timidus, ac vitae diffidens, veluti hostibus sese praetoribus dedit.

XLVI. Quibus rebus confectis omnia propere per nuncios consuli declarantur. At illum ingens cura atque laetitia simul occupavere. Nam laetabatur, intelligens conjuratione patefacta civitatem periculis ereptam esse : porro autem anxius erat, dubitans, in maximo scelere tantis civibus deprehensis, quid facto opus esset; poenam illorum sibi oneri, impunitatem perdendae reipublicae credebat. Igitur confirmato animo vocari ad sese jubet Lentulum, Cethegum, Statilium, Gabinium, item Q. Coeparium quemdam, Terracinensem, qui in Apuliam ad concitanda servitia proficisci parabat. Ceteri sine mora veniunt: Coeparius, paullo ante domo egressus, cognito indicio, ex urbe profugerat. Consul Lentulum, quod praetor erat, ipse manu tenens perducit; reliquos cum custodibus in aedem Concordiae venire jubet. Eo senatum advocat, magnaque frequentia ejus ordinis Volturcium cum legatis introducit; Flaccum praetorem scrinium cum litteris, quas a legatis acceperat, eodem adferre jubet.

XLVII. Volturcius interrogatus "de itinere, de litteris, postremo quid, aut qua de caussa, consilii habuisset?" primo fingere alia, dissimulare de conjuratione; post, ubi fide publica dicere jussus est, omnia uti gesta erant aperit, docetque, "se paucis ante diebus a Gabinio et Coepario socium adscitum nihil amplius scire quam legatos; tantummodo audire solitum ex Gabinio, P. Autronium, Servium Sullam, L. Vargunteium, multos praeterea in ea conjuratione esse." Eadem Galli fatentur; ac Lentulum dissimulantem coarguunt praeter litteras sermonibus, quos ille habere solitus erat: "ex libris Sibyllinis, regnum Romae tribus Corneliis portendi; Cinnam atque Sullam antea; se tertium esse, cui fatum foret urbis potiri; praeterea ab incenso Capitolio illum esse vigesimum annum, quem saepe ex prodigiis haruspices respondissent bello civili cruentum fore." Igitur perlectis litteris, quum prius omnes signa sua cognovissent, senatus decernit, "uti abdicato magistratu Lentulus, item ceteri in liberis custodiis haberentur." Itaque Lentulus P. Lentulo Spintheri, qui tum aedilis erat, Cethegus Q. Cornificio, Statilius C. Caesari, Gabinius M. Crasso, Coeparius, nam is paullo ante ex fuga retractus erat, Cn. Terentio senatori traduntur.

XLVIII. Interea plebes, conjuratione patefacta, quae primo cupida rerum novarum nimis bello favebat, mutata mente Catilinae consilia exsecrari, Ciceronem ad caelum tollere; veluti ex servitute erepta, gaudium atque laetitiam agitabat. Namque alia belli facinora praedae magis quam detrimento fore; incendium vero crudele, immoderatum, ac sibi maxime calamitosum putabat; quippe cui omnes copiae in usu quotidiano et cultu corporis erant. Post eum diem quidam L. Tarquinius ad senatum adductus erat, quem ad Catilinam proficiscentem ex itinere retractum aiebant. Is cum se diceret indicaturum de conjuratione, si fides publica data esset, jussus a consule quae sciret edicere, eadem fere quae Volturcius de paratis incendiis, de caede bonorum, de itinere hostium senatum edocet: praeterea "se missum a M. Crasso, qui Catilinae nunciaret, ne eum Lentulus et Cethegus aliique ex conjuratione deprehensi terrerent, eoque magis properaret ad urbem accedere, quo et ceterorum animos reficeret, et illi facilius e periculo eriperentur." Sed ubi Tarquinius Crassum nominavit, hominem nobilem maximis divitiis, summa potentia, alii rem incredibilem rati, pars, tamen etsi verum existimabant, tamen quia in tali tempore tanta vis hominis lenienda quam exagitanda videbatur, plerique Crasso ex negotiis privatis obnoxii, conclamant, "indicem falsum," deque ea re postulant uti referatur. Itaque consulente Cicerone frequens senatus decernit: "Tarquinii indicium falsum videri; cumque in vinculis retinendum, neque amplius potestatem faciendam, nisi de eo iudicaret, cujus consilio tantam rem mentitus esset." Erant eo tempore qui existimarent illud a P. Autronio machinatum, quo facilius, appellato Crasso, per societatem periculi reliquos illius potentia tegeret. Alii Tarquinium a Cicerone immissum aiebant, ne Crassus more suo suscepto malorum patrocinio, rempublicam conturbaret. Ipsum Crassum ego postea praedicantem audivi, tantam illam contumeliam sibi ab Cicerone impositam.

XLIX. Sed iisdem temporibus Q. Catulus et C. Piso neque gratia, neque precibus, neque pretio Ciceronem impellere potuere, uti per Allobroges aut per alium indicem C. Caesar falso nominaretur. Nam uterque cum illo graves inimicitias exercebant; Piso oppugnatus in judicio repetundarum, propter cujusdam Transpadani supplicium injustum; Catulus ex petitione pontificatus odio incensus, quod extrema aetate, maximis honoribus usus, ab adolescentulo Caesare victus discesserat. Res autem opportuna videbatur, quod, privatim egregia liberalitate, publice maximis muneribus grandem pecuniam debebat. Sed ubi consulem ad tantum facinus impellere nequeunt, ipsi singulatim circumeundo, atque ementiendo quae se ex Volturcio aut Allobrogibus audisse dicerent, magnam illi invidiam conflaverant; usque adeo, ut nonnulli equites Romani, qui praesidii caussa cum telis erant circum aedem Concordiae, seu periculi magnitudine, seu animi nobilitate impulsi, quo studium suum in rempublicam clarius esset, egredienti ex senatu Caesari gladio minitarentur.

L. Dum haec in senatu aguntur, et dum legatis Allobrogum et Tito Volturcio, comprobato eorum indicio, praemia decernuntur, liberti et pauci ex clientibus Lentuli, diversis itineribus, opifices atque servitia in vicis ad eum eripiendum sollicitabant, partim exquirebant duces multitudinum, qui pretio rempublicam vexare soliti erant. Cethegus autem, per nuncios, familiam atque libertos suos, lectos et exercitatos in audaciam, orabat, ut grege facto cum telis ad sese irrumperent. Consul ubi ea parari cognovit, dispositis praesidiis ut res atque tempus monebat, convocato senatu refert, "quid de his fieri placeat, qui in custodiam traditi erant." Sed eos paullo ante frequens senatus judicaverat, "contra rempublicam fecisse." Tum D. Junius Silanus, primus sententiam rogatus, quod eo tempore consul designatus erat, de his qui in custodiis tenebantur, praeterea de L. Cassio, P. Furio, P. Umbreno, Q. Annio, si deprehensi forent, supplicium sumendum decreverat; isque postea, permotus oratione C. Caesaris, pedibus in sententiam Tib. Neronis iturum se dixerat; quod de ea re, praesidiis additis, referendum censuerat. Sed Caesar, ubi ad eum ventum est, rogatus sententiam a consule hujuscemodi verba locutus est:

LI. "Omnes homines, Patres conscripti, qui de rebus dubiis consultant, ab odio, amicitia, ira atque misericordia vacuos esse decet. Haud facile animus verum providet ubi illa obficiunt; neque quisquam omnium lubidini simul et usui paruit. Ubi intenderis ingenium, valet: si lubido possidet, ea dominatur, animus nihil valet. Magna mihi copia est memorandi, Patres conscripti, qui reges atque populi ira aut misericordia impulsi male consuluerint; sed ea malo dicere, quae majores nostri contra lubidinem animi recte atque ordine fecere. Bello Macedonico quod cum rege Perse gessimus Rhodiorum civitas, magna atque magnifica, quae populi Romani opibus creverat, infida atque adversa nobis fuit; sed postquam, bello confecto, de Rhodiis consultum est, majores nostri, ne quis divitiarum magis quam injuriae caussa bellum inceptum diceret, impunitos eos dimisere. Item bellis Punicis omnibus, quum saepe Carthaginienses et in pace et per inducias multa nefaria facinora fecissent, nunquam ipsi per occasionem talia fecere; magis, quid se dignum foret, quam quid in illis jure fieri posset quaerebant. Hoc idem providendum est, Patres conscripti, ne plus valeat apud vos P. Lentuli et ceterorum scelus, quam vestra dignitas; neu magis irae vestrae quam famae consulatis. Nam si digna poena pro factis eorum reperitur, novum consilium approbo; sin magnitudo sceleris omnium ingenia exsuperat, his utendum censeo quae legibus comparata sunt. Plerique eorum, qui ante me sententias dixerunt, composite atque magnifice casum reipublicae miserati sunt; quae belli saevitia esset, quae victis acciderent, enumeravere; rapi virgines, pueros; divelli liberos a parentum complexu; matres familiarum pati quae victoribus collibuissent; fana atque domos exspoliari; caedem, incendia fieri; postremo, armis, cadaveribus, cruore atque luctu omnia compleri. Sed per deos immortales! quo illa oratio pertinuit? an, uti vos infestos conjurationi faceret?

Scilicet quem res tanta atque tam atrox non permovit, eum oratio accendet! Non ita est: neque cuiquam mortalium injuriae suae parvae videntur: multi eas gravius aequo habuere. Sed alia aliis licentia est, Patres conscripti. Qui demissi in obscuro vitam habent, si quid iracundia deliquere, pauci sciunt; fama atque fortuna eorum pares sunt; qui magno imperio praediti in excelso aetatem habent, eorum facta cuncti mortales novere. Ita in maxima fortuna minima licentia est; neque studere, neque odisse, sed minime irasci decet; quae apud alios iracundia dicitur, in imperio superbia atque crudelitas appellatur. Equidem ego sic existimo, Patres conscripti, omnes cruciatus minores quam facinora illorum esse; sed plerique mortales postrema meminere, et in hominibus impiis sceleris obliti de poena disserunt, si ea paullo severior fuit. D. Silanum virum fortem atque strenuum certo scio quae dixerit studio reipublicae dixisse, neque illum in tanta re gratiam aut inimicitias exercere; eos mores, eam modestiam viri cognovi. Verum sententia non mihi crudelis, quid enim in tales homines crudele fieri potest? sed aliena a republica nostra videtur. Nam profecto aut metus aut injuria te subegit, Silane, consulem designatum, genus poenae novum decernere. De timore supervacaneum est disserere, quum praesertim diligentia clarissimi viri, consulis, tanta praesidia sint in armis. De poena possumus equidem dicere, id quod res habet, in luctu atque miseriis mortem aerumnarum requiem, non cruciatum esse; eam cuncta mortalium mala dissolvere; ultra neque curae neque gaudio locum esse. Sed, per deos immortales! quamobrem in sententiam non addidisti, uti prius verberibus in eos animadverteretur? An, quia lex Porcia vetat? at aliae leges item condemnatis civibus animam non eripi, sed in exilium permitti jubent. An, quia gravius est verberari quam necari? quid autem acerbum, aut grave nimis in homines tanti facinoris convictos? Sin, quia levius? qui convenit in minore negotio legem timere, quum eam in majore neglexeris? At enim quis reprehendet, quod in parricidas reipublicae decretum erit? Tempus, dies, fortuna, cujus lubido gentibus moderatur. Illis merito accidet, quidquid evenerit: ceterum vos, Patres conscripti, quid in alios statuatis, considerate. Omnia mala exempla ex bonis orta sunt; sed, ubi imperium ad ignaros, aut minus bonos pervenit, novum illud exemplum ab dignis et idoneis ad indignos et non idoneos transfertur. Lacedaemonii devictis Atheniensibus triginta viros imposuere, qui rempublicam eorum tractarent. Hi primo coepere pessimum quemque et omnibus invisum indemnatum necare: ea populus laetari et merito dicere fieri. Post, ubi paullatim licentia crevit, juxta bonos et malos lubidinose interficere, ceteros metu terrere. Ita civitas servitute oppressa stultae laetitiae graves poenas dedit. Nostra memoria victor Sulla quum Damasippum et alios hujusmodi, qui malo reipublicae creverant, jugulari jussit, quis non factum ejus laudabat? homines scelestos, factiosos, qui seditionibus rempublicam exagitaverant, merito necatos aiebant. Sed ea res magnae initium cladis fuit. Nam uti quisque domum aut villam, postremo aut vas aut vestimentum alicujus concupiverat, dabat operam, uti in proscriptorum numero esset. Ita illi, quibus Damasippi mors laetitiae fuerat, post paullo ipsi trahebantur; neque prius finis jugulandi fuit, quam Sulla omnes suos divitiis explevit. Atque ego haec non in M. Tullio, neque his temporibus, vereor: sed in magna civitate multa et varia ingenia sunt. Potest alio tempore, alio consule, cui item exercitus in manu sit, falsum aliquid pro vero credi; ubi hoc exemplo per senati decretum consul gladium eduxerit, quis finem statuet, aut quis moderabitur? Majores nostri, Patres conscripti, neque consilii neque audaciae unquam eguere; neque illis superbia obstabat, quo minus aliena instituta, si modo proba erant, imitarentur. Arma atque tela militaria ab Samnitibus, insignia magistratuum ab Tuscis pleraque sumpserunt; postremo quod ubique apud socios aut hostes idoneum videbatur, cum summo studio domi exsequebantur; imitari quam invidere bonis malebant. Sed eodem illo tempore, Graeciae morem imitati, verberibus animadvertebant in cives, de condemnatis summum supplicium sumebant. Postquam respublica adolevit, et multitudine civium factiones valuere, circumveniri innocentes, alia hujuscemodi fieri coepere; tum lex Porcia aliaeque leges paratae sunt, quibus legibus exilium damnatis permissum est. Hanc ego caussam, Patres conscripti, quo minus novum consilium capiamus in primis magnam puto. Profecto virtus atque sapientia major in illis fuit, qui ex parvis opibus tantum imperium fecere, quam in nobis, qui ea bene parta vix retinemus. Placet igitur, eos dimitti, et augeri exercitum Catilinae? minime; sed ita censeo: publicandas eorum pecunias, ipsos in vinculis habendos per municipia quae maxime opibus valent; neu quis de his postea ad senatum referat, neve cum populo agat; qui aliter fecerit, senatum existimare, eum contra rempublicam et salutem omnium facturum."

LII. Postquam Caesar dicendi finem fecit, ceteri verbo alius alii varie adsentiebantur; at M. Porcius Cato, rogatus sententiam, hujuscemodi orationem habuit: "Longe mihi alia mens est, Patres conscripti, quum res atque pericula nostra considero, et quum sententias nonnullorum mecum ipse reputo. Illi mihi disseruisse videntur de poena eorum, qui patriae, parentibus, aris atque focis suis bellum paravere: res autem monet, cavere ab illis, quam, quid in illis statuamus, consultare. Nam cetera maleficia tum persequare, ubi facta sunt; hoc nisi provideris ne accidat, ubi evenit frustra judicia implores; capta urbe nihil fit reliqui victis. Sed, per deos immortales! vos ego appello, qui semper domos, villas, signa, tabulas vestras pluris quam rempublicam fecistis: si ista, cujuscumque modi sunt, quae amplexamini, retinere, si voluptatibus vestris otium praebere vultis, expergiscimini aliquando, et capessite rempublicam. Non agitur de vectigalibus, neque de sociorum injuriis: libertas et anima nostra in dubio est. Saepenumero, Patres conscripti, multa verba in hoc ordine feci; saepe de luxuria atque avaritia nostrorum civium questus sum, multosque mortales ea caussa adversos habeo. Qui mihi atque animo meo nullius unquam delicti gratiam fecissem, haud facile alterius lubidini malefacta condonabam. Sed, ea tametsi vos parvi pendebatis, tamen respublica firma erat; opulentia negligentiam tolerabat. Nunc vero non id agitur, bonisne an malis moribus vivamus, neque quantum, aut quam magnificum imperium populi Romani sit, sed cujus haec cumque modi videntur, nostra, an nobiscum una hostium futura sint. Hic mihi quisquam mansuetudinem et misericordiam nominat. Jam pridem equidem nos vera rerum vocabula amisimus; quia bona aliena largiri, liberalitas; malarum rerum audacia, fortitudo vocatur: eo respublica in extremo sita est. Sint sane, quoniam ita se mores habent, liberales ex sociorum fortunis, sint misericordes in furibus aerarii; ne illi sanguinem nostrum largiantur, et dum paucis sceleratis parcunt bonos omnes perditum eant. Bene et composite C. Caesar paullo ante in hoc ordine de vita et morte disseruit, credo, falsa existimans ea quae de inferis memorantur; diverso itinere malos a bonis loca tetra, inculta, foeda atque formidolosa habere. Itaque censuit "pecunias eorum publicandas, ipsos per municipia in custodiis habendos;" videlicet timens, ne, si Romae sint, aut a popularibus conjurationis aut a multitudine conducta, per vim eripiantur. Quasi vero mali atque scelesti tantummodo in urbe, et non per totam Italiam sint; aut non ibi plus possit audacia, ubi ad defendendum opes minores sunt. Quare vanum equidem hoc consilium est, si periculum ex illis metuit: sin in tanto omnium metu solus non timet, eo magis refert me mihi atque vobis timere. Quare, quum de P. Lentulo ceterisque statuetis, pro certo habetote, vos simul de exercitu Catilinae et de omnibus conjuratis decernere. Quanto vos attentius ea agetis, tanto illis animus infirmior erit: si paullulum modo vos languere viderint, jam omnes feroces aderunt. Nolite existimare, majores nostros armis rempublicam ex parva magnam fecisse. Si ita res esset, multo pulcherrimam eam nos haberemus; quippe sociorum atque civium, praeterea armorum atque equorum, major nobis copia quam illis est. Sed alia fuere, quae illos magnos fecere, quae nobis nulla sunt; domi industria, foris justum imperium, animus in consulendo liber, neque delicto neque lubidini obnoxios. Pro his nos habemus luxuriam atque avaritiam; publice egestatem, privatim opulentiam; laudamus divitias, sequimur inertiam; inter bonos et malos discrimen nullum; omnia virtutis praemia ambitio possidet. Neque mirum; ubi vos separatim sibi quisque consilium capitis, ubi domi voluptatibus, hic pecuniae, aut gratiae servitis; eo fit, ut impetus fiat in vacuam rempublicam. Sed ego haec omitto. Conjuravere nobilissimi cives patriam incendere; Gallorum gentem infestissimam nomini Romano ad bellum accersunt; dux hostium supra caput est: vos cunctamini etiam nunc, quid intra moenia deprehensis hostibus faciatis? Misereamini censeo,—deliquere homines adolescentuli per ambitionem,—atque etiam armatos dimittatis. Nac ista vobis mansuetudo et misericordia, si illi arma ceperint, in miseriam vertet. Scilicet res ipsa aspera est; sed vos non timetis eam. Immo vero maxime; sed inertia et mollitia animi alius alium exspectantes cunctamini, dis immortalibus confisi, qui hanc rempublicam in maximis saepe periculis servavere. Non votis neque suppliciis muliebribus auxilia deorum parantur: vigilando, agendo, bene consulendo, prospera omnia cedunt: ubi secordiae te atque ignaviae tradideris, nequidquam deos implores; irati infestique sunt. Apud majores nostros T. Manlius Torquatus bello Gallico filium suum, quod is contra imperium in hostem pugnaverat, necari jussit; atque ille egregius adolescens immoderatae fortitudinis morte poenas dedit: vos de crudelissimis parricidis quid statuatis, cunctamini? Videlicet vita cetera eorum huic sceleri obstat. Verum parcite dignitati Lentuli, si ipse pudicitiae, si famae suae, si dis aut hominibus unquam ullis pepercit: ignoscite Cethegi adolescentiae, nisi iterum jam patriae bellum fecit. Nam quid ego de Gabinio, Statilio, Caepario loquar? Quibus si quidquam unquam pensi fuisset, non ea consilia de republica habuissent. Postremo, Patres conscripti, si mehercule peccato locus esset, facile paterer vos ipsa re corrigi, quoniam verba contemnitis; sed undique circumventi sumus. Catilina cum exercitu faucibus urget: alii intra moenia, in sinu urbis sunt hostes: neque parari, neque consuli quidquam occulte potest: quo magis properandum est. Quare ita ego censeo: quum nefario consilio sceleratorum civium respublica in maxima pericula venerit, hique indicio T. Volturcii et legatorum Allobrogum convicti confessique sint caedem, incendia, alia foeda atque crudelia facinora in cives patriamque paravisse, de confessis, sicuti de manifestis rerum capitalium, more majorum, supplicium sumendum."

LIII. Postquam Cato adsedit, consulares omnes itemque senatus magna pars sententiam ejus laudant, virtutem animi ad caelum ferunt; alii alios increpantes timidos vocant; Cato clarus atque magnus habetur; senati decretum fit, sicuti ille censuerat. Sed mihi multa legenti, multa audienti, quae populus Romanus domi militiaeque, mari atque terra praeclara facinora fecit, forte lubuit attendere, quae res maxime tanta negotia sustinuisset. Sciebam saepenumero parva manu cum magnis legionibus hostium contendisse; cognoveram, parvis copiis bella gesta cum opulentis regibus; ad hoc, saepe fortunae violentiam toleravisse; facundiâ Graecos, gloriâ belli Gallos ante Romanos fuisse. Ac mihi multa agitanti constabat, paucorum civium egregiam virtutem cuncta patravisse; eoque factum, uti divitias paupertas, multitudinem paucitas superaret. Sed postquam luxu atque desidia civitas corrupta est, rursus respublica magnitudine sua imperatorum atque magistratuum vitia sustentabat; ac, sicuti effeta aetate parentum, multis tempestatibus haud sane quisquam Romae virtute magnus fuit. Sed, memoria mea, ingenti virtute, diversis moribus fuere viri duo, M. Cato, et C. Caesar; quos, quoniam res obtulerat, silentio praeterire non fuit consilium, quin utriusque naturam et mores, quantum ingenio possem, aperirem.

LIV. Igitur his genus, aetas, eloquentia, prope aequalia fuere; magnitudo animi par, item gloria; sed alia alii. Caesar beneficiis ac munificentia magnus habebatur, integritate vitae Cato. Ille mansuetudine et misericordia clarus factus, huic severitas dignitatem addiderat. Caesar dando, sublevando, ignoscendo, Cato nihil largiendo gloriam adeptus. In altero miseris perfugium, in altero malis pernicies; illius facilitas, hujus constantia laudabatur. Postremo Caesar in animum induxerat laborare, vigilare; negotiis amicorum intentus, sua negligere, nihil denegare, quod dono dignum esset; sibi magnum imperium, exercitum, novum bellum exoptabat, ubi virtus enitescere posset. At Catoni studium modestiae, decoris, sed maxime severitatis erat. Non divitiis cum divite, neque factione cum factioso, sed cum strenuo virtute, cum modesto pudore, cum innocente abstinentia certabat; esse, quam videri, bonus malebat: ita, quo minus gloriam petebat, eo magis sequebatur.

LV. Postquam, ut dixi, senatus in Catonis sententiam discessit, consul optimum factum ratus noctem quae instabat antecapere, ne quid eo spatio novaretur, triumviros quae supplicium postulabat, parare jubet; ipse, dispositis praesidiis, Lentulum in carcerem deducit; idem fit ceteris per praetores. Est locus in carcere, quod Tullianum appellatur, ubi paullulum ascenderis ad laevam, circiter duodecim pedes humi depressus. Eum muniunt undique parietes, atque insuper camera, lapideis fornicibus vincta; sed incultu, tenebris, odore foeda atque terribilis ejus facies est. In eum locum postquam demissus est Lentulus, vindices rerum capitalium quibus praeceptum erat laqueo gulam fregere. Ita ille patricius ex clarissima gente Corneliorum, qui consulare imperium Romae habuerat, dignum moribus factisque suis exitium vitae invenit. De Cethego, Statilio, Gabinio, Caepario eodem modo supplicium sumptum est.

LVI. Dum ea Romae geruntur, Catilina ex omni copia, quam et ipse adduxerat et Manlius habuerat, duas legiones instituit, cohortes pro numero militum complet: deinde, ut quisque voluntarius aut ex sociis in castra venerat, aequaliter distribuerat, ac brevi spatio legiones numero hominum expleverat, quum initio non amplius duobus millibus habuisset. Sed ex omni copia circiter pars quarta erat militaribus armis instructa; ceteri, ut quemque casus armaverat, sparos aut lanceas, alii praeacutas sudes portabant. Sed, postquam Antonius cum exercitu adventabat, Catilina per montes iter facere, modo ad urbem, modo in Galliam versus castra movere; hostibus occasionem pugnandi non dare; sperabat prope diem magnas copias sese habiturum, si Romae socii incepta patravissent. Interea servitia repudiabat, cujus initio ad eum magnae copiae concurrebant, opibus conjurationis fretus; simul alienum suis rationibus existimans, videri caussam civium cum servis fugitivis communicavisse.

LVII. Sed postquam in castra nuncius pervenit Romae conjurationem patefactam, de Lentulo, Cethego, ceteris, quos supra memoravi, supplicium sumptum, plerique, quos ad bellum spes rapinarum aut novarum rerum studium illexerat, dilabuntur; reliquos Catilina per montes asperos magnis itineribus in agrum Pistoriensem abducit, eo consilio, uti per tramites occulte perfugeret in Galliam. At Q. Metellus Celer cum tribus legionibus in agro Piceno praesidebat, ex difficultate rerum eadem illa existimans, quae supra diximus, Catilinam agitare. Igitur ubi iter ejus ex perfugis cognovit, castra propere movit, ac sub ipsis radicibus montium consedit, qua illi descensus erat in Galliam properanti. Neque tamen Antonius procul aberat; utpote qui magno exercitu, locis aequioribus expeditus, in fuga sequeretur. Sed Catilina, postquam videt montibus atque copiis hostium sese clausum, in urbe res adversas, neque fugae neque praesidii ullam spem, optimum factum ratus in tali re fortunam belli tentare, statuit cum Antonio quamprimum confligere. Itaque concione advocata, hujuscemodi orationem habuit:

LVIII. "Compertum ego habeo, milites, verba

virtutem non addere, neque ex ignavo strenuum, neque
fortem ex timido exercitum oratione imperatoris fieri.
Quanta cujusque animo audacia natura aut moribus
inest, tanta in bello patere solet : quem neque gloria,
neque pericula excitant, nequidquam hortere ; timor
animi auribus obficit. Sed ego vos quo pauca monerem
advocavi ; simul uti caussam consilii aperirem. Scitis
equidem, milites, secordia atque ignavia Lentuli quan-
tam ipsi cladem nobisque attulerit ; quoque modo, dum
ex urbe praesidia opperior, in Galliam proficisci nequi-
verim. Nunc vero quo in loco res nostrae sint, juxta
mecum omnes intelligitis. Exercitus hostium duo,
unus ab urbe, alter a Gallia obstant : diutius in his
locis esse, si maxime animus ferat, frumenti atque aliarum rerum egestas prohibet. Quocumque ire placet,
ferro iter aperiendum est. Quapropter vos moneo, uti
forti atque parato animo sitis ; et quum proelium
inibitis memineritis vos divitias, decus, gloriam, praeterea libertatem atque patriam in dextris portare. Si
vincimus omnia nobis tuta erunt ; commeatus abunde.
coloniae atque municipia patebunt : sin metu cesseri-
mus eadem illa adversa fient ; neque locus, neque
amicus quisquam teget quem arma non texerint.
Praeterea, milites, non eadem nobis et illis necessitudo impendet : nos pro patria, pro libertate, pro vita
certamus ; illis supervacaneum est pugnare pro potentia paucorum. Quo audacius aggredimini, memores
pristinae virtutis! Licuit nobis cum summa turpi-
tudine in exilio aetatem agere ; potuistis nonnulli
Romae, amissis bonis, alienas opes exspectare. Quia
illa foeda atque intoleranda viris videbantur, haec
sequi decrevistis. Si haec relinquere vultis, audacia

opus est : nemo nisi victor pace bellum mutavit. Nam in fuga salutem sperare, quum arma, quibus corpus tegitur, ab hostibus averteris, ea vero dementia est. Semper in proelio iis maximum est periculum, qui maxime timent : audacia pro muro habetur. Quum vos considero, milites, et cum facta vestra aestimo, magna me spes victoriae tenet. Animus, aetas, virtus vestra me hortantur; praeterea necessitudo quae etiam timidos fortes facit. Nam multitudo hostium ne circumvenire queat, prohibent angustiae loci. Quod si virtuti vestrae fortuna inviderit, cavete inulti animam amittatis; neu capti potius sicuti pecora trucidemini, quam virorum more pugnantes cruentam atque luctuosam victoriam hostibus relinquatis."

LIX. Haec ubi dixit, paullulum commoratus, signa canere jubet, atque instructos ordines in locum aequum deducit; dein, remotis omnium equis, quo militibus exaequato periculo animus amplior esset, ipse pedes exercitum pro loco atque copiis instruit. Nam, uti planities erat inter sinistros montes et ab dextra rupes aspera, octo cohortes in fronte constituit; reliqua signa in subsidio arctius collocat. Ab his centuriones omnes lectos et evocatos, praeterea ex gregariis militibus optimum quemque armatum in primam aciem subducit. C. Manlium in dextera, Faesulanum quemdam in sinistra parte curare jubet; ipse tum libertis et colonis propter aquilam adsistit, quam bello Cimbrico C. Marius in exercitu habuisse dicebatur. At ex altera parte C. Antonius, pedibus aeger, quod proelio adesse nequibat M. Petreio legato exercitum permittit. Ille cohortes veteranas, quas tumulti caussa conscripserat, in fronte, post eas ceterum exercitum in subsidiis locat. Ipse equo circumiens unumquemque nominans appellat, hortatur, rogat, uti meminerint, se contra latrones inermes, pro patria, pro liberis, pro aris atque focis suis cernere. Homo militaris, quod amplius annos triginta tribunus, aut praefectus, aut legatus, aut praetor cum magna gloria fuerat, plerosque ipsos factaque eorum fortia noverat: ea commemorando militum animos accendebat.

LX. Sed ubi omnibus rebus exploratis Petreius tuba signum dat, cohortes paullatim incedere jubet; idem facit hostium exercitus. Postquam eo ventum est, unde a ferentariis proelium committi posset, maximo clamore cum infestis signis concurrunt; pila omittunt; gladiis res geritur. Veterani, pristinae virtutis memores, cominus acriter instare; illi haud timidi resistunt; maxima vi certatur. Interea Catilina cum expeditis in prima acie versari, laborantibus succurrere, integros pro sauciis accersere, omnia providere, multum ipse pugnare, saepe hostem ferire; strenui militis et boni imperatoris officia simul exsequebatur. Petreius ubi videt Catilinam, contra ac ratus erat, magna vi tendere, cohortem praetoriam in medios hostes inducit, eosque perturbatos atque alios alibi resistentes interficit; deinde utrimque ex lateribus aggreditur. Manlius et Faesulanus in primis pugnantes cadunt. Postquam fusas copias, seque cum paucis relictum videt Catilina, memor generis atque pristinae dignitatis, in confertissimos hostes incurrit, ibique pugnans confoditur.

LXI. Sed confecto proelio, tum vero cerneres, quanta audacia quantaque vis animi fuisset in exercitu Catilinae. Nam fere, quem quisque vivus pugnando locum ceperat, cum amissa anima corpore tegebat. Pauci autem, quos medios cohors praetoria disjecerat, paullo diversius, sed omnes tamen adversis vulneribus conciderant. Catilina vero longe a suis inter hostium cadavera repertus est, paullulum etiam spirans ferociamque animi, quam habuerat vivus, in vultu retinens. Postremo ex omni copia, neque in proelio neque in fuga quisquam civis ingenuus captus est; ita cuncti suae hostiumque vitae juxta pepercerant. Neque tamen exercitus populi Romani laetam aut incruentam victoriam adeptus erat; nam strenuissimus quisque aut occiderat in proelio, aut graviter vulneratus discesserat. Multi autem qui de castris visendi aut spoliandi gratia processerant, volventes hostilia cadavera, amicum alii, pars hospitem aut cognatum, reperiebant: fuere item, qui inimicos suos cognoscerent. Ita varie per omnem exercitum laetitia, moeror, luctus atque gaudia agitabantur.

NOTES.

CHAPTER I.

1. Omnes] The MSS. generally read *omnis*, and this in the age of Cicero and Sallust, according to the grammarians, was the usual orthography of the nom. and accus. plur. of nouns in *is*, gen. sing. not increasing gen. plur. in *ium*. Copyists frequently changed the termination to *es*, the later form, for the sake of clearness: in some instances they left *is*, mistaking it perhaps for a nom. or gen. sing. as *Catil.* 18. nonas Decembris, and 31. omnis tristitia invasit. Probably the usage always fluctuated. In this edition the later form in *es* is preserved throughout to obviate any difficulty in construction.

2. Sese student: i. q. simply student] This construction is not unusual with verbs of *wishing*, *seeking*, &c. Compare Cic. *de Off.* i. 19. principem se esse mavult quam videri; ii. 20. ille gratum se videri studet; for princeps, gratus videri. Corn. Nepos, *in Vit. Eumen.* 8. illa phalanx non parere se ducibus sed imperare postulabat. Compare another instance in Sallust, *Jug.* 14. vellem potius ob mea quam ob majorum meorum beneficia posse me a vobis auxilium petere. And again, *Catil.* 7. certamen...se quisque hostem ferire.

3. Ceteris animalibus] Ovid contrasts man with the other animals in similar language, *Metam.* i. 84:

> Pronaque cum spectent animalia caetera terram
> Os homini sublime dedit.

Sil. Ital. xv. 84:

> Nonne vides hominum ut celsos ad sidera vultus
> Sustulerit Deus, ac sublimia finxerit ora,
> Cum pecudes volucrumque genus formasque ferarum
> Segnem atque obscoenam passim stravisset in alvum?

Compare Persius, *Sat.* ii. 61:

> O curvae in terras animae et coelestium inanes.

Varro: Fabre compactum animal hominem quis ferat sic pecuatim ire? Seneca: Nemo usque adeo tardus et hebes et demissus in terram est, ut ad divina non erigatur. Juvenal, xv. 147. of animals, prona et terram spectantia.

4. Transeant] "Pass through life:" passively, as opposed to *agant vitam*, "transact, do the business of life." Seneca, *Epist.* 93. hoc a me exigo ne velut per tenebras aevum emetiar; ut agam vitam, non ut praetervehar. *De Prov.* 4. transisti sine adversario vitam. Pers. *Sat.* v. 60:

> Tum crassos transisse dies, lucemque palustrem,
> Et sibi jam seri vitam ingemuere relictam.

5. Ventri obedientia] Aurel. Victor, of the Emperor Claudius, ventri foede obediens : venter, the natural appetites. Persius, *Prol. in Sat.* 12. Magister artis ingenique largitor Venter.

6. Animi imperio] The soul is commonly represented as the ruler of the body. Comp. Cic. *de Rep.* iii. Deus homini, animus imperat corpori. Senec. *Nat. Quaest.* vii. 24. habere nos animum cujus imperio et impellimur et revocamur. *Epist.* 114. rex noster est animus. Claudian, *iv. Cons. Hon.* 234:

> hanc alta capitis fundavit in arce
> Mandatricem operum, prospecturamque labori.

7. Utimur] *Uti* generally in a good sense, to employ to a good purpose, to enjoy the use of. Here the verb belongs strictly to *imperio* only, but governs *servitio* also indirectly by the figure zeugma : i.e. "we enjoy the government of the soul, but suffer the servitude of the body." Comp. Lucan, ii. 131 :

> Ille fuit vitae Mario modus, omnia passo
> Quae pejor fortuna potest, atque omnibus uso
> Quae melior.

8. Quo mihi rectius videtur] "Wherefore it seems to me the more right." Or more exactly, "so much the more right does it seem to me." Comp. eo profusius, c. 13.

9. Ingenii] Varro, contemporary with Sallust, introduced the double *ii* in these genitives. Later writers, imitating ancient spelling, frequently resorted to the single *i*. Hence the MSS. fluctuate. See Spengel on Varro, *de Lingua Lat.* p. 10. In this edition the double *ii* is preserved throughout, as the usual form.

10. Opibus] "Resources." *Vires* semper apud Sall. sunt corporis vires. Dietsch.

11. Maxime] Caesar wrote *maximus*, *optimus*. Quintil. *Inst.* i. 7. Before him the *u* was commonly written, but not always: *maximos* is found in the inscription of the Duilian column. In this edition the form in *i* is retained.

12. Nam divitiarum] Compare Sallust, *Jugur.* 2. igitur praeclara facies, magnae divitiae, ad hoc vis corporis et alia hujusmodi omnia alicui dilabuntur; at ingenii egregia facinora, sicuti anima, immortalia sunt. Cf. Tac. *Agric.* 46.

NOTES. 51

13. Fluxa] "Fleeting," "fading;" *fluidus*, that which fleets or flows naturally; *fluxus*, that which becomes so by corruption or degeneracy, therefore generally of artificial things: but this distinction is not uniformly preserved. Here translate "fading," or "evanescent," as opposed to *clara*. "Beauty fades and decays, virtue shines and endures."

14. Habetur] Not "is esteemed," as implying men's opinion of it, but in its more proper sense: "virtue is a noble and eternal possession." So again *Catil.* 58. audacia pro muro habetur. Sallust often gives this force to the active also, as *Jugur.* 94. toto die intentos praelio Numidas habuerat. Dietsch.

15. Inter mortales] More emphatic, as being more universal, than *homines*; as we say *mankind* for *men*. Comp. A. Gellius, xiii. 28. who gives a whole chapter to the consideration of these words, taking for his text an expression of the old writer Claudius Quadrigarius; concione dimissa Metellus in Capitolium venit cum mortalibus multis; inde domum proficiscitur; tota civitas eum reduxit.

16. Procederet] "Advanced, succeeded;" *procedere*, i. q. ex voto evenire. Comp. Liv. i. 57. ubi id parum processit. ii. 44. velut processisset Sp. Licinio. Of persons, as Terent. *Adelph.* v. 9. 22. processisti hodie pulchre. Plaut. *Trucul.* ii. 6. 35. tu recte provenisti. Another sense of the word is "to march," "walk in a solemn or measured step." Terent. *Andr.* i. 1. 100. funus procedit. Lucan, speaking of the conquering progress of the Roman republic, vii. 422. Te geminum Titan procedere vidit in axem. *Incedere* has the sense, Virg. *Aen.* i. 50. quae Divum incedo regina.

17. Mature facto opus est] "'Twere well it were done quickly." *Maturus* and *mora* opposed, Ovid, *Metam.* xiii. 300. Si mora pro culpa est, ego sum maturior illo.

18. Alterum alterius auxilio eget] Horat. alterius sic Altera poscit opem res. *Indigens...eget.* This tautology has given offence: many editions read *veget*, but without authority. *Indigens* may be taken absolutely for *mancum*, *debile*.

CHAPTER II.

1. Igitur] This particle is placed first in a sentence by Sallust, except in interrogation, but generally later by Cicero and subsequent writers. Sallust is said to use it seventy five times, *itaque* seventy seven, and *ergo* four times only. Dietsch.

4—2

2. **Initio**] Comp. Cic. *de Leg.* iii. omnes antiquae gentes regibus quondam paruerunt.

3. **Reges diversi**] i. e. *in contrarium abeuntes,* "taking opposite courses."

4. **Etiam tum**] "Still;" "in those times men still lived without ambition."

5. **Periculo atque negotiis**] Some explain *periculo* i. q. *experimento, experiendo.* Others explain the phrase by the fig. hendiadys, for *periculosis negotiis.* Rather, *periculo,* "danger;" *negotiis,* "grave and difficult affairs;" therefore, "dangers and troubles."

6. **Quodsi**] *Quod* is not pronominal (i. q. *propter quod*), but merely marks a transition, "but:" quodsi, in conjunction, "but if."

7. **Animi virtus**] "The courage of kings and captains."

8. **Artibus**] i. q. *studiis,* "means," "methods," or "habits of acting," or i. q. *moribus,* "dispositions." The word is commonly used by Sallust in these senses. Comp. *Catil.* 3. insolens malarum artium: *Jugur.* 82. vir egregius in aliis artibus.

9. **Invasere**] Absolute; as *Catil.* 10. *Jugur.* 41. Liv. v. 13. dulcedo invasit plebeios creandi.

10. **Quae homines etc.**] scil. *omnia quae homines faciunt arando, navigando, aedificando,* "men's ploughing, sailing, building," *parent,* i. q. *ex virtute pendent,* "all depend upon the exercise of their energies, moral and physical." Comp. Hor. *Sat.* ii. 3. 94. omnis enim res Virtus, fama, decus, divina humanaque pulcris Divitiis parent.

11. **Transegere**] Or *transiere,* for which there is also good authority, and which seems to consort better with *peregrinantes.*

12. **Contra naturam**] "The reverse of what nature intended."

13. **Juxta aestimo**] "I value both alike," i. e. "as equally despicable." For *juxta* in the sense of equality, comp. Sallust, *Catil.* 37. 51. 61. *Jugur.* 85. 88. Generally of two things connected with the copula; but otherwise *Catil.* 58.

14. **Verum enim vero**] More forcible than the simple *verum:* frequent in Livy and Sallust, more rare in Cicero. Ruhnken, *Dictata in Terent. Adelph.* ii. 3. 2.

15. **Is demum**] "He of all men." Comp. *Catil.* 20. idem velle atque idem nolle ea demum firma amicitia est.

16. **Aliquo...intentus**] Not "intent upon," which would

require the *dat.*, but "occupied with," "kept on the stretch by:" the *ablat. modi*, or *instrumenti*. Comp. *scientia confisus*, "satisfied with, encouraged by the consciousness of knowledge:" *pede nixus*, "using the foot as the means or instrument whereby to support oneself."

CHAPTER III.

1. **Bene facere reip.**] "To act for the advantage of the state." Comp. *Jugur.* 85. quippe bene facta mea reipublicae procedunt.

2. **Haud absurdum**] "No mean thing;" "not unworthy:" Tacitus uses the word to express his contempt for the Jewish rites: Judaeorum mos absurdus sordidusque, *Hist.* v. 5. *absurdus*, not derived probably from *surdus*. Festus cites a word *sardare*, *intelligere*, from Naevius. So *insulsus* from *salsus*, *insulto* from *salto*.

3. **Multi**] Placed towards the end of the sentence, *emphasis gratia;* "many such, I say."

4. **Haudquaquam par gloria**] So Cicero *pro Mur.* 9. dicendum est quod sentio, rei militaris virtus praestat ceteris omnibus.

5. **Auctorem**] "The doer of deeds," i. q. *actorem*. So Vell. ii. 10. praeclari facinoris auctor. Virgil, *Aen.* v. 748. vulneris auctor. But *auctor rerum* frequently i. q. *scriptor rerum*. Comp. Tac. *Ann.* iii. 30. C. Sallustius rerum Rom. florentissimus auctor: and, apud auctores rerum reperio. Modern editors read *actorem*. The contrast between the *writer* and the *doer* may be traced to Homer. *Iliad* 9. 443.

μύθων τε ῥητῆρ' ἔμεναι πρηκτῆρά τε ἔργων.

6. **Arduum**] So Justin, *in praef.* calls writing history, opus ardui laboris.

7. **Facta dictis exaequanda**] So Livy, vi. 20. facta dictis aequando: the difficulty consists in writing worthily of noble actions. Pliny, *Ep.* viii. 4. una sed maxima difficultas quod haec aequare dicendo arduum.

8. **Ubi de magna virtute**, etc.] The sentiment is directly imitated from Thucyd. ii. 35. (the funeral speech of Pericles): χαλεπὸν γὰρ τὸ μετρίως εἰπεῖν κ. τ. λ.

9. **Aequo animo accipit**] "Acquiesces in."

10. **Supra ea**] i. e. *quae quisque supra ea putat*.

11. **Studio latus sum**] "I applied myself earnestly to public affairs:" *studio* i. q. *amore, cupidine*. Comp. Sall. *Fr.*

Hist. iii. 11. ad bellum majore studio quam consilio profectus. So *odio, iracundia, avaritia ferri*.

12. Insolens malarum artium] "Unaccustomed to evil practices."

13. Eadem qua ceteros, etc.] "The pursuit of public honours subjected me to the same abuse and envy as the rest of my competitors." *Fama* in the sense of *mala fama*, whence *famosus*, "infamous."

CHAPTER IV.

1. Ex multis] "From and after many troubles, etc." Comp. Cic. *pro Arch.* 1. ex gravi morbo recreari, *Brut.* 92. ex consulatu profectus in Galliam. Nepos, *Timol.* 3. ex maximo bello otium conciliavit.

2. Habendam] *Habere aetatem*, "to keep a certain tenor of life." Comp. *Catil.* 51. qui demissi in obscuro vitam habent.

3. Decrevi] Comp. *Jugur.* 4. decrevi procul a republ. agere aetatem.

4. Servilibus officiis] "Unworthy employments," fit only for slaves, inasmuch as they occupy the body only, not the mind. The great estates of the nobles at this time were generally cultivated and even superintended by slaves.

5. Ambitio mala] i.e. *quae malum affert*, or, *malos facit*. So Horace, *Sat.* i. 6. 129. misera ambitio, i.e. quae miseros reddit. Mala pugna (*Jugur.* 56), an unsuccessful engagement.

6. Carptim] "Piecemeal;" "to write the history of Rome in monographs." Comp. Plin. *Ep.* vi. 22. ego carptim et κατὰ κεφάλαια. Tac. *Hist.* iv. 46. dimissi carptim ac singuli.

7. Absolvam] scil. *narrationem*, "I will execute a narrative:" or more generally, "I will discuss," i.q. agam, disseram. Comp. Ammian. Marc. xxiii. 6. locorum situm, quantum ratio sinit, absolvam.

8. Prius...quam...faciam] The conjunctive unusual. *Jugur.* 5. priusquam initium expedio. It implies more hesitation: "before I think of beginning." Cic. *de Orat.* 1. 39. tragoedi quotidie, antequam pronuncient, vocem sensim excitant.

CHAPTER V.

1. Catilina] This cognomen is connected with the words *catillus*, "a dish;" *catillo*, "one who licks dishes;" and may be a cant term for a pilferer.

2. Nobili genere] The *gens Sergia*, a patrician house

which claimed Trojan descent. Accordingly Virgil introduces a Sergestus in company with Aeneas, *Aen.* v. 121. Sergestusque, domus tenet a quo Sergia nomen. The name occurs in the *Fasti* from the year A.C. 303. There exists a coin of M. Sergius, with the cognomen Silus. One of this gens was distinguished for his valour in the war with Hannibal. Pliny, *Hist. Nat.* vii. 29. M. Sergio, ut quidem arbitror, nemo quenquam hominum jure praetulerit, licet pronepos Catilinae gratiam nomini deroget. Secundo stipendio dexteram manum perdidit, stipendiisque duobus ter et vicies vulneratus est...sinistra manu sola quater pugnavit,...dextram sibi ferream fecit, eaque alligata praeliatus, etc. Pliny mentions another Sergius, with the cognomen Orata, *Hist. Nat.* ix. 79. ostrearum vivaria primus omnium invenit Sergius Orata in Baiano, aetate L. Crassi oratoris, ante Marsicum bellum ; nec gulae causa sed avaritiae, magna vectigalia tali ex ingenio suo percipiens...is primus omnium saporem ostreis Lucrinis adjudicavit. It seems not unlikely that the nickname Catilina may have been given him on this account.

3. **Malo pravoque**] *Malus*, bad in essence, *pravus*, bad in form. Hence pravus, i. q. curvus, deformis, perversus: opposed to rectus. Hor. *Sat.* ii. 3. 87. Sive ego prave seu recte hoc volui. Hence *malus*, bad in morals, *pravus*, perverse in judgment. Doederlein, *Synon.* i. 60.

4. **Ibi**] scil. *iis rebus.* Comp. *Catil.* 20. divitiae apud illos sunt, ubi (sc. apud quos) illi volunt.

5. **Corpus patiens**] Comp. Cicero, *in Catil.* i. 10. praeclaram tuam patientiam famis, frigoris, inopiae rerum omnium : and ii. 5. iii. 7. Comp. further the character of Catiline given by Cicero, *pro Caelio*, 6. illa vero in homine mirabilia fuerunt ...versare suam naturam, et regere ad tempus, atque huc et illuc torquere et flectere: cum tristibus severe, cum remissis jucunde, cum senibus graviter, cum juventute comiter, cum facinorosis audaciter, cum libidinosis luxuriose vivere. Haec ille tam varia multiplicique natura cum omnes omnibus ex terris homines improbos audacesque collegerat, tum etiam multos fortes viros et bonos specie quadam virtutis assimulatae tenebat.

6. **Cujus rei libet**] i. q. *cujuslibet rei*. So *Catil.* 52. sed cujus haec cunque modi videntur.

7. **Vastus animus**] "Prodigious or monstrous spirit." *Vastus:* 1 vacant; 2 desert; 3 wild; 4 shocking, monstrous; 5 vast.

8. **Post dominationem**] "No man since the usurpation of Sulla had been so ambitious of power." Comp. *Jugur.* 5. Hannibal post magnitudinem nominis Romani Italiae opes

maximo adtriverat, "more than any invader since the Roman power had become great."

9. **Sullae**] Not *Syllae*, as appears from inscriptions, and from the derivation of the word from *sura*. The one form represents the Latin *u*, the other the Greek *v*, which might be adopted by a scribe who had a Greek text before him. Sulla composed his own memoirs in Greek. The pronunciation would probably be alike in either case.

10. **Dum sibi regnum pararet**] "While he was bringing his usurpation to effect." Comp. *Jugur.* 31. regni paratio.

11. **Quidquam pensi habebat**] Comp. *Catil.* 12. 23. 31. *Jugur.* 41. nihil pensi neque sancti habere. Liv. xlii. 23. *pensum*, i. q. *perpensum, consideratum.*

12. **Diversa**] "Contrary one to the other."

13. **Supra repetere**] "To trace from a higher source:" the object is *instituta*, or rather *res Romanas* generally, understood in *inst. maj. disserere;* "to discuss," with or without an accus. of the object. Comp. Cic. *de Nat. Deor.* iii. 40. ea disserere malui. Tac. *Ann.* i. 4. bona libertatis disserere. This passage involves both these constructions: scil. *disserere instituta*, and *disserere quomodo*, etc.

CHAPTER VI.

1. **Sicuti ego accepi**] Implying that upon this point, namely, the foundation of Rome itself, there were different opinions. Tacitus commences his *Annals* with the words, Urbem Romam a principio reges habuere; as a matter upon which there is no question.

2. **Aborigines**] Dionysius of Halicarnassus, in the last century B. C., is the first writer who mentions this tradition. Misled perhaps by his imperfect acquaintance with Latin he calls this people 'Αβερρίγενες ὥστε δηλοῦσθαι πλανήτας, from whence Festus some centuries later, though spelling the name correctly, repeats the absurd interpretation: Aborigines appellati sunt quod errantes convenerint in agrum qui nunc est populi Rom. Suidas again misspells it 'Αβωρίγενες. A work of Varro on the "Antiquities of Man" bore the title *Aborigines*.

3. **Sine legibus, sine imperio**] "Neither with a free constitution, nor under authorized rule."

4. **Una moenia**] *Unus* in plur. only joined with plural nouns; as *nuptiae, litterae*, etc. *Jugur.* 60. unae atque alterae scalae.

5. **Alius alio more viventes**] Comp. *Catil.* 52. alius alium expectantes. *Jugur.* 53. alius alium appellant.

NOTES. 57

6. **Res**] i.q. *civitas.* So *res Romana, res Latina,* etc.

7. **Civibus, moribus, agris**] "Population, institutions, and territory."

8. **Sicuti pleraque mortalium habentur**] i.e. *habent se, sunt.* Comp. the Greek idiom ὡς ἔχει τὰ πλεῖστα τῶν θνητῶν, "as is the case generally with human affairs." *Mortalium* may be gen. of *mortalia,* or of *mortales,* i.e. *homines.*

9. **Metu perculsi**] The common notion that *percussus* refers to the body, *perculsus,* to the mind, is erroneous. Either word is used indifferently of body or mind; but *percussus* of the mind when the affection is slight, *perculsus* when it is grave. Bentley on Hor. *Ep.* vii. 15. Ruhnken on Terent. *Andr.* i. 1. 98. This distinction however is not always preserved.

10. **Domi militiaeque intenti**] "Always actively engaged, whether in peace or in war."

11. **Obviam ire**] "To oppose, resist." *Jugur.* 5. Liv. ix. 14.

12. **Patriam parentesque**] "Their country and their parents." This is the sense of *parentes* in this place, and in Catil. 52. *Jugur.* 87. Tac. *Ann.* i. 59. But *parentes* from *parēre,* "subjects," is also combined with *patriam,* and is only to be distinguished by the context. So *Jugur.* 3. vi quidem regere patriam aut parentes importunum est. Comp. *Jugur.* 102. parentes abunde habemus, amicorum nunquam satis fuit. Vell. ii. 108. Maroboduus ex voluntate parentium inter suos occupavit principatum.

13. **Portabant**] This word used (for *ferebant*) of *weighty,* and fig. of *important* things. Ruhnken *ad Terent. Andr.* ii. 2. 1. See note 1 on c. 30.

14. **Imperium legitimum**] *Imperium* is absolute, irresponsible authority, within certain limits of time, place and circumstances, as that of a general over his soldiers in the field, of the consul in certain particulars, as of levying soldiers, taking the auspices, etc. *Legitimum,* "restricted by law." Comp. note 3.

15. **Delecti**] "Selected;" *legere* and *eligere,* "to take," generally, out of a number: *deligere,* "to select for peculiar fitness." Thus in Caes. *B. G.* vii. 76. huic rei idoneos homines deligebat.

16. **Regium imperium quod initio conservandae libertatis fuerat**] "Regal authority which had originally conduced to the maintenance of liberty." Comp. Liv. iii. 39. quod unum exaequandae sit libertatis. xxxviii. 50. nihil tam aequandae libertatis esse. xxvii. 9. ea prodendi imperii Rom. tradendae

Hannibali, victoriae esse. Varro, *de Re Rust.* i. 19. ea sola quae agri tuendi erunt. In all these cases the subject of the sentence conduces to, or has for its object, that which is put in the genit. with the future participle; and the genitive attributes to it a certain quality, function or tendency. But where the genitive is connected with another verb than the verb substantive *causa* or *consilio* must be supplied, like the Greek ἕνεκα or χάριν. Thus Sallust, *Fr. Hist.* i. 19. exercitum opprimendae libertatis habet. Liv. viii. 6. placuit averruncandae Deum irae victimas caedi. That these are not genitives of quality (e. g. victims fit for averting divine wrath) appears from such passages as Tac. *Ann.* ii. 59. Germanicus Aegyptum proficiscitur cognoscendae antiquitatis, iii. 27. multa populus paravit tuendae libertatis et firmandae concordiae.

17. **Dominationem**] "Ab aliis scriptoribus et a Sall. semper de potentia et imperio non legitimo dicitur." Dietsch.

18. **Convertit**] "Turned itself," *intrans.* or more properly *reflexive*.

19. **Insolescere**] i. q. *superbire*.

CHAPTER VII.

1. **Formidolosa**] "Terrible," as in Cic. *pro Cluen.* 3, *pro leg. Man.* 21, and always in Sallust; but sometimes it has a passive signification, terrified, fearful, timid; as Tac. *Ann.* i. 62. Terent. *Eun.* iv. 6. 19.

2. **Adepta libertate**] The perf. partic. of the deponent used passively. *Jugur.* 101. dum prope jam adeptam victoriam retinere cupit. So, *amplexus, confessus, expertus, moderatus, pactus, partitus, ultus,* and others.

All these deponents had in past ages an active form; the passive use of *adipiscor* is preserved in the indicative and infinitive, in Plaut. *Trinum.* ii. 2. 28. non aetate verum ingenio adipiscitur sapientia. Q. Fabius Maximus, quoted by Priscian, viii. 4. 16. amitti quam apisci.

3. **Lubidinem habebant**] "Placed their satisfaction."

4. **Labos**] This form used by Sallust, according to the testimony of Servius on *Aen.* i. 253. Sallustius paene ubique *labos* posuit, quem nulla necessitas (sc. metri) coegit.

5. **Domuerat**] *Domare,* poetice, "to level the rough and soften the hard." Virg. *Aen.* ix. 608. rastris terram domat. Silius, iii. 499. magna vi saxa domantem.

6. **Se**] Redundant, after the verb desiring, *properabat.* Comp. note 2 on ch. 1.

NOTES. 59

7. **Eas**] For *id*, agreeing by attraction with *divitias;* therefore the emendation *ea* (neut. plur.) is unnecessary. Comp. Plaut. *Trinum.* iii. 2. 71. is est honos meminisse officium suum. Liv. ii. 38. si haec profectio et non fuga est. Cic. *Somn. Scip.* hic fons, hoc principium est movendi; and the Virgilian, Hic labor, hoc opus est.

CHAPTER VIII.

1. **Ex lubidine magis quam ex vero**] The adverb *magis* is rejected by many MSS. Comp. *Catil.* 48. tanta vis hominis lenienda quam exagitanda videbatur. 9. beneficiis quam metu; and 52. Tac. *Ann.* i. 58. pacem quam bellum probatam. iii. 17. iv. 61.

2. **Celebrat**] "Renders famous or celebrated." Comp. *Jugur.* 85. haec atque talia majores vestri faciendo seque remque publicam celebravere.

3. **Aestimo**] *Aestimo* has generally the primary sense of "counting," "reckoning," while *existimo* is confined to the secondary sense of "thinking," "supposing:" but where *aestimo* has the secondary or reflective sense, as in this passage, it is more direct and decided than *existimo*. Here, "I calculate," that is, on precise authentic data: *existimo* would be "I suppose, infer, imagine."

4. **Aliquanto**] i.e. *aliqua ex parte,* "a good deal;" *aliquantum* is not *paullum*, but *satis multum.*

5. **Scriptorum magna ingenia**] "Writers of great genius." Comp. Catul. lxiv. 4. Argivae robora pubis i.q. pubes robusta.

6. **Eorum qui ea fecere**] This inelegant repetition occurs again, *Jugur.* 31. neque eos qui ea fecere pudet.

7. **Ea copia**] "Such means, opportunities, or advantages." The Romans had not the advantage of such excellent writers, because their ablest men were most engaged in affairs. For *copia* in this primary sense, comp. *Catil.* 17. quibus molliter vivere copia erat. Plaut. *Capt.* ii. 1. 21. quum quod volumus nos copia est. *Mil.* iv. 6. 11. copia vix fuit eum adeundi. Terent. *Heaut.* ii. 3. 41. ea res dedit tum existimandi copiam. For the sentiment compare Ovid, *Fast.* iii. 101:

> Nondum tradiderat victas victoribus artes
> Graecia, facundum sed male forte genus,
> Qui bene pugnabat Romanam noverat artem,
> Mittere qui poterat pila disertus erat.

CHAPTER IX.

1. **Jus bonumque**] "Right and good," "lawful and expedient:" *jus* i. q. *rectum, aequum; bonum* i. q. *utile reipublicae.*

For the sentiment comp. Tac. *Ann.* iii. 26. init. *Germ.* 19. plus ibi boni mores valent quam alibi bonae leges.

2. **In suppliciis deorum**] "In the solemn services of the gods," *supplicium* i. q. *supplicatio*, a bending of the knee in prayer, adoration, or thanksgiving. Comp. Liv. xxvii. 50. matronae suppliciis votisque fatigare Deos. Tac. *Ann.* iii. sed tunc supplicia Dis ludique magni decernuntur. Festus says further, *supplicia* veteres quaedam *sacrificia* a supplicando vocabant. As applied to "punishment," (usually "capital punishment,") it means, kneeling to be beheaded, or scourged.

3. **In amicis fideles**] "Faithful in regard to their friends," not *in amicos*, the reading of some MSS. and many editions. Comp. *Catil.* 11. in civibus facinora fecere. 51. quid in illis jure fieri posset. Cic. *de Off.* i. 14. qui aliis nocent ut in aliis liberales sint. The same construction is frequent in verse, where the metre shews this case to be ablat. and not accus. Ovid, *Met.* vii. 22. quid in hospite regia virgo Ureris? *Trist.* v. 2. 26. lenis in hoste fuit. Virg. *Aen.* ii. 541. Talis in hoste fuit Priamo. The accus. would signify, "towards," the ablat. "in the matter of," "in regard to." The construction with the ablat. is not confined, as some have maintained, to expressing *love* or *hate*.

4. **Artibus**] "Dispositions." Comp. *Jugur.* 90. luxuria et ignavia pessimae artes. Or "principles," *Catil.* 10. fidem, probitatem, ceteras artes bonas. See above, c. 2.

5. **Evenerat**] For the turn of construction comp. Tacitus, *Hist.* i. 10. nimiae voluptates cum vacaret, quotiens expedierat magnae virtutes.

6. **Qui contra imp.**] Comp. *Catil.* 52. the case of Manlius's son; and of Postumius Tubertus, Val. Max. ii. 7. 6.

7. **Pulsi loco**] i. e. *loco suo*. Comp. *Jugur.* 38. 52.

8. **Beneficiis quam metu**] In this place most MSS. omit *magis*. See note 1 on c. 8.

9. **Agitabant**] "Exercised," "practised:" Plin. *Ep.* viii. 2. agitare justitiam.

10. **Ignoscere quam persequi**] *Ignoscere* might stand absolutely, as Sall. *Fr. Hist.* i. 19. ignoscendo populi Romani magnitudinem auxisse: but *persequi* requires an object. Supply *eam* from *injuria;* and comp. *Jugur.* 14. tuasne injurias persequar? Cic. *pro Mur.* 21. acceptam injuriam persequi non placet.

CHAPTER X.

1. **Nationes ferae et populi**] Comp. Cic. *de Off.* ii. 8. regum, populorum, nationum portus erat. *Gens* and *natio*, *gens* and *populus*, are frequently combined without precise distinctions of signification. But properly *gens* and *natio* refer to community of origin, *populus* to community of institutions. Where *gens* and *natio* are distinguished *gens* has the wider signification, as Tac. *Germ.* 2. ita nationis nomen non gentis evaluisse.

2. **Patebant**] "Were accessible." Cities and territories are said *patere* to a people that has subdued and acquired the *right* to enter them; honours and offices to the citizen who has a *right* to sue for them, Liv. iv. 25. ne cui patricio plebeii magistratus paterent; private possessions to the owner, or the friend who has a *right* to use them as his own, Cic. *ad Div.* vi. 10. ut intelligant omnia Ciceronis patere Trebiano.

3. **Optandae**] "Desirable." For this adjectival sense of the fut. part. pass., comp. *Jugur.* 64. virtus, gloria, atque alia optanda bonis.

4. **Subvertit**] "Has overthrown." The historic perfect: or the present, implying a general remark. In that case *edocuit* is aoristic, i. q. *edocere solet; subegit*, i. q. *subigere solet.*

5. **Invasit**] "Rushed in," in an absolute sense. Comp. *Catil.* 2. lubido atque superbia invasere. So *incessit. Catil.* 7. 13. *Jugur.* 13. 41.

CHAPTER XI.

1. **Propius virtutem**] "Nearer to virtue." Comp. *Jugur.* 18. propius mare Africum. 19. proxime Hispaniam. Liv. ii. 48. proxime formam latrocinii.

2. **Vera via**] "Genuine," "honest;" opposed to *dolis atque fallaciis.* Comp. Cic. *Philipp.* i. 14. vereor ne ignorans verum iter gloriae. *Vera via* is also i. q. *recta*, opposed to *prava*, "crooked." Sall. *de Rep. Ordin.* animus ferox prava via ingressus.

3. **Avaritia pecuniae studium habet**] "Avarice implies a devoted pursuit of money." For the force of *habet*, beyond the simple *est*, comp. Cic. *in Catil.* iv. 4. habere videtur ista res iniquitatem, "seems to smack of injustice;" *de Off.* iii. 2. alterum potest habere dubitationem, "may admit of doubt."

4. **Neque copia neque inopia**] "Avarice is assuaged

neither by wealth nor want;" i. e. "the desire of money which is inflamed by want is not less inflamed even by acquisition."

5. **Armis recepta republ.**] "When he had recovered possession of the government by force of arms." Comp. Cic. *pro Sex. Rosc.* 45, speaking of Sulla, imperii majestatem quam armis receperat. Sulla pretended to wrest the government from an usurping faction. His first professions were studiously mild. Comp. Vell. ii. 25. putetis Sullam venisse in Italiam non belli vindicem sed pacis auctorem; tanta cum quiete exercitum per Calabriam Apuliamque cum singulari cura frugum, agrorum, hominum, urbium perduxit. Cic. *de Off.* ii. 8. in illo secuta est honestam causam non honesta victoria.

6. **Neque modum neque modestiam**] A cant phrase; see the same reversed c. 38.

7. **In civibus**] "In regard to the citizens." Comp. note on ch. 9. *in amicis*.

8. **Habuerat**] "Had treated." Habere aliquem bene, male liberaliter, etc. i. q. *tractare*. Comp. *Jugur.* 103. Liv. xxix. 8; xxxvii. 34; xxxix. 1.

9. **Amare, potare**] A jingling expression, equivalent to the English, "to indulge in wine and women." Comp. *Jugur.* 85. quin ergo ament, potent. *Potare* has a frequentative sense, "to drink freely."

10. **Privatim ac publice**] "Whether they were private or public property."

11. **Delubra**] "Shrines," in which votive offerings were dedicated. To rob a *temple* might imply only stripping it of its furniture or materials; but to rob a shrine is to carry off what has been peculiarly consecrated to the deity. Varro's derivation of the word may be true as far as it goes: sicut locum in quo figeret candelam candelabrum appellarunt, ita in quo deum ponerent nominarunt delubrum.

12. **Nihil reliqui victis fecere**] "Left nothing remaining to the conquered." The construction is similar in the phrases, lucri, compendi, aequi, boni facere.

13. **Animos fatigant**] "Shake their principles."

14. **Ne**] In the sense of *nedum*, which indeed is given in many MSS., and is cited here by Priscian, "much less."

15. **Ne illi...temperarent**] "Much less could they, the Roman soldiers, with their corrupt habits, be expected to

refrain from abusing their victory." Comp. Tac. *Hist.* iii. 31. qui semper Bedriaci victoriae temperassent; i. e. victoria moderate usi fuissent.

CHAPTER XII.

1. **Hebescere]** "The brilliancy of virtue grew dim." Comp. Sall. *de Rep. Ordin.* ii. 6. postquam divitiae clarae haberi.

2. **Pro malevolentia duci]** "Was reputed to be envy or spite towards the rich and successful."

3. **Ex divitiis]** The prep. indicates the *cause* or *origin*. *Catil.* 14. uti cujusque studium ex aetate flagrabat. *Jugur.* 32. timido et ex conscientia diffidenti.

4. **Pudorem, pudicitiam]** "Modest principles and personal chastity."

5. **Pensi...moderati]** "Weighed and measured," "considered and regulated."

6. **Verum illi]** "But the ancients indeed;" with emphasis: *rerum* is not opposed to the preceding words, but to the inference understood. Supply, "You will then see how great is the difference," i.e. between the temples of ancient days and modern mansions.

7. **Injuriae licentiam]** "Licence to oppress their own neighbours." The Romans excused their own aggressions on the plea of defending weaker nations against the tyranny of their neighbours. Comp. Rutilius, i. 64. profuit injustis te dominante capi.

8. **Sociis; hostibus]** The same opposition expressed in different words by Cicero, *in Verr.* iv. honestius est reipublicae... imperatorem ea in bello reliquisse, quam praetorem in pace abstulisse.

9. **Proinde quasi]** "Exactly as if." Ruhnken on Ter. *Heaut.* i. 1. 13.

10. **id demum esset]** the demonstrative introduced for emphasis. Comp. 20. idem velle atque nolle ea demum firma amicitia est. 58. in fuga salutem sperare ea vero dementia est.

CHAPTER XIII.

1. **Subversos montes, maria constructa]** Mountains overthrown (excavated) to make seas (lakes or fish-ponds). Comp. Tac. *Ann.* xii. 56. structo cis Tiberim stagno. This refers particularly to Lucullus, into whose fish-ponds at Bauli sea-

water was admitted by a dyke cut through a hill. Pompey called him the Xerxes togatus. Vel. ii. 33. Pliny, *Hist. Nat.* ix. 54. Lucullus exciso monte euripum et maria admisit. Varro, *de Re Rust.* iii. 17. Lucullus postquam perfodisset montem ac maritima flumina immisisset in piscinas. But the word constructa may refer to moles or villas projected into the sea, as in Horace *Od.* iii. 1. 33. jactis in altum molibus, and iii. 24. 3. caementis licet occupes Tyrrhenum omne tuis. Again *Catil.* 20. in exstruendo mari et montibus cooequandis.

2. **Quas...abuti**] scil. *iis.* Comp. Cic. *ad Div.* ii. 3. quae... facultas data erit utemur, scil. ea. *Jugur.* 54. universos... atque agit gratias, scil. iis.

3. **Cultus**] "Refinement," in either a good or a bad sense; as Horace, *Sat.* ii. 2. 65. Mundus erit qui non offendat sordidus atque In neutram partem cultus miser. Liv. xxix. 21. de cultu ac desidia imperatoris.

4. **Terra marique omnia exquirere**] Imitated by Lucan, iv. 375. quaesitorum terra pelagoque ciborum Ambitiosa fames. Petron. Arb. *Spec. Bell. Civ.* 40. Ingeniosa gula est, et seqq. See Aul. Gellius, vii. 16, about the foreign luxuries of the Roman table; and Seneca, *Ep.* 89. Compare also for the general scope of the passage, Lucan, i. 163 :

> Non auro tectisve modus, mensasque priores
> Aspernata fames ; cultus gestare decoros
> Vix nuribus rapuere mares ; foecunda virorum
> Paupertas fugitur, totoque accersitur orbe
> Quo gens quaeque perit, etc.

5. **Luxu antecapere**] "To anticipate with voluptuous indulgence."

6. **Haud facile carebat**] "Could not easily control or forego the gratification of its appetites;" therefore, "could not *be free from* them." Carere i. q. vacare, liber esse ab aliqua re.

CHAPTER XIV.

1. **Flagitiorum atque facinorum**] The abstract "crimes" for the concrete "criminals;" as *scelus, pestis*, etc. are frequently used. The reading, *flagitiosorum, facinorosorum,* is a mistaken attempt to correct this legitimate figure of speech. With regard to the distinction between the words, *flagitium* conveys the idea of "disgraceful," *facinus* of what is "amazing," or "monstrous."

NOTES.

2. **Stipatorum**] "Attendants," "body-guards." *Stipator*, from *stipa*, one who packs goods, fills up interstices, &c.

3. **Nam quicumque impudicus, etc.**] Comp. Cicero, *in Catil.* ii. 4. quis tota Italia veneficus, quis gladiator, quis latro, quis sicarius, quis parricida, quis testamentorum subjector, quis circumscriptor, quis ganeo, quis nepos, quis adulter, quae mulier infamis, quis corruptor juventutis, quis corruptus, quis perditus inveniri potest, qui se cum Catilina non familiarissime vixisse fateatur?

4. **Aes grande conflaverat**] "Had contracted great debt." Conflare (1) to blow up or kindle fire, (2) to forge with fire, (3) to create, make or raise.

5. **Omnes undique**] A poetical repetition, as Virg. *Aen.* ii. 498. quos omnes undique Graiae Circum errant acies.

6. **Catilinae**] Gen. case governed by *proximi*, "the nearest and most intimate friends of Catilina." Comp. *Jugur.* 80. Bocchi proximos.

7. **Incidere**] "To fall into," used generally, as the English, in a bad sense. So incidere in morbum, in insidias, &c. We say, "to fall into bad habits," not "into good habits."

8. **Animi...fluxi**] "Pliant" or "ductile." Comp. Tac. *Ann.* vi. 38. fluxam senio mentem. Suet. *Tib.* 52. Drusus animi fluxioris.

CHAPTER XV.

1. **Jam primum**] "To begin then:" not with reference to the youth of Catiline, but to the narrative in hand. Comp. Tac. *Ann.* iv. 6. congruens crediderim recensere ceteras quoque reipubl. partes quibus modis ad eam diem habitae sint...jam primum &c.

2. **Cum virgine nobili**] The person is not indicated, but Cicero blurts out the monstrous charge, ex eodem stupro tibi et uxorem et filiam invenisti, which Plutarch *Vit. Cic.* c. 10, adopts. Asconius says that he married a woman who was actually his daughter by an illicit connexion. Such loose charges would deserve no attention except for the ready acceptance they met with.

3. **Cum sacerdote Vestae**] This is said to have been Fabia, sister of Cicero's wife Terentia. Asconius, on Cicero's speech *in toga candida*. She was acquitted of the charge. Cicero makes no direct mention of it, but may allude to it in the passage cited by his commentator: quum ita vixisti ut non

esset locus tam sanctus quo non adventus tuus, etiam si nulla culpa subesset, crimen afferret : on which Asconius remarks ; ita et suis pepercit et nihilo levius inimico summi opprobrii turpitudinem objecit.

4. **Alia**] Without the copula, as *Catil.* 21, 48, 57.

5. **Orestillae**] Probably of the family of L. Aurelius Orestes, L. f. L. n. who was consul A.U. 597. An Aufidius Orestes was consul A.U. 683.

6. **Necato filio**] Comp. Cic. *in Catil.* i. 6. quum morte superioris uxoris novis nuptiis domum vacuam fecisses. The story is repeated by Valerius Maximus, ix. 1. 9. Cicero tells a similar story of one Oppianicus, in the speech for Cluentius, c. 9.

7. **Infestus**] "Hateful," *passive ;* more commonly *active*, "hostile." Infestisque obvia signis signa, Lucan i. 6.

8. **Quietibus**] So the plural in Cicero, *de Off.* i. 29. somno et quietibus caeteris ; though it is there used not for sleep, but for other modes of refreshing the body.

9. **Vastabat**] "Spoiled, ravaged," i. q. *diripiebat*. This is the reading of a majority of MSS.: the editions very commonly adopt the easier reading *vexabat*. Comp. *Jugur.* 41. avaritia polluere et vastare omnia.

10. **Foedi oculi**] "Discoloured," "bloodshot."

11. **Prorsus**] "In short." Joined with a verb at the end of a sentence, i. q. *ut paucis complectar*. Comp. *Catil.* 25. prorsus multae facetiae leposque inerat.

CHAPTER XVI.

1. **Signatores**] Persons who attested wills with their seals. Comp. Suet. *Tib.* 23. Also witnesses to marriage rites: Juvenal x. 336. veniet cum signatoribus auspex. Non nisi legitime vult nubere.

2. **Commodare**] "From among these persons he was wont to offer the services of false witnesses." *Commodare.* the historic infin.

3. **Habere...majora alia**] Both the infin. and the subst. governed by *imperabat*. Comp. Hor. *Od.* i. 2. 50. Hic magnos potius *triumphos*, Hic ames *dici* pater atque princeps; i. 1. 19. Est qui nec veteris *pocula* Massici, Nec partem solido *demere* de die Spernit. For the change from the infin. to the imperf. comp. *Catil.* 54. nihil *denegare*...sibi magnum imperium *exoptabat ;* and c. 56. occasionem...non dare ; sperabat quoque.

4. Gratuito] "Wantonly," i.e. with no immediate motive or temptation: hence, "in vain," "to no purpose:" Liv. i. 47. jam enim a scelere ad aliud spectare mulier scelus...ac gratuita praeterita parricidia essent. For the sentiment compare Cic. *de Off.* ii. 24. of Caesar, ut hoc ipsum eum delectaret, peccare, etiam si causa non esset.

5. Quod aes alienum per omnes terras ingens erat] "Because in every country there were men deeply in debt;" and therefore interested in the success of a social revolution. This may refer to the state of the empire generally and distress throughout the provinces, but it seems to point more particularly to Italy and to Sulla's veterans. See below.

6. Sullani milites] The veterans of Sulla's legions, many thousands of whom he had settled in colonies throughout Italy. These fortunate soldiers soon squandered the produce of their estates, contracted debts, and having no habits of peaceful industry, only looked to new commotions to retrieve themselves. Comp. *Catil.* 37. and Cic. *in Catil.* ii. 9. in tantum aes alienum inciderunt, ut si salvi esse velint Sulla sit iis ab inferis excitandus.

7. In Italia] The Republic never maintained a standing army in Italy: its legions were all occupied in the provinces. The police of Rome and the large towns was kept by the citizens themselves, and the consuls and chief magistrates had only a few lictors and archers in attendance upon them.

8. In extr. terris] Pompey was engaged, under the provisions of the Manilian bill, which gave him proconsular power over all the provinces of the east, in subduing Mithridates, king of Pontus, and in ordering the affairs of the eastern frontier. Comp. Virg. *Geor.* ii. 171. Qui nunc extremis Asiae jam victor in oris Imbellem avertis Romanis arcibus Indum; and the same expression in Lucan iv. 1. referring to Spain.

9. Consulatum petenti] Catiline first stood for the consulship A.U. 688. Being thwarted in this attempt he still hoped to succeed at a subsequent opportunity: his suit for the consulship is therefore spoken of as still proceeding.

10. Nihil] "In no respect at all:" more emphatic than the simple *non*.

CHAPTER XVII.

1. Kal. Junias] The first of June: A.U. 690, B.C. 64.

2. L. Caesare] i.e. L. Julius Caesar, a connexion, but distant, of C. Caesar the dictator, and uncle by his sister Julia of M. Antonius the triumvir.

3. **C. Figulo**] i.e. C. Marcius Figulus: adopted into the Marcian gens, his original name being C. Minucius Thermus.

4. **Singulos appellare**] "He addressed various persons separately:" *appellare*, "to appeal with urgency." Comp. *Jugur.* 14. exsul patria, domo, solus atque omnium honestarum rerum egens, quo accedam, aut quos appellem?

5. **Ubi satis explorata sunt quae voluit**] "When he had fully discovered all he wanted," i. e. the temper and disposition of the persons he sounded. To express, "when others had discovered what he wanted," would require *quae vellet*.

6. **In unum**] "Together," "so as to meet one another." Locum, spatium, or other words may be supplied.

7. **Necessitudo**] Not "connexion" in this place, but "necessity," "straits." After *necessitudo* supply *erat*, which is comprehended in *inerat*.

8. **P. Lentulus Sura**] Of the Cornelian gens: consul A. U. 683. He had been expelled from the senate for licentious conduct. He was induced by pretended Sibylline oracles to believe that three Cornelii should be sovereigns of Rome, two of whom, Cinna and Sulla, had fulfilled their destiny, and that he was himself fated to be the third. See Plutarch, *Vit. Cicer.* 17. The cognomen *Sura*, means "an ankle." *Sulla* is a diminutive of the same meaning.

9. **P. Autronius**] Surnamed *Paetus;* see the following chapter.

10. **L. Cassius Longinus**] This man was a competitor with Cicero in suing for the consulship: he was remarkable for his corpulence. See Cic. *in Catil.* iii. 7. nec mihi esse P. Lentuli somnum, nec L. Cassii adipem, nec Cethegi furiosam temeritatem pertimescendam. He undertook the charge of setting the city on fire.

11. **C. Cethegus**] One of the Cornelian gens. He was, next to Catiline, the prime mover of the conspiracy, and was notorious for his ferocity and boldness. He is called by Lucan, "Cethegus of the bared arm." ii. 544. exsertique manus vesana Cethegi. vi. 794. Mariique truces, nudique Cethegi.

12. **P. and Serv.**] Cornelius Sulla were nephews of the dictator, sons of his brother Servius. Publius was absolved from the charge of conspiracy with Catiline, being defended by Cicero.

13. **L. Vargunteius**] This man undertook to assassinate Cicero in his house. He had been Cicero's colleague in the

quaestorship: accused of bribery and defended by Hortensius, but condemned. See Cic. *pro Sulla*, 2, 5.

14. **Q. Annius**] This person is unknown; but Cicero mentions an uncle of Catiline's named L. Annius, who had been condemned judicially in the year 690.

15. **M. Porcius Laeca**] At whose house the conspirators met, *Catil.* 27. Comp. Cic. *pro Sull.* 2. and *in Catil.* i. 4.

16. **L. Bestia**] Of the gens Calpurnia. He was tribune of the people in the year of the conspiracy. Escaping condemnation, he became afterwards aedile, A.U. 696.

17. **Q. Curius**] Of this man see further, *Catil.* 23, 28. The senate voted him a reward as the discoverer of the conspiracy; but Cicero was induced to declare that it had been first disclosed to him by C. Caesar, and the reward was taken from Curius. See Suet. *Jul.* 17.

18. **Domi nobiles**] "Noble," i. e. "distinguished by their family honours and magistracies in their native cities." At Rome a man became *nobilis* by serving a curule magistracy; i. e. becoming consul, praetor, aedile, or censor.

19. **M. Licinium Crassum**] This Crassus belonged to a branch of the family surnamed Dives. He was himself proverbially the richest of the Romans. He was ambitious of becoming the chief of the commonwealth, and trimmed between the Marians and the senate. Finding himself outstripped in popularity and fame by Pompey, he leagued with him and Caesar, and formed an alliance which received the name of a triumvirate; implying an extraordinary public commission. He took the government of Syria A. U. 700, intending to make war upon the Parthians, and acquire great military resources for the furtherance of his schemes; but was slain after the fatal battle of Carrhae, A.U. 701. There is no proof of his supposed connexion with the conspiracy of Catiline.

20. **Apud illos**] By the figure *anacoluthon* or *non-sequence*, the grammatical construction of a sentence is sometimes broken, and the sense carried on as it were from a new starting-point. Here *illos* agrees with *conjuratos* understood in conjuratio. A similar irregularity occurs at the beginning of the next chapter.

CHAPTER XVIII.

1. **De qua**] scil. conjuratione. The reading *de quo* in many editions has less authority, and seems to have arisen from an attempt to elude the difficulty.

2. **L. Tullo, M' Lepido coss.**] A. U. 688, B. C. 66. L. Volcatius Tullus and M' Aemilius Lepidus consuls. "Manius;" sic scripsi Fastos cum Orellio secutus. Dietsch in loc.

3. **Legibus ambitus**] "By the laws relating to canvassing for office." Of these the principal was the *lex Calpurnia* (more correctly, *Acilia Calpurnia*, from the consuls of the year 687, by whom it was passed), confirmed and extended by the *lex Tullia* of Cicero (691), against bribery. See Cic. *pro Murena*, 23, 32.

4. **Interrogati**] "Accused," i. q. *postulati*.

5. **Pecun. repetundarum**] Or simply, *repetundarum*, "convicted of extortion in provincial administration." Catiline had served the praetorship in Africa.

6. **Profiteri**] scil. *se candidatum*. He could not declare himself a candidate to the Rogator within the proper time, because he had not been absolved from the charge which incapacitated him. Comp. Vell. Paterc. ii. 92. quaesturam petentes quos indignos putavit profiteri prohibuit.

7. **Cn. Piso**] A young noble of the Calpurnian gens. He is to be distinguished from his contemporaries, 1. C. Piso, consul A. U. 687, proconsul of the Province in Gaul, where he reduced the Allobroges, a staunch supporter of the senate; 2. C. Piso Frugi, first husband to Cicero's daughter Tullia; 3. L. Piso Caesorinus, consul A. U. 696, when Cicero was driven into banishment, the subject of his furious invective *in Pisonem:* (Caesar married his daughter Calpurnia); 4. M. Pupius Piso Calpurnianus, a Calpurnius adopted by M. Pupius; consul A. U. 693.

8. **In Capitolio Kal. Jan.**] On the first of January, when the new consuls assumed the fasces, they convened the senate in the Capitol, and were saluted by the nobles and magistrates. The conspirators intended to take advantage of this solemnity to effect their assassination. L. Aurelius Cotta and L. Manlius Torquatus were consuls A. U. 690.

9. **Fascibus correptis**] "Seizing the fasces," i. e. the consular power, which they represented.

10. **Duas Hispanias**] At this time Spain was divided into two provinces, the Hither and the Further, afterwards Tarraconensis and Baetica. The former extended from the Pyrenees to the Sinus Urcitanus (modern Almeria) on the south, to Gallaecia and the mouth of the Douro on the west; the latter was supposed to comprehend the rest of the peninsula, but beyond the Guadiana the country was only partially subdued

till the praetorship of Caesar, A.U. 694. Between the Guadiana and the Douro a third province was afterwards formed called Lusitania.

11. Rursus transtulerant] This repetition is not unfrequent. Comp. Florus, i. 3. in suum corpus rediisse rursus. Terence, *Adelph.* iv. 1. 9. quam huc reverti posset iterum.

12. Maturasset...dare] "Had given too soon," i. q. maturius dedisset. *Pro curia*, in front of the senate-house.

13. Ea res] i. e. his having given the signal too soon.

CHAPTER XIX.

1. Quaestor pro praetore] "A quaestor with praetor's rank." Having served the inferior office of quaestor, commissioner of the treasury, at Rome, Piso was sent to govern the Hither Spain, with the superior rank of propraetor, ordinarily given only to such as had served the praetorship at home. But, as Sallust insinuates, the senate stretched a point in order to get quit of a dangerous enemy. Comp. Suet. *Jul.* 9. Pisoni ob suspicionem urbanae conjurationis provinciam Hispaniam ultro *extra ordinem* datam esse. The phrases pro praetore, pro consule, are equivalent to the substantives propraetor, proconsul. Some of the provinces were praetorian, others consular; the latter were for the most part frontier provinces, or such as required large armies for their defence; e. g. the two Gauls, Syria, Cilicia, and Macedonia. On the other hand, Asia, Achaia, Bithynia, and the three provinces of Spain, were praetorian.

2. Adnitente] "Lending all his influence thereto."

3. Infestum inimicum] "A bitter personal enemy." The former word is omitted in several MSS. as apparently redundant.

4. Simul] Sallust frequently uses this copulative to connect a second less important reason with the principal reason already given. Comp. *Catil.* 16, 17, 20, 56, and *Jugur.* 4. cujus de virtute quia multi dixere praetereundum puto, simul ne per insolentiam quis existimet memet studium meum laudando extollere.

5. Complures] i. q. *nonnulli*, in a positive sense, "several;" *plures* always comparative, with reference to another smaller number.

6. Ab equit. Hisp.] For the motive of this assassination, compare Dion, xxxvi. 27. ὁ μὲν ἐνταῦθα ὑπὸ τῶν ἐπιχωρίων ἀδικήσας τι αὐτοὺς ἐσφάγη. And Asconius, *ad Cic. Orat. cont. Ant. et L. Catil.* Piso perierat in Hispania, ibique dum injurias provincialibus facit, occisus est. Sallust's insinuation against Pompeius is not credible; he had not sufficient motive, besides being far absent and occupied with other affairs. If there was any domestic treachery, it lies with the Senatorial party itself.

7. **Iter faciens]** "On a march;" not, on his way into the country, where he had already arrived, as appears from Dion and Asconius.

8. **Sunt qui ita dicunt]** Some read *dicant*. The distinction, if correctly observed, comes to this, *sunt qui dicunt*, "there are some, I know, who say;" *sunt qui dicant*, "some, perhaps, may be found who say."

9. **Cnaei Pompeii veteres fidosque clientes]** An accidental hexameter. Many such have been discovered in the Latin prose-writers. Comp. *Jugur.* 5. Bellum scripturus sum quod populus Romanus. Tac. *Ann.* i. 1. Urbem Romam a principio reges habuere. *Germ.* 39. Sylvam auguriis patrum et prisca formidine sacram. Quintilian has remarked, *Inst. Orat.* ix. 4, that Livy's preface begins with a portion of an hexameter: Facturusne operae pretium sim. Drakenborch, on this passage, collects similar instances. See Liv. vii. 11, 13, 14; xxi. 9; xxii. 50; xxiii. 18. It is said that the only bit of prose that may pass for a pentameter is in Cicer. *de Off.* iii. 23. Quid dominus navis? eripietne suum?

10. **Clientes]** Persons whom Pompeius had attached to himself in the province when he commanded there against Sertorius: such as Caesar (*Bell. Civ.* i. 75) calls beneficiarii. See Caes. *Bell. Civ.* ii. 11. magna esse Pompeii beneficia et magnas clientelas in provincia citeriore sciebat.

CHAPTER XX.

1. **In rem fore]** "To the purpose," "advantageous." In the same sense ob rem, *Jugur.* 31; and ex re, Terent. *Phorm.* v. 7. 76.

2. **Universos]** "The whole number collectively."

3. **Spectata]** For the use of the neuter plur. compare below "sita sunt."

4. **Res cecidisset]** Metaphor from the fall of dice.

5. **Per ignaviam, etc.]** "By means of," "through the instrumentality of." Comp. below, emori per virtutem, vitam per dedecus amittere. *Catil.* 12. per summum scelus omnia sociis adimere. 42. inconsulte ac velut per dementiam agere.

6. **Tempestatibus**] "Seasons of peril or trouble." *Tempestas*, in its primary sense, is "a period of time," opposed to *tempus*, "a moment of time." Hence it is sometimes used for a favourable or fitting season, as Cic. *ad Div.* xiv. 4. si esset licitum per nautas qui tempestatem praetermittere nolebant. But more commonly for an unfavourable or perilous season.

7. **Incipere**] "To undertake."

8. **Idem velle, etc.**] Comp. *Jugur.* 31. quos omnes eadem cupere, eadem odisse, eadem metuere in unum coegit, sed haec inter bonos amicitia inter malos factio est. The same sentiment is found in some places of Cicero, and echoed by Seneca *de Ira*, iii. 34. vinculum amoris idem velle.

9. **Ea demum**] "That after all."

10. **Agitavi**] The indic. represents that his views were already made known to them by personal communication.

11. **Diversi**] "Each severally."

12. **Concessit in**] "Has fallen under."

13. **Tetrarchae**] Properly, "rulers of quarters of kingdoms," applied to some oriental potentates, among whom the father often divided his dominions between his sons. But this signification was dropped, and the word was applied to certain petty or dependent sovereigns in the East, to whom the republic would not concede the kingly title. It has been remarked that the word *tetrarchae* is generally found in combination with *reges*. Comp. Sall. *Fr. Hist.* iv. 26. tetrarchas regesque territos animi firmavit. Cic. *pro Mil.* 28. omitto socios, exteras nationes, regem, tetrarchas. *In Vatin.* 12. foedere cum civitatibus, cum regibus, cum tetrarchis. Vel. ii. 51. regum, tetrarcharum, simulque dynastarum copiis. Horat. *Sat.* i. 3. 12. modo reges atque tetrarchas, Omnia magna, loquens.

14. **Vulgus**] "A mere rabble." Comp. Justin. xli. 1. Parthi veluti vulgus sine nomine praeda victorum fuere. (Observe the hexametrical flow.) Hor. *Carm.* ii. 16. malignum spernere vulgus. Here it is opposed to the respectable class of citizens, such as have legitimate influence and authority in the state.

15. **Sine gratia, sine auctoritate**] "Without interest or influence."

16. **Iis obnoxii**] "Under obligation to them," and therefore "at their mercy." Comp. *Catil.* 48. plerique Crasso ex negotiis privatis obnoxii.

17. **Pericula, etc.**] The dangers which the weak incur in

political competition with the powerful, which he goes on to specify, the loss of their elections, charges of bribery preferred against them by their opponents, poverty from the disappointment of their hopes of office and emolument, and from the judicial fines which may be inflicted upon them.

18. **Consenuerunt**] "Grown weak," metaphorically. Comp. Liv. xxxv. ne cunctando senescerent concilia, i. 22. senescere civitatem otio ratus.

19. **Cetera res expediet**] "Circumstances will effect the rest."

20. **Superare**] i. q. *abunde esse*. Comp. *Jugur.* 64.

21. **In exstruendo mari et montibus coaequandis**] "In raising seas and levelling mountains," i. e. excavating fish-ponds on shore, and cutting through land to admit the water of the sea. Comp. above, c. 13. subversos montes, maria constructa.

22. **Continuare**] i. q. *domos domibus adjicere*. "To join two or more houses together." Comp. Liv. xxxiv. 4. ingens cupido agros continuandi. Tac. *Ann.* xv. 39. domo palatium et hortos continuare. Comp. Lucan, i. 170. Longa sub ignotis extendere rura colonis.

23. **Larem familiarem**] "A domestic genius," or "family divinity;" implying "a home."

24. **Nova diruunt**] "Destroy," from mere caprice, "what has been just built." Compare the story of Caesar in Suet. *Jul.* 46. munditiarum lautitiarumque studiosissimum multi prodiderunt: villam in Nemorensi a fundamentis inchoatam magnoque sumptu absolutam, quia non tota ad animum ei responderet, totam diruisse, quanquam tenuem adhuc et obaeratum.

25. **Pecuniam trahunt, vexant**] "They spoil and plunder," i. e. "squander and dissipate their means;" *vexo*, according to A. Gell. ii. 6, is from *vehor*; and *trahere*, *vexare* have much the same meaning as the military terms *agere, ferre*, "to drive and carry off;" thereby effecting a devastation.

26. **Decus, gloria in oculis sita sunt**] "Are set before your eyes," as prizes or other objects set before you. Comp. *Jugur.* 51, 54.

CHAPTER XXI.

1. **Quieta movere**] i. q. *turbare*. Comp. Tac. *Ann.* iii. 30. mota Africa. Imitated by Ammianus Marcellinus, xv. 5. composita turbare; quieta perturbare.

2. **Merces**] "Reward," "gain;" frequently in a bad sense

3. **Condicio belli**] "Condition, or terms on which they were to engage." *Conditio* and *condicio* may be regarded as originally different words, the first from *condere*, "making" or "construction," the second from *dicio* (connected with *dice*), "terms," "circumstances," "state of life," &c., but these merged eventually into one, which was spelt according to the more obvious derivation, conditio.

4. **Quid ubique**] This may be explained *quid opis, et ubi id haberet.* Comp. 47. quid aut qua de causa consilii habuisset.

5. **Tabulas novas**] "Fresh tablets," i. e. an abolition of debts. The metaphor is taken from the use of waxed tablets for scoring accounts. When the account was cleared, by payment or otherwise, the wax might be smoothed with the blunt end of the stylus, in readiness to begin a new score.

6. **Proscriptionem**] A placard by which notice is publicly given of a sale, &c. Ulpian, in the Digest, gives the name to the announcement over a shop: Proscribere palam sic accipimus, claris literis ut de plano recte legi possint, ante tabernam scilicet, vel ante eum locum, in quo negotiatio exercetur, nec in loco remoto, sed in evidenti. Hence the proclamation by which the lives or properties of citizens were declared forfeited were called proscriptions. Sulla was the first to placard *tabulas proscriptionis*. Afterwards the second triumvirate, Antonius, Lepidus, and Octavius.

7. **Fert**] "Has for its own," or "makes its own." Ter. *Heaut.* ii. 1. 3. rerum quas fert adolescentia. Or in the sense of *aufert*: as Horace, Omnia fert aetas.

8. **P. Sittium Nucerinum**] Sittius derived his name from Nuceria (Nocera) a city of Campania. He had fled to Mauretania to escape an accusation at Rome, and maintained himself in distinction there by siding alternately with the petty chiefs of the country in their intestine feuds. He took Caesar's side after the battle of Thapsus, and intercepted Scipio and other fugitives of the senatorial party. Caesar made him a grant of territory from the possessions of Juba king of Numidia, where he was ultimately killed in a quarrel with a native chief.

9. **C. Antonium**] This Antonius had the cognomen Hybrida. He was the son of the famous orator M. Antonius, and brother of M. Antonius Creticus, who was father of Antony the triumvir. He became consul in the year 691, and was Cicero's colleague.

10. **Omnibus necessitudinibus circumventum**] "Distressed by exigencies of various kinds."

11. **Praedae fuerat**] "Had been an occasion of booty, illegitimate gain." Comp. c. 48. nam alia belli facinora praedae magis quam detrimento fore.

12. **Petitionem**] "Suit for the consulship."

CHAPTER XXII.

1. **Populares**] Properly, "of his own nation:" hence, "associates," as *Catil.* 24. quod factum primo populares conjurationis concusserat. Terent. *Phorm.* i. 1. 1. amicus summus meus et popularis Geta. Donatus on Ter. *Adelph.* ii. 1. 1. popularitas in omnis rei consortium sumitur.

2. **Adigeret**] This reading (for *adiceret* or *addiceret*) guessed by Cortius, has been confirmed by MSS. The phrase is common: adigere without the prep. occurs: as Caes. *Bell. Cic.* i. 76. ipse idem jusjurandum adigit Afranium; and ii. 28.

3. **Humani corporis sanguinem**] The redundant expression seems intended for emphasis. This ceremony is mentioned by the historians, Florus, iv. 1; Dion Cass. xxxvii. 20, who adds that a boy was slain for the purpose. But the custom of ratifying an oath by drawing blood from the body and drinking it existed among the Scythians and Dacians, and was probably in this case a remnant of an old Italian superstition. The Christian apologists pointed with triumph to this horrid rite. Minucius, *Octav.* 30. et quod Saturni filio dignum est...ipsum credo docuisse sanguinis foedere conjurare Catilinam. Cicero may possibly allude to it *in Catil.* 1. sica. quae quidem quibus abs te initiata sacris et devota sit...; but Sallust himself insinuates that it was at least unknown to Cicero. Perhaps it was a single drop of blood mixed in a bowl of wine to preserve the shadow of an antique ceremonial.

4. **Atque eo dictitare fecisse quo**] "And they went on to say, he did so in order that," &c. *Dictitare.* The historic infin.; the subject being the same as to *fuere qui dicerent*. So Dietsch and others, after the common reading, which however seems hardly admissible. The MSS. vary, e.g. *dictante, dictare, dictitavere,* but present nothing satisfactory. *Dictitarent,* "they repeated," or "asseverated," would give sense, but has no authority. *Eo...quo,* "in order that."

5. **Alius alii...conscii**] The dat.; as in the construction, *conscire sibi*. Terent. *Heaut.* i. 1. 69. qui fuere et conscii. Tac. *Ann.* i. 43. flagitiorum exercitui meo conscius.

6. **Ciceronis invidiam**] Passive, "the odium against Cicero," when he was afterwards accused by the tribune

Clodius of getting Roman citizens punished with death without an appeal to the people. For this sense of the word comp. c. 6. invidia ex opulentia orta est; and c. 23. nobilitas invidia (Ciceronis) aestuabat. Cicero himself thus defines it (*Tusc. Disp.* iv. 7. 16) invidia non in eo qui invidet solum dicitur, sed etiam in eo cui invidetur.

7. **Pro magnitudine**] "Considering its importance."

CHAPTER XXIII.

1. **Coopertus**] "Overwhelmed." We say, "covered with infamy," or "with ridicule;" the Romans applied the metaphor to the deeds themselves, as Cic. *in Ver.* i. 4. sceleribus coopertum. Liv. xxxix. 15. cooperti stupris. Horace's use of the phrase approaches nearer to ours: *Sat.* ii. 1. 68. Famosisque Lupus coopertus versibus.

2. **Senatu...moverant**] This is the phrase for "expelling from the senate," which was done by the censor omitting the name on reading the list of the order at the *lustrum*. Comp. Liv. xxvii. 11. xxxiv. 44. xxxviii. 28. The same phrase is applied more generally, *statu, possessione movere*. *Amoverant*, the reading of one MS. and several editions, is incorrect.

3. **Suamet**] The termination *met*, is generally confined to *ego, tu*, and *sui;* occasionally however we find *meummet, meamet, meimet*.

4. **Prorsus**] "In short." See note on c. 15.

5. **Neque dicere neque facere, etc.**] "Reckless in every thing he said or did:" not merely careless, but wanton and desperate: as Vell. ii. 95. Clodius qui neque dicendi neque faciendi ullum nisi quem vellet nosset modum. Compare the same phrase in Liv. xxvi. 15.

6. **Consuetudo**] "Intimacy," more particularly "sexual;" Lucr. v. 1279 consuetudo concinnat amorem: then "criminal," as in this place: *stupri*, though supplied in some editions, is not required.

7. **Maria montesque**] The commentators have collected passages where "seas and mountains of gold" are spoken of hyperbolically: as e.g. montes auri polliceri, χρυσίου πόντος, &c. Persius, ii. 65. uses *montes*, absolutè, for "heaps of gold;" Cratero magnos promittere montes.

8. **Obnoxia**] scil. *amori, affectui:* as Tac. *Ann.* xvi. 6: i. q. *morigera*, "obedient." So in Seneca, *obnoxius domino*.

9. **Insolentiae**] "Unusual audacity." Comp. Hor. *Epod.* 16. extr. Meaeque terra cedat insolentiae.

10. **Haud occultum habuit**] "Did not keep it secret:" the phrase expresses continuance of action, and so far differs from the simple *haud occultavit*.

11. **Sublato auctore**] "Leaving out the name of her informant." (In English the pres. part. is preferred in such phrases to the past, which latter is usual in Latin.) Comp. Cic. *ad Att.* xiii. 44. id nomen ex omnibus libris tollatur. ii. 24. Caepionem de oratione sua sustulit.

12. **Quae quoque modo**] For *quae et quo modo:* as in *Jugur.* 39. Comp. also *quid ubique*, *Catil.* 21. Or it may be taken for *quocunque modo*, implying the shifts she used to indicate her means of information while concealing the real fact which would have compromised Curius.

13. **Aestuabat...credebant**] Observe the sing. and plur. both connected with the same noun of number; and comp. Tac. *Ann.* ii. 24. ut quis et longinquo advenerat miracula narrabant.

14. **Quamvis egregius**] "Ever so excellent:" i.e. in the estimation of the hearer, not of the speaker, so as to retain the force of *vis* from *volo:* "as excellent as ever you please."

15. **Homo novus**] "A new man:" a term of disparagement applied to candidates for public office, whose families were not ennobled by having attained any of the curule magistracies. Plutarch, *Cat. Min.* οἱ ἀπὸ γένους δόξαν οὐκ ἔχοντες, ἀρχόμενοι δὲ γνωρίζεσθαι δι' αὑτῶν. Cicero frequently refers to his own want of nobility, and to the slur it entailed upon him, as *Phil.* vi. 6. quid enim non debeo vobis, Quirites, quem vos, a se ortum, hominibus nobilissimis omnibus honoribus praetulistis. Comp. the celebrated panegyric upon him in Juvenal, viii. 226:

Hic novus Arpinas, ignobilis et modo Romae
Municipalis eques.

16. **Post fuere**] "Were postponed." The words should be written separately, as in *Catil.* 53. ante Romanos fuisse.

CHAPTER XXIV.

1. **Comitiis habitis**] The consular comitia, or assembly of the centuries for the election of consuls, were held generally in June or July, six months before the consuls-designate entered upon their office. After the assembly had been held and the votes given the consuls-designate were declared: *declarabantur*, or *renuntiabantur*.

NOTES. 79

2. Populares conjurationis] "The associates in the plot;" *popularis* has no bad sense, and should not be rendered by "accomplices." See above, c. 22.

3. Pecuniam...sumptam mutuam] Money taken up by way of loan. *Mutuus*, from *muto*, used in its primary meaning, i. e. "exchanged."

4. Faesulae] The modern Fiesole, an ancient Etruscan city on a hill, two miles to the north of the modern Florence.

5. Princeps] "The first to commence military operations." Caes. *Bell. Gall.* vii. 2. Carnutes principes se ex omnibus bellum facturos pollicentur.

6. Sumptus...toleraverant] "Had met, though with difficulty, their lavish expenditure by," &c.

7. Modum fecerat] i. q. *finem attulerat*, "had put an end to."

8. Servitia] "Slaves." The abstract for the concrete: used always by Sallust for slaves as a class: individual slaves he calls *servi*. Dietsch.

CHAPTER XXV.

1. Virilis audaciae] Comp. Vell. i. 1. virilis animi foemina. Flor. iv. 5. virilis militiae uxor.

2. Viro] *scil.* Decimus Junius Brutus (see *Catil.* 40); he had been consul A. U. 677.

3. Liberis] One of her sons was D. Junius Brutus Albinus, *legatus* to Julius Caesar in Gaul, and afterwards one of his assassins.

4. Docta] Observe the triple construction, with the abl., the infin., and the accus.: unless *psallere, multa alia (facere)*, depend upon *solebat*, or some such verb understood. Compare *posse versus facere*, below.

5. Psallere, saltare] Some MSS. read also *canere* or *cantare*. *Canere* to sing, *psallere* to sing to the lyre.

6. Elegantius quam necesse est probae] The ancient Romans regarded dancing and singing as accomplishments exhibited for the entertainment of others. Hence they were always connected in their minds with servile or histrionic performances. The fashion of dancing for amusement, or to contribute to social festivity among themselves, was learnt at a later period from the Greeks. In the last century of the republic some of the most distinguished senators were noted for their excellence in dancing, but not without exciting much contempt from grave censors (see the chapter of Macrobius (*Saturn.* ii. 10) upon the subject) : and Horace stigmatizes the fashion of teaching young women the soft Ionian dances. Motus doceri gaudet Ionicos Matura virgo, et fingitur artubus. *Carm.* iii. 6. 26. Sallust by the word *necesse* seems to admit that the practice was tolerated in his time, but regarded with jealousy. *Probae :* i. q. *pudicae.* Hor. *Epod.* 17. 40. tu pudica, tu proba. If there is any distinction *proba* may refer to manners, *pudica* to morals, as in Sall. *Fr. Hist.* oris probi, animi invereeundi.

7. **Multa alia**] The ablat. litteris, the infin. psallere, and the acc. alia, seem all to depend upon docta, "taught or skilled in."

8. **Instrumenta luxuriae**] "The means of corruption," or " vice."

9. **Decus**] "Good name, honour." Comp. *Jugur.* 4. decus atque libertatem gratificari.

10. **Fuit**] Many MSS. read *fuere;* which is an attempt to correct a supposed incorrectness in the construction of the sense. The sing. *fuit* is defended by *Jugur.* 18. ea loca quae proxime Carthaginem Numidia appellatur, not appellantur. Ovid, *Art. Am.* iii. 222. Quas geritis vestes sordida lana fuit.

11. **Lubidine sic accensa**] Scil. *Sempronia*, not the abl. abs., though the phrase *accendi* may be applied to passions, as well as to persons. *Jugur.* 6. accensa studia.

12. **Peteret**] "Courted." Comp. Propert. ii. 16. 27. Quum te jam multi peterent tu me una petisti. Senec. *Medea*, 218. petebant tunc meos thalamos proci, Qui nunc petuntur.

13. **Creditum abjuraverat**] "Had forsworn a trust." Among the Romans, the absence of facilities for bartering and exchange rendered it necessary to keep hoards of gold and silver, and these it was often requisite to entrust to the care of friends. The facility of breaking such engagements caused their faithful fulfilment to be regarded as an eminent virtue. Comp. Juvenal, xiii. 60 :

> Nunc si depositum non infitietur amicus,
> Si reddat veterem cum tota aerugine follem,
> Prodigiosa fides et Tuscis digna libellis,
> Quaeque coronata lustrari debeat agna.

14. **Praeceps abierat**] A combination of two phrases; *praeceps ire*, "to fall headlong ;" but *abire*, "to stray from the right path." A man is said *in alia omnia abire*, who digresses from the subject under discussion. *Abire* is also connected with *praeceps* in its ordinary sense in Livy, xli. 10. praeceps in provinciam abiit.

15. Haud absurdum] "Not contemptible." Comp. Tac. *Ann.* xiii. 45. of Poppaea, the wife of Nero, a passage evidently imitated from this: sermo comis, nec absurdum ingenium; modestiam praeferre et lascivia uti; rarus in publicum egressus, idque velata parte oris. See above note 2. on *Catil.* 3.

16. Posse] Supply *inerat*, or some similar verb, which the writer omits in order to pass abruptly to the summing up of the whole character: *prorsus...inerat.*

17. Jocum movere] "To raise a laugh." Comp. Hor. *Epist.* i. 19. 19. O imitatores, servum pecus, ut mihi saepe Bilem, saepe jocum vestri movere tumultus. So, stomachum, fletum alicui movere, "to cause anger, draw tears," &c.

18. Vel molli, vel procaci] Both words of bad signification, the latter the stronger of the two, "either amatory or meretricious." Indeed Cicero says, *pro Caelio*, 20. ut non solum meretrix sed etiam procax videretur.

19. Facetiae...lepos] "Wit and grace."

CHAPTER XXVI.

1. Nihilo minus] "Having thus made his preparations for seizing power by force, if necessary, Catiline, *although repulsed in his previous attempt*, nevertheless sued again for the consulship of the year following," i. e. of the year 692. Kritz. Or, "although he had made preparations for seizing power, nevertheless he sued for the next year's consulship in the legitimate way:" Gerlach and others: which gives a simpler meaning. If he became consul-designate, he expected to have much influence with one of the actual consuls, viz. Antonius; for the actual consuls were in a great degree dependent upon their successors for the salary, retinue, and military force, with which they were sent to their provinces.

2. Dolus aut astutiae] No slur is intended in the word *dolus*, which meant, in the best Latinity, "contrivance," whether in a good or a bad sense. Afterwards the sense became restricted. Comp. Ulpian, *Dig.* iv. 3. veteres dolum etiam bonum dicebant, et pro solertia hoc nomen accipiebant, maxime si adversus hostem latronemve aliquis machinetur. Comp. also Gellius, xii. 9; and Festus, who thus explains the law phrase, *sine dolo malo.*

3. Ad hoc] "In addition."

4. Pactione provinciae] The consuls generally chose by lot between the provinces of the Cisalpine Gaul and Macedonia. The former was important from its proximity to the city, but the latter more attractive from its greater extent and wealth. Cicero having obtained Macedonia transferred it to his colleague, which was considered an act of great generosity. But Cicero did not intend to take a province at all: he preferred remaining in the city, where his engagements as an advocate ensured him riches and consideration. Antonius eventually succeeded to the province of Macedonia, which he governed for two years, and was recalled and impeached for extortion, and also charged with complicity with Catiline. He was defended by Cicero, but condemned and banished.

5. **In campo**] "In the campus Martius," where the election was held. This attempt is referred to by Cicero, *in Catil.* i. 5, where he says that Catiline sought to kill not only him, as actual consul, but also the competitors for the ensuing consulship.

6. **Aspera foedaque evenerant**] "Had turned out to his injury and his shame." The adject. for the adverb. Comp. *Jugur.* 63. cuncta prospera eventura; but *Catil.* 52. bene consulendo prospere omnia cedunt.

CHAPTER XXVII.

1. **C. Manlium...dimisit**] Manlius must have returned to Rome, for he is mentioned c. 24, as already at Faesulae, unless the writer has forgotten himself.

2. **Camertem**] Of Camerinum, a town in Umbria, near the borders of Picenum.

3. **Picenum**] A district between the Apennines and the Adriatic, from the river Aternus on the south to the Aesis on the north.

4. **C. Julium**] About this Julius nothing more is known: he was probably not a Caesar. The Julian gens was already widely spread by clientship.

5. **Apuliam**] A region south-east of Picenum, bordering on the Adriatic, and extending to the Iapygian promontory, the eastern extremity of Italy.

6. **Quem ubique**] See notes on c. 21, and 23.

7. **Cum telo esse**] "To wear arms:" forbidden by the Twelve Tables, and by later laws. It became, however, common in these times, and was again prohibited by a law of Pompeius in his sole consulship, A.U. 702. The conspirators who murdered Caesar carried daggers in the case which belonged to the *stylus*. *Cum telo esse* is the antique formula. Cic. *pro Milon.*

4. ipsa lex esse cum telo hominis occidendi causa vetat. Comp. *in Catil.* i. 6; and the phrases *esse cum toga, cum imperio*.

8. **Jubere**] scil. *cum telo esse*.

9. **Festinare**] "He was busy."

10. **Intempesta nocte**] "Late at night." Servius, in Virg. *Aen.* iii. 587, explains this phrase, nox intempesta dicta est media, tanquam inactuosa; "unseasonable for action." Macrob. *Sat.* i. 3. non idonea rebus gerendis.

11. **Per M. Porcium Laecam**] It appears from Cicero that the meeting was held in the house of Lacca. The time of meeting is indicated by Cicero *pro Sulla*, 18. ea nocte quae consecuta est posterum diem nonarum Novembris, 6—7 Nov. 691 = 11 Jan. B.C. 62, allowing for the error in the calendar before its reformation by Julius Caesar.

12. **Ibi**] May mean *apud eum*, or better, *eo conventu*. Comp. *Catil.* 5. ibique juventutem exercuit: scil. in illis rebus.

CHAPTER XXVIII.

1. **L. Vargunteius senator**] Cicero says they were both knights; *in Catil.* i. 4. reperti sunt duo equites Rom. qui te ista cura liberarent, et sese illa ipsa nocte paullo ante lucem me in meo lectulo interfecturos pollicerentur. Appian and Plutarch both give different names from Sallust. This discrepancy in the evidence is not unimportant, as regards the credibility of the story as told by Sallust and Cicero.

2. **Paullo post**] scil. *post intempestam noctem:* i.e. *primo mane*, "very early in the morning." Clients and dependents who came to salute their patrons placed themselves at their doors before day-break in their eagerness to anticipate one another. Virgil says simply, Mane salutantes; but Juvenal, Sideribus dubiis aut illo tempore quo se Frigida circumagunt pigri sarraca Bootae. Cic. *ad Attic.* i. 18. quum bene completa domus esset tempore matutino. Symmachus in the 4th century speaks of keeping awake all night for the purpose: nondum ante januam eminentium potestatum vigilem noctem salutator expertus es. *Epist.* viii.

3. **Confodere**] i.e. multis ac gravibus vulneribus enecare. Dietsch. So, *concidere* Juv. xiv. 291. Concisum argentum in titulos faciesque minutas.

4. **Janua prohibiti**] Comp. *Jugur.* 21. Numidas insequentes moenibus prohibuit: "kept out of the city by means of the walls."

5. **In Etruria**] The Etruscans had been spoiled and massacred by Sulla, for their adherence to the Marian party. See Florus, iii. 21. Cic. *ad Att.* i. 19. They had risen against the Senate immediately after Sulla's death, when Lepidus headed a movement against the existing government. See Florus, iii. 22. Sall. *Fr. Hist.* i. 14. Etruria et omnes reliquiae belli arrectae.

6. **Sollicitare**] Always in Sallust of exciting people to do something. See *Catil.* 36, 39, 50. *Jugur.* 19. Dietsch.

7. **Ex Sullanis colonis**] "Of the Sullan colonists," i.e. the veterans planted by Sulla on the estates of dispossessed Italian communities to the number of 120,000 or more. See Cicero, *in Catil.* ii. 9.

CHAPTER XXIX.

1. **Ancipiti malo**] "The double calamity;" i.e. the plot within the city, and the insurrection in Etruria, &c. Comp. *Jugur.* 67. neque caveri anceps malum posse.

2. **Rem ad senatum refert**] A technical phrase; "he moves a resolution in the senate concerning the affair:" the more usual form being *referre de aliqua re ad sen.*, with the same meaning. Comp. a third form, *Catil.* 50. consul convocato senatu refert quid de his fieri placeat qui in custodiam traditi erant: "submits a resolution to the pleasure of the senate." This was a. d. xii. Kal. Nov. Cic. *in Catil.* i. 3. meministine me ante diem xii. Kal. Nov. dicere in senatu certo die fore in armis qui dies futurus esset a. d. viii. Kal. Novembres? The decree which followed was given on xi. Kal. Nov. = 22 Oct. 691 = 26 Dec. 63 B.C., as appears from the notice of Asconius, who says that the first oration against Catiline was delivered, cum octavus decimus dies esset postquam factum est senatus consultum, etc. The *Orat. in Catil.* 1. was delivered on vi. Id. Nov. = 8 Nov. 691 = 12 Jan. 62 B.C. This, it will be seen, was some days before the meeting in Porcius Laeca's house, and the attempt to murder the consul.

3. **Solet**] Absol. for *fieri solet:* as *Catil.* 30. *Jugur.* 15, 25, 66.

4. **Ea potestas...maxima, etc.**] Observe the place which *maxima* holds in this sentence, removed from its substantive, and give it a *pregnant* sense: "This power, which is paramount to all, the Roman law allows the senate to confer upon the magistrate: the power, namely, of raising an army, &c." Such a decree was denominated *Senatus consultum ultimum.* This was equivalent to giving the consuls dictatorial power, and was

far more convenient to the nobles than creating a dictator, which they had not ventured to do for 150 years, except in the case of Sulla.

5. **Domi militiaeque**] Ordinarily the consul exercised no military imperium within the city, but only in the camp: on these occasions the imperium was added to the judicium or jus juris dicendi, within the city also, i.e. the city was put under military law.

6. **Nullius**] There is MS. authority for the genitive, and the common reading, *nulli*, can hardly stand, whether it be connected with *rerum*, or *consuli*. The meaning of the passage is: "except in the case of the senate using its prerogative to issue its ultimate decree, the consul has no *jus* of any kind, either separate or conjoined, but what he derives from the appointment of the people." The phrase *populi jussus* is equivocal. Properly it means the decree of the curies, by which, in early times, the imperium was conferred upon the kings, and after the establishment of the republic, upon the consuls, posterior to their election by the centuries. In process of time this became a mere form. But the phrase may be used loosely for the election itself, by which the consul became virtually invested with the jus juris dicendi, and jus imperandi beyond the walls. Sallust means perhaps to reserve to the people the right of extending this jus in extreme cases to paramount authority within the city; which however they never ventured to claim, though they strongly objected to its exercise by the senate.

CHAPTER XXX.

1. **Arma portari**] Gaius distinguishes *ferre*, *portare* and *agere*: Ferri proprie dicimus quae quis suo corpore bajulat, portari ea quae quis in jumento secum ducit, agi ea quae animalia sunt: *portare* is also emphatic or poetic for *ferre*. So ferre, vehere, portare are used with some distinction by Statius, *Theb.* viii. 315, in an address to the Earth which had swallowed up Amphiaraus:

domos Atlanta supernas
Ferre laborantem nullo vehis ipsa labore:
Nos tantum portare negas? nos, Diva, gravaris?

scil. "to bear," "to carry," "to support."

2. **Senati decreto**] This ancient form of the genitive is sanctioned by Nonius, viii. 10; and Donatus on Terence *Andr.* ii. 2. 28. notices that Sallust used it. Tumulti also occurs, *Catil.* 59.

3. **Q. Marcius Rex**] Consul with L. Caecilius Metellus, A.U. 686, and afterwards proconsul in Cilicia. Cicero praises his courage and military skill, *in Pison. 23.* Ab Anco Marcio sunt Marcii Reges. Suet. *Cal.* 6. Marcius and Martius are probably the same word.

4. **Q. Metellus Creticus**] Consul with L. Hortensius A.U. 685: he subdued Crete as proconsul.

5. **Circumque loca**] "The neighbouring regions:" *circum* and *circa* are thus used absolutely for *quae circ. sunt*, very commonly in Livy. See ix. 11; xxiv. 3. The MSS. read *circumque ea loca*, and the emendation is due to Cortius, who saw that the reading must have arisen from the transcribers' ignorance of the idiom. *Ea*, meaning Apulia, would make the passage absurd. *Loca* is governed by *in*.

6. **Hi utrique**] For the more correct form, *horum uterque*. So *Catil.* 5. quae utraque. Tac. *Ann.* xvi. 11. pater filiam, avia neptem, illa utrosque intuens, for utrumque.

7. **Ad urbem imperatores**] These words are to be connected together: generals returned from their provinces, and waiting outside the walls for the day of their triumph, before which they were not allowed to enter the city; or who, having received the imperium, had not yet completed their levies. Asconius explains the phrase, *Act. in Verr.* i. 15. sic dici solet de iis qui cum potestate provinciali aut nuper a provincia revertissent, aut nondum in provinciam profecti essent.

8. **Calumnia**] "Machination, cabal," from an old word *caluo, decipio*, Priscian; who cites a passage from the *Historiae* of Sallust: contra ille calui ratus.

9. **Q. Pompeius Rufus**] This man, who was praetor A.U. 691, is to be distinguished from another bearing the same names, tribune of the people A.U. 702, who made himself conspicuous as a turbulent partizan of Cn. Pompeius, in that year sole consul. Rufus, the praetor, is praised by Cicero for his moderation and integrity. After serving the state in the affair of Catiline, he obtained the proconsular government of Africa. There were two families belonging to the *gens Pompeia*, distinguished by the surnames Rufus and Strabo. Cn. Pompeius Magnus was son of Cn. Pompeius Strabo. The praenomens of the Rufi, so far as they are known to us, were Aulus and Quintus; those of the Strabones, Cnaeus and Sextus.

10. **Q. Metellus Celer**] Of the *gens Caecilia*, one of the most numerous and widely ramified of the great Roman houses. One great branch of it bore the surname Metellus; but this family again was subdivided, and its various offsets were dis-

tinguished by additional surnames; such as *Pius*, *Nepos* and *Celer*. Metellus Celer and Metellus Nepos were brothers, both sons of a Nepos. A story is told by Plutarch, that this Celer received his surname for the celerity with which he provided a show of gladiators for the solemnity of his father's funeral. But the surname Celer was borne by another Metellus before him, by whom he was probably adopted. The praetor Celer became afterwards consul, A. U. 694.

11. **Permissum**] "Authority was given." Comp. Cic. *in Catil.* i. 2. senatusconsulto consulibus permissa respublica, "put in charge of the consuls." Lucan, i. 595. Pontifices, sacri quibus est permissa potestas.

12. **Sestertia centum**] "One hundred sestertia," i.e. "one hundred thousand sestertii (sesterces)." The *sestertius* was a Roman coin, one-fourth of the denarius (10 asses), and therefore equal to $2\frac{1}{2}$ asses. Hence the name, which is an abbreviation of *semis tertius* (scil. *nummus*); i.e. 1 an as, 2 an as, and 3 a half as. "Hence the symbol HS or IIS, which is used to designate the sestertius. It stands for either LLS. (Libra Libra et Semis) or for IIS, the two I's merely forming the numeral *two* (scil. *asses* or *librae*), and the whole being, in either case, equivalent to *dupondius et semis*."

"The value of the sestertius up to the time of Augustus . . . . . . = 0 0 2 ·5
—— of the sestertium . . . . . = 8 17 1
After Augustus,
the sestertius . . . . . . = 0 0 1 3·5
the sestertium . . . . . . = 7 16 3."

£ s. d. f.

See Smith's *Dictionary of Gr. and Rom. Antiquities*, Art. Sestertius.

13. **Gladiatoriae familiae**] "Troops of gladiators." It was a commercial speculation to maintain a number of swordsmen, trained in schools (*ludi*) by masters of the art (*lanistae*), and to let these out to the magistrates for public shows. The gladiators were at first captives or criminals; but persons were found to offer themselves voluntarily for pay; and it became usual to affix a period (three years) for their service; after which, if they survived, they received a staff (*rude donati*) in token of their discharge. The large numbers of these gladiators collected, particularly at Capua, became an object of alarm to the government in times of disturbance. On this occasion their schools were dispersed in various towns as a measure of precaution.

14. **Minores magistratus**] The aediles, quaestors and triumvirs, appointed for various purposes. The inferior magistrates were elected by the comitia tributa, the superior by the

centuriata. Aul. Gell. xiii. 15. The tribunes of the people were not strictly magistrates. The establishment of the watch is mentioned by Cicero, *in Catil.* i. 1. Augustus first instituted a regular police, *cohors vigilum*, in Rome.

CHAPTER XXXI.

1. **Quae**] The neut. plur. "which things." Comp. *Jugur.* 41. scilicet ea, quae secundae res amant, lascivia atque superbia incessere.

2. **Reipublicae magnitudine**] "From the greatness of the Republic," the ablat. of the cause, i. q. *propter reip. magnitudinem.* Comp. *Jugur.* 42. Gracchis cupidine victoriae haud satis moderatus animus fuit.

3. **Incesserat**] Omitted without reason in most editions on account of the dat. *quibus.* But comp. Caes. *B. C.* iii. 74. exercitui Caesaris tantus incessit dolor. Liv. iv. 57. cura patribus incessit. Tac. *Ann.* iii. 36. incedebat enim deterrimo cuique licentia. Cicero, *ad Div.* xvi. 12, says, mirus invaserat furor improbis. Translate: "assailed by fear of war, to which from the greatness of the republic they had long been unaccustomed."

4. **Afflictare**] Properly, "to dash against," as of ships driven on shore, the conflict of armies, &c.; but it does not seem to occur in the sense of *plangere* or *prosternere*, as an act of lamentation. Construe it metaphorically, "were afflicted," "distressed."

5. **Miserari**] "Lamented over." *Misereri*, "to feel compassion in the mind;" *miserari*, "to express compassion."

6. **Eadem illa movebat**] "Continued plotting as before."

7. **Lege Plautia**] A law *de vi*, i. e. against public violence, carried by M. Plautius Sylvanus, a tribune of the plebs, A. U. 665. It made the offence of wearing arms in the city, and occupying the public places with an armed force, capital, in the Roman sense, i. e. involving loss of *caput*, or civil condition, whether by death, or, as an alternative, by self-banishment.

8. **L. Paullo**] This was L. Aemilius Lepidus Paullus, brother of the triumvir M. Lepidus, consul A. U. 704. He was proscribed by the triumvirs A. U. 711, but escaped death.

9. **Et ut sui**] The MSS. fluctuate between this and the much easier readings, *aut sui; ac sui; vel sui; quasi sui.* In such cases the harder construction is generally to be preferred,

as the more likely to have been altered by the transcribers. Construe: "And as if to clear himself." *Ut* is thus used for *quasi* by Cicero, *de Orat.* i. 50. neque ea ut sua possedisse, sed ut aliena libasse: and elsewhere.

10. Sui expurgandi] A gerund in the genit. agrees in case gender and number with its noun if sing. as sui expurgandi, invidiae ferendae &c. but a noun in the plural may be governed in case by genit. of gerund in sing. as: poenarum solvendi tempus. Cic. *de Invent.* ii. 2. ex magna copia nobis fuit exemplorum eligendi potestas.

11. Jurgio] "A frivolous and malicious charge." Comp. Cic. *pro Cael.* 13. omnia sunt alia, non crimina, sed maledicta jurgii petulantis magis quam publicae quaestionis.

12. Luculentam] "Splendid, admirable:" used of orations in this sense by Cicero, *ad Att.* xii. 21. Cato verbis luculentioribus et pluribus rem eandem prehenderat.

13. Utilem] "That did good service." *Utilis* has frequently an emphatic sense, "of admirable service." Comp. Ovid, *Metam.* v. 212. Et pedibus Pterelas et naribus utilis Agre. Propert. iii. 7. 19. Hic satus ad pacem, hic castrensibus utilis armis. In the same manner, *non utilis*, "pernicious." Ovid, *Met.* xv. 103. postquam non utilis auctor Victibus invidit. Lucan, x. 26. (Alexander) non utile mundo Editus exemplum, terras tot posse sub uno Esse viro. There is therefore no cold disparagement, as has been supposed, implied in the phrase, luculentam atque utilem reipubl. Sallust here refers to the first speech against Catiline.

14. Quam postea scriptam edidit] Sallust does not pretend to give Cicero's speeches, because they were published by himself.

15. Ubi ille assedit] "Stantes enim dicebant, ubi judicum erat sedere." Kritz. "assidere," in forensic language, to sit down in one's place beside others. Cic. *pro Rosc. Amerin.* peroravit aliquando, assedit; surrexi ego.

16. Ut erat paratus ad dissimulanda] i. q. *pro dissimulatione sua.* Comp. *Jugur.* 7. Jugurtha ut erat impigro atque acri ingenio. Ovid, *Metam.* xiii. 3:

<blockquote>
Utque erat impatiens irae Sigeia torvo
Litora respexit, classemque in litore, vultu.
</blockquote>

17. Inquilinus civis] From *incolo,* "a sojourner in a city;" as a lodger in a house, one who has no rights of possession. This is an unjust sarcasm on Cicero, who was a genuine citizen of Rome; but the proud patrician sneers at the plebeians generally, as an adventitious class.

18. **Ad hoc**] "Hereto," "in addition," as in c. 26, note 3. not, ad hoc maledictum.

19. **Parricidam**] "Unnatural murderer." This epithet is applied to any monstrous criminal: as *Catil.* 14. omnes undique parricidae, sacrilegi, convicti judiciis: but more particularly to traitors against the state, slayers of their country, Cic. *in Catil.* i. 7. te patria odit ac metuit, ac jam diu te nihil judicat nisi de parricidio suo cogitare. Comp. Tac. *Hist.* i. 85. hostem et parricidam Vitellium vocantes.

20. **Ruina restinguam**] Just as a conflagration may be extinguished by the falling or pulling down of the house. Cicero, *pro Murena*, 25, cites the same phrase as used by Catiline: quum Catoni respondisset si quod esset in suas fortunas incendium excitatum, id se non aqua sed ruina restincturum. This reply, according to Cicero, was made not to himself, but to Cato, who probably had followed him in the debate.

CHAPTER XXXII.

1. **Quod neque insidiae consuli procedebant**] *Consuli* is governed by procedebant, the *dativus commodi*, rather harshly applied; "since his plans did not succeed with regard to the consul." The same construction follows immediately, *insidias consuli maturent.*

2. **Optimum factum**] Simply, "the best thing;" *factu*, which many MSS. read, would express more fully, "the best thing to be done." So *bonum factum* "good!" Comp. Suet. *Jul.* Bonum factum : ne quis Senatori novo curiam monstrare velit. It was a common heading for proclamations. Plaut. *Poen.* prolog. Bonum factum : edicta ut servetis mea.

3. **Nocte intempesta**] See note 10, Chap. xxvii. This was the night of the 8th—9th of November, A.U. 691=12, 13 Jan. B.C. 62. Cicero delivered the second Catilinarian postridie quam Catilina profugit, v. Id. Nov.=9 Nov.

4. **Prope diem**] "Shortly:" scil. *ad prope diem*, i.e. *ad diem qui prope est; ad proximum diem.* For this adjectival use of the prep. comp. Hor. *Od.* iv. 6. 3. Trojae prope victor altae Phthius Achilles, "the nearly-conqueror of Troy." Lucan, vi. 363. tuus, Oeneu, Pene gener, "thy almost-son-in-law."

5. **Accessurum**] Understand, *pollicetur.*

6. **Ex suo numero**] "Of his band:" *numerus* in its

figurative sense of order, rank, class, &c., as in *numerus deorum*, *numerus beatorum*. Comp. Lucr. v. 180:

> Qui nunquam vero vitae gustavit amorem,
> Nec fuit in numero (scil. viventium).

Virg. *Aen.* v. 305:

> Nemo ex hoc numero mihi non donatus abibit.

7. **Cum mandatis**] "With instructions." The *command* refers to the person charged to deliver the message, not to the person to whom the message is to be delivered.

CHAPTER XXXIII.

1. **Feneratores**] More correct than *foeneratores*, as derived from *feo*, i.e. *gigno*.

2. **Patriae**] The same double construction with gen. and dat. occurs *Jugur.* 84. plerosque militiae paucos fama cognitos accire. Comp. above c. 25. note on multa alia.

3. **Lege uti**] "To have the benefit of the law." The laws of the Twelve Tables fixed the highest rate of interest at $\frac{1}{12}$th per ann. of the sum borrowed, = 8⅓ per cent. This was called *unciarium fenus*, the *uncia* being $\frac{1}{12}$th of the *as*. This was reduced to one half by the consuls Manlius and Plautius, A.U. 407. Liv. vii. 27. These enactments were generally disregarded: in the time of Horace money could fetch as much as 5 per cent. per month. See *Sat.* i. 2. 14. Quinas hic capiti mercedes exsecat. Comp. Tac. *Ann.* vi. 16. But the passage in the text refers more particularly to the lex Paetelia Papiria, A.U. 428, by which imprisonment for debt was forbidden. See Liv. viii. 28. At an earlier period the creditor had power not only to confine his debtor, but to sell him into slavery. Aulus Gellius, xx. 1, cites a law of the Twelve Tables which enacted that if there were more creditors than one they might cut up the debtor's body in due proportion: partes secanto: si plus minusve secuerunt se fraude esto. Gellius understood this law literally, and it has generally been interpreted accordingly. Some, however, maintain that the *sectio* refers only to a division of the debtor's effects. Perhaps it was a rude way of expressing the idea of strict retribution, like the provisions of the Mahometan law of retaliation, not meant to be actually enforced.

4. **Atque praetoris**] The praetor urbanus was the principal judge in all civil processes, and the poor debtors complained that he favoured their wealthier creditors. In the *edictum* which he issued on assuming his office, he declared the

principles on which he should administer justice, and frequently trenched upon the provisions of actual law.

5. **Vestrum**] The passage was thus read by A. Gellius (xx. 6), though many MSS. give *vestri*. Observe that *nostri*, *vestri* are genitives sing. of the possessives *noster*, *vester*, not genitives plural of *nos*, *vos*, as the grammars for the most part assert. In partition *nostrum* must be used, as *primus nostrum*, *multi nostrum*, not *nostri*. On the other hand, *amor nostri*, where "being or condition," *negotii*, may be understood. So where *nos* is the subject, *pars nostrum amat:* but *vivas memor nostri*, *noster* being the object.

6. **Boni**] "Good citizens."

7. **Argentum aere solutum est**] The silver coin, the *sestertius*, was paid with the brass coin, the *as*. This refers to an adjustment of debts made by the government in the year U.C. 668, when obligations were cancelled by the payment of one-fourth of the amount (quadrante capitis, Vell. ii. 23). The sestertius (i. e. semistertius) originally = $2\frac{1}{2}$ asses: but after the second Punic war it was made = 4 asses. See Plin. *Hist. Nat.* xxxiii. 13. Hannibale urgente, Q. Fabio Maximo dictatore asses unciales facti, placuitque denarium sedecim assibus permutari, sestertium quaternis. The weight of the as was gradually reduced from its original 12 ounces to 1; and the denarius, properly ten asses, was made = sixteen, the sestertius = four asses.

8. **Secessit**] On three or more occasions the plebs removed in a body from the city. See Livy, ii. 32 (A. U. 260); iii. 50 (A. U. 305); *Epit.* xi. (A. U. 466); Sallust, *Jugur.* 31, speaks of two secessions to the Aventine. They were prevailed upon to return by concessions accorded them by the patricians.

9. **Amittit**] "Parts with;" *amittere*, to let a thing be taken from one, *perdere*, to throw it away.

10. **Quonam modo**] "How we may sell our lives as dearly as possible."

CHAPTER XXXIV.

1. **Vellent...discedant**] Observe the change of construction. "Marcius said, If they *wished* to make any suit to the senate, *let* them lay down their arms." Comp. c. 32. quibus rebus possent opes factionis confirment.

2. **Ab armis discedant**] i. e. a bello, "abandon their hostile attitude."

3. **Optimo cuique**] "The most distinguished among the nobles." So the highest aristocracy were called the *optimates*.

4. **Massiliam in exilium**] Comp. Cicero, *in Catil.* ii. 6. Massilia, the modern Marseilles, was founded by the Phocaeans (Thucyd. i. 13) on the south coast of Gaul, about 600 B.C., and became celebrated for its commerce and civilization. When the Romans gained a footing on the further side of the Alps, they formed an alliance with Massilia, and allowed it to retain a nominal independence and sovereignty over a small district on the coast. The Roman province being governed by proconsuls sent there by the oligarchical party, and all their influence brought to bear upon the allies of the republic, Massilia became firmly attached to the senate; and Catiline, in pretending to choose it for his place of exile, intimated that he was falsely accused of hostility to the ruling faction. Exile among the Romans was banishment to a place beyond the direct control of the commonwealth, but any allied city was allowed to receive exiles, however near it might be to Rome. Gradually all the free states were absorbed into the provinces, and there ceased to be any place of asylum for exiles within the frontiers of the empire.

5. **Non quo**] An elliptic expression for *non eo quod*.

6. **Q. Catulus**] The princeps or premier of the senate, consul A. U. 676. He was the most illustrious of the oligarchical party both in rank and reputation. Catulus was of the Lutatian, properly Luctatian, *gens*.

7. **Exemplum**] "A copy."

CHAPTER XXXV.

1. **Commendationi meae**] "To this recommendation of my interests to your care."

2. **Defensionem**] "Judicial defence;" *satisfactionem*, "private explanation."

3. **In novo consilio**] "Under the circumstances of my new design;" i.e. his repairing to the camp of Manlius, and professing to assert the claims of the injured debtors.

4. **Conscientia de culpa**] "Consciousness of guilt;" as Cic. *ad Att.* ii. 24 : his de rebus conscium esse Pisonem.

5. **Me dius fidius**] i. e. *ita me Deus* (i. e. *Jovis*) *filius* (*Hercules*) *juvet*. Some suppose there to be a Deus Fidius, from a passage in Plautus, *Asin.* i. 1. 8. per Dium Fidium quaeris: but this appears to be a mock personification.

6. Licet cognoscas] "You may ascertain if you please."

7. Statum dignitatis] Cortius observes that *status* is the position a man holds, *gradus* that which he seeks, therefore proposes to substitute the latter for the former here; on the supposition that *status dignitatis* means the consulship which Catiline failed to *obtain*. It refers, however, to the position which Catiline already occupied. Translate: "I could not *maintain* the privilege of my high position, which authorized me to expect success in suing for the consulship." Comp. c. 18. Catilina, pecuniarum repetundarum reus, prohibitus erat consulatum petere. *Obtinere;* most properly to hold, keep, preserve: only in a secondary sense, to acquire, obtain.

8. Meis nominibus] *Sumptum*, which occurs here in some MSS., is a gloss, to explain the construction: "debts contracted on my own account," "inscribed in the ledger with my name:" (*nomen* or *nomina* may be used indifferently), *alienis nom.* sub. *aes alienum sumptum*, "debts incurred as surety for others," "inscribed with others' names."

9. Honore honestatos] Comp. Plaut. *Capt.* ii. 2. 106. quum me tanto honore honestas. Honestare laude occurs in Cicero; honestare gloria in the *Jugur.* c. 10.

10. Alienatum] "Cast out." *Alienare* significat alienos reddere et e familia ejicere. Ruhnken on Ter. *Heaut.* v. 2. 20.

11. Hoc nomine] "Having made this undertaking," i.e. to defend the cause of the oppressed. *Nomen*, the subscription of one's name, implying a pledge.

CHAPTER XXXVI.

1. In agro Arretino] Arretium, mod. Arezzo, lay almost on the direct road from Rome to Faesulae. This reading is therefore preferred to *Reatino*, which most editions follow. *Reate*, in the country of the Sabines, was far to the right.

2. Exornat] "Furnishes:" so, *classem exornare*, "to equip a fleet."

3. Cum fascibus] The *fasces*, i.e. an axe in a bundle of rods, was the ensign of the higher magistracies of the city. This was accordingly an usurpation of official rank: as Plutarch says in his life of Cicero, c. 16. Cicero *in Catil.* ii. 6. quum arma, quum secures, quum fasces, quum tubas, quum signa militaria, quum aquilam illam argenteam scirem esse praemissam.

4. **Hostes**] "Public enemies," more properly *perduelles*. The word meant originally no more than "strangers," (comp. *hospes*). Cicero says of this change of signification, *de Off.* i. 12. illud etiam animadverto, quod qui proprio nomine perduellis esset is hostis vocaretur, lenitate verbi tristitiam rei mitigante. Hostis enim apud majores is dicebatur quem nunc peregrinum dicimus. Gaius, in *Digest.* quos nos hostes appellamus eos veteres perduelles appellabant, per eam adjectionem indicantes, cum quibus bellum erat. *Perduellis* then means a foreign enemy with whom there may be *bellum*, legitimate warfare; but the pirate non est ex perduellium numero sed communis *hostis* omnium. Cic. *Off.* iii. 29. This is a further distinction, and in this sense the outlawed conspirator might be designated *hostis* more correctly than *perduellis*. *Duellum*, i.q. *bellum*, from the same root as *duo*, etc., signifying "division."

5. **Sine fraude**] i.e. *sine damno*. Comp. Liv. i. 24. quod sine fraude mea populique Rom. fiat, facio. Doederlein, *Latein. Synonym.*, connects *fraus* with ψεῦδος, as *frigus* with ψῦχος, *fricare* with ψάω, *frendere* with ψίνδεσθαι (i.q. κλαίειν, Hesychius), *friare* with ψίειν.

6. **Praeter...condemnatis**] The part. depends upon *liceret*, after which understand *iis: praeter* adverbial, i. q. *praeterquam*. Comp. Justin. xiii. 5. omnium civitatium exsules, praeter caedis damnati, restituebantur. Suet. *Ner.* 56. religionum contemptor praeter unius Deae Syriae.

7. **Delectum**] Levy of troops, not *dilectum*. The MSS. of Latin authors fluctuate in the orthography of this word. In this place, with one exception, they concur in *delectus*. But if there were such a word as *dilectus*, we should surely meet with it in the sense of *love*, as *dilectio*, in which it never occurs.

8. **Persequi maturet**] Comp. Tac. *Hist.* v. 18. si Romana classis sequi maturasset, i.c. celeriter secuta esset, *Jugur.* 36, 39.

9. **Ad occasum ab ortu**] Quintilian remarks of the proper order of words: est et naturalis ordo, ut viros ac foeminas, diem ac noctem, ortum et occasum dicas, potius quam retrorsum. *Inst. Orat.* ix. 4. 23. But the reverse order occurs sometimes, as in Lucr. and Virg. noctes atque dies: Stat. *Sylv.* iii. 3. 47. Sed quibus occasus pariter famulantur et ortus.

10. **Perditum irent**] "Sought to destroy:" implying wish and endeavour to effect an object. Comp. *Catil.* 52. *Jugur.* 31, 68, 85.

11. **Duobus senati decretis**] "Notwithstanding the existence of two decrees:" the ablat. absol. expressing a condition

or state. Comp. Cic. *ad Div.* iv. 6. nunc autem hoc tam gravi vulnere etiam illa quae consenuisse videbantur recrudescunt. *Pro Arch.* 3. hac tanta celebritate famae. Sallust, *Fr. Hist.* cetera secundis rebus oriri sueta mala.

12. **Uti tabes**] "Like a contagion." Some MSS. read *atque uti tabes:* "and as it were contagion."

CHAPTER XXXVII.

1. **Aliena**] "Estranged, hostile."

2. **Id adeo**] The force of *adeo* is here emphatic, "in fact:" being a stronger affirmation of a previous proposition. So again, id adeo malum, at the end of this chapter. Comp. *Jugur.* 66. eum imperium Numidiae sine mora habiturum : id adeo mature posse evenire ; and again 110, 111.

3. **Aluntur, etc.**] "They get their living without anxiety in tumults and seditions, because poverty wants little, and has nothing to lose." *Habetur,* i.q. *toleratur.*

4. **Ea vero**] A demonstration, introduced for emphasis, changes the construction. Comp. for the force of the pronoun, *Catil.* 58. in fuga salutem sperare ea vero dementia est. Cic. *Nat. Deor.* ii. 10. reliqua pars mundi ea et ipsa tota natura fervida est. See note 10 on *Catil.* 12.

5. **Praeceps ierat**] "Had become utterly demoralized, or reckless." Comp. *Catil.* 25. luxuria atque inopia praeceps abierat. Persius, iii. 41. imus, imus praecipites.

6. **Praestabant**] "Exceeded:" rarely used as here in a bad sense; but comp. Cic. *de Leg.* i. 19. qui singulis vitiis excellunt.

7. **Sentinam**] *Sentina,* a sink, cesspool, hold of a ship. So Cic. *ad Att.* i. 19, speaking of the good effects anticipated from settling some of the urban population on public domains in Italy: et sentinam urbis exhauriri et Italiae solitudinem frequentari posse arbitrabar. Also, *in Catil.* i. 5.

8. **Ex gregariis militibus**] "Of the common soldiers."

9. **Ita divites**] Comp. *Catil.* 51. neque prius finis jugulandi fuit quam Sulla omnes suos divitiis explevit.

10. **Regio victu atque cultu.**] "In regal luxury." The term *rex* was applied invidiously to citizens of extraordinary wealth and ostentatious manner of living. So *regum pueri:* the delicate children of the nobility. Pers. iii. 17.

11. Manuum mercede] "With the wages of manual labour." Comp. Virg. *Aen.* viii. 409. Cui tolerare colo vitam tenuique Minerva.

12. Privatis atque publicis largitionibus] i. e. distributions of corn, oil, or wine, made by rich patrons to their clients; or by candidates for office, or actual magistrates, to the people. Thus Crassus, after the defeat of Spartacus, when suing for the consulship, A. U. 683, feasted the Roman people at ten thousand tables. Public largesses had been given occasionally, and C. Gracchus introduced the sale of corn at low fixed prices to the citizens; but M. Cato first advised a regular gratuitous distribution, in the hope of withdrawing the needy citizens from the influence of the demagogues. The largess (five bushels, Sall. *Fr. Hist.*) was given monthly, Suet. *Oct.* 40.

13. Praetulerat] Depending upon *quae*, as *toleraverat*.

14. Eos] Scil. *juvenes*, understood in *juventus*: the construction is broken, *juventus* being a nomin. absolute.

15. Juxta] "Not more for the advantage of the one than the other, but equally ill for both." Comp. *Catil.* 61. ita cuncti suae atque hostium vitae juxta pepercerant.

16. Jus libertatis imminutum] "Treated as if they were neither citizens nor freemen," i. e. deprived of the privileges of the constitution. The families of the proscribed were incapacitated for holding public office by a Lex Cornelia, A. U. 673. Vell. ii. 28. exclusique paternis opibus liberi etiam petendorum honorum jure prohiberentur, simulque quod indignissimum est, senatorum filii et onera ordinis sustinerent et jura perderent. The rehabilitation of these persons was agitated for many years; defeated by Cicero in his consulship; and at last effected by Caesar as dictator. See Plutarch, *Caes.* 37 (A. U. 705); Suet. *Jul.* 75.

17. Aliarum atque senati] *Atque* and *ac* are used after words of comparison, e. g. *idem, pars, similis, alius, aeque, perinde, aliter, secus;* where the sense can only be rendered in English by "as," or "than." *Ut*, however, sometimes occurs with *atque*, as Cic. *in Verr.* i. 46. aliter atque ut edixerat; from which it may be surmised that the copula of comparison has dropped out of the idiom; and that *atque* had originally its proper sense of "immediately," "just;" e. g. *hic facit idem atque (quod) ego*, "he does just the same as I do."

18. Id adeo malum] Emphatic, "that evil, then;" or "that evil, great as it was:" namely, the inveterate jealousy of the commons towards the senate, dating at least from the times of the Gracchi sixty or seventy years before.

S.   7

CHAPTER XXXVIII.

1. **Cn. Pompeio et M. Crasso coss.**] A. U. 684.

2. **Tribunicia potestas restituta est**] Among the principal measures of Sulla for curbing the pretensions of the Marian or popular party at Rome, and securing to the senate the administration of affairs, was the restriction he placed upon the prerogative of the tribunes of the plebs. Comp. Appian, *Bell. Civ.* i. 100. τὴν δὲ τῶν δημάρχων ἀρχὴν ἴσα καὶ ἀνεῖλεν, ἀσθενεστάτην ἀποφήνας, καὶ νόμῳ κωλύσας μηδεμίαν ἄλλην τὸν δήμαρχον ἀρχὴν ἔτι ἄρχειν. Liv. *Epit.* lxxxix. tribunorum plebis potestatem minuit et omne jus ferendarum legum ademit. The ancient right of *intercessio*, or a veto on motions in the senate, still remained to them. At the same time Sulla confined the comitia of the tribes to the election of the inferior magistrates, forbidding it to enact laws or receive criminal appeals. All these prerogatives were restored by a *Lex Pompeia*, in the year above mentioned. Vell. ii. 30. Pompeius tribuniciam potestatem restituit, cujus Sulla imaginem sine re reliquerat.

3. **Adolescentes**] Properly *adolescentia* extended from 15 to 30 years of age. But the term was frequently applied to persons of more advanced age. Thus Cicero, *Philipp.* ii. 46, calls himself an *adolescens* in the time of his consulship, when he was 44 years of age. Sallust, speaking of Caesar in his thirty-seventh year, calls him *adolescentulus, Catil.* 49. In this place *homines adolescentes* may be rendered "rising men;" that is, men who were beginning to become important political characters.

4. **Summam potestatem**] Meaning the tribunate, which since the *lex Pompeia* had become the most influential office in the state.

5. **Senati specie**] "Under pretence of supporting the authority of the senate," but really to maintain their own ascendancy. Comp. Lucan, ix. 206. non jam regnare pudebit, Nec color imperii, nec frons erit ulla senatus: "henceforth men will act the king without scruple, there will be no colour of legitimate command, nor pretence of senatorial authority."

6. **Sicuti**] "As though." Comp. *Catil.* 31. sicuti jurgio lacessitus foret.

7. **Potentia**] Power, without respect to its legality, and generally in opposition to legitimate authority, *potestas*. Comp. *Catil.* 39. paucorum potentia crevit. Lucan, iv. *in fin.*:

> Jus licet in jugulos nostros *sibi fecerit ense*
> Sylla *potens*, Mariusque ferox, et Cinna cruentus,
> Caesareaeque domus series, cui *tanta potestas*
> *Concessa est;* emere omnes, hic vendidit urbem.

8. **Neque modestia, neque modus]** Comp. note c. 11.

CHAPTER XXXIX.

1. **Ad bellum maritimum atque Mithridaticum]** The "maritime war" was that against the Cilician pirates, who infested the whole of the Mediterranean, and often made descents on land, even in Italy. Gabinius, a creature of Pompey, proposed a law for conferring upon him extraordinary command for their suppression, A. U. 687. The speed and efficiency with which Pompey put down these marauders was deservedly celebrated. See Cic. *pro leg. Manil.* 12, Plutarch, *Pomp.* 24, and the historians Appian, Florus, and Velleius Paterculus.

The "Mithridatic war" was the long contest waged by the republic against Mithridates, the renowned king of Pontus. Sulla had defeated, and was supposed to have crushed him; but he rose again, and wrested the province of Asia from the Romans. Lucullus again defeated him, but he was still unconquered; and at last, at the motion of Manilius, the Roman people appointed Pompey to carry on the war against him, with full powers throughout the eastern possessions of the republic. This extraordinary commission was regarded by the senate with great jealousy. It was apprehended that Pompey would never consent to return to Rome as a private man. Nevertheless, after the successful completion of his task, and the addition of extensive provinces to the empire, he disbanded his legions, and was content to be the first citizen in the free state. But he afterwards repented, and tried, by a league with Caesar and Crassus, (the first triumvirate,) to acquire a more decided supremacy in the commonwealth. The Manilian law was carried A. U. 688.

2. **Plebis opes imminutae]** "The power of the commons was curtailed." During Pompey's absence the nobles strove to recover their ascendancy, which he had considerably reduced in his consulship, A. U. 684.

3. **Innoxii]** Passive, "secure from attack." Comp. Lucan, ix. 891:

> Gens unica terras
> Incolit a saevo serpentum innoxia morsu.

Columella, v. 9. innoxius ab injuria pecorum.

4. **Ceteros]** Comp. c. 51: juxta bonos et malos lubidinose interficere, ceteros metu terrere.

5. **Quo plebem etc.]** There is great confusion in this passage. Understand *hi*, the nobility, both patrician and plebeian; *ipsi*, such of them as actually occupied the public

offices at any time; *ceteri*, the rest of them, who were at the same time not in office, such as the defeated candidates; but more especially the *tribunes of the people*, who are said to be *in magistratu*, incorrectly, because the tribunate was not strictly a magistracy, but who frequently used their power, as such, to harass the real magistrates, the consuls and praetors. Disappointed candidates, especially if they were tribunes, excited the people against their rulers; but by an unscrupulous use of the *judicia* the magistrates, secure themselves, terrified them into moderation. *Placidius tractarent*, "keep them quiet," as opposed to *accenderent* or *exagitarent*. But this sense is questionable. *Placidius tractarent* should rather mean, "treat with kindness;" and Kritz's emendation, *qui* for *quo*, seems preferable.

6. **Dubiis rebus**] "At a period of public peril." Comp. Tac. *Hist.* i. 31. cetera cohors, ut turbidis rebus evenit, parat signa. *Ann.* ii. 62. Catualda, dubiis rebus ejus, ultionem ausus. So *rebus perditis*, *rebus secundis*, etc. The reading *novandi* is supported by some MSS., while *novandis*, which is commonly adopted, is bad both in sense and grammar.

7. **Eorum**] Scil. *plebis*.

8. **Exsanguibus**] i. e. *invalidis*. Comp. Cic. *pro Sest.* 10. hominibus enervatis atque exsanguibus.

9. **A. Fulvius**] Comp. Val. Max. v. 8. 5, who makes this the name of the father. The father, by the old Roman law, had power of life and death over his child up to any age. Instances are given of parents calling their relations together and sitting in judgment on their sons for public crimes. But this right had become obsolete, and its exercise would not have been endured in this case, but for the prejudice of the government against Catiline and his abettors.

10. **Quod modo bello usui foret**] "As long as they could be of any service, at least for fighting, if for nothing else."

CHAPTER XL.

1. **Legatos Allobrogum**] The Allobroges, a tribe between the Rhone and Isère, had sent envoys to Rome to complain of the exactions of the provincial government, and to sue for a remission of their public debts. They had been with difficulty conquered, and had more than once revolted. Cicero says of them, *in Catil.* iii. 6. quam gentem unam restare (of all the southern Gauls) quae populo Romano bellum facere et posse, et non nolle videretur. Comp. Caes. *B. G.* i. 6. Q. Fabius

Maximus obtained the surname *Allobrogicus* for his victory over them as far back as A. U. 634. Juvenal, viii. 13:

> Cur Allobrogicis et magna gaudeat ara
> Natus in Herculeo Fabius lare.

2. **Negotiatus erat**] "Was established in trade," and had therefore *resided* among them. The *negotiator* was a Roman citizen settled as a trader in the provinces and generally a money-lender.

3. **Videt**] i.q. *cognoscit, accipit, audit.* Comp. Liv. xxxiv. 31. nunc tyrannum me vocari video. Cic. *pro Arch.* 8. quoties ego hunc Archiam vidi magnum numerum optimorum versuum dicere ex tempore.

4. **Tanta ista mala**] Comp. c. 48. tantam illam contumeliam.

5. **In domum D. Bruti**] Cicero says, ad Gabinium legatos esse perductos; but this does not mean "to the house of Gabinius," but "to meet him," as Sallust also says afterwards.

6. **Neque aliena consilii**] i.e. *opportuna consilio.* "convenient for the meetings of the conspirators." For the construction comp. Cic. *de Fin.* i. 4. quis alienum putet ejus esse dignitatis.

7. **Cujusque generis**] "Persons of every class."

8. **Innoxios**] "Innocent of the conspiracy."

CHAPTER XLI.

1. **Studium belli**] "Their national disposition for war." Comp. Lucan, vii. 694:

> Non jam Pompeii nomen populare per orbem,
> Nec studium belli, sed par quod semper habemus
> Libertas et Caesar erunt.

2. **Majores opes**] "Ampler resources;" i.e. the whole strength of the republic, as compared with the forces on which the conspirators relied.

3. **Tuta consilia**] "A secure course;" taking the side of the government they risked nothing.

4. **Q. Fabio Sangae, cujus patrocinio, etc.**] Comp. Cic. *de Off.* i. 11. tantopere apud nostros justitia culta est, ut ii qui civitates aut nationes devictas bello in fidem recepissent, earum patroni essent more majorum. Hence we may infer that this Fabius inherited the office of *patronus* from the conqueror Fabius Allobrogicus.

5. **Praecepit ut**] The perf. is found in the majority of MSS.: the change of tense is much in the author's manner. Comp. *Jugur.* 28. his praecepit omnes mortales pecunia aggrediantur. 111. regi patefecit quod polliceatur. The conjunction is found in all the MSS. but two.

6. **Manifestos**] *Manifestus* from *manus* and *fendo*, as *infestus* from *in* and *fendo*; properly, "what can be taken in the hand;" hence, "caught in the fact." So manifestus rerum capitalium. below, c. 52.

CHAPTER XLII.

1. **Gallia**] At this time the republic possessed two provinces named Gaul: the "hither," *citerior*, south of the Alps, bounded by the rivers Rubicon and Aesar, and the "further," *ulterior*, north of the Alps, extending to the Rhone and the Cevennes. The hither province was divided into Cispadane and Transpadane, with reference to the river Po (Padus) which intersected it.

2. **Bruttio**] The western peninsular extremity of Italy was called Bruttium: here the word is an adjective, agreeing with *agro*. So, Bruttia saxa, Pers. vi. 27.

3. **Cuncta simul**] "Everything at once," as madmen might do.

4. **Consiliis**] "Meetings for deliberation;" *concilia* has generally a bad sense, "clandestine meetings," which is not required here.

5. **Caussa cognita**] "After examination."

6. **Ulteriore G.**] This emendation for *Citeriore* is rendered necessary by the statement of Cicero that Murena was in the transalpine province. Cic. *pro Mur.* 41. Metellus Celer was in the cisalpine or hither province. See Cic. *in Catil.* ii. 12, and above, c. 30.

7. **Legatus**] A lieutenant of the imperator, or governor of a province. Sometimes the governor being himself absent deputed his charge to a *legatus*. But in this case the legatus was sent by the senate itself, and no proconsul appointed. Comp. Cic. *de Prov. Cons.* 3. atque hanc Macedoniam...etiam sine imperio per legatos tuebamur.

CHAPTER XLIII.

1. **Ut videbantur magnis**] "Such as appeared to be considerable." The impersonal form *videbatur*, is more usual. But comp. Cic. *ad Div.* xvi. 4. teque, ut mihi visus est, diligit, instead of, visum est.

2. **Constituerant]** The plur. supported by many of the best MSS. is referred irregularly to *Lentulus cum ceteris*, as though it were *Lentulus ceterique*. Comp. *Jugur*. 101. Bocchus cum peditibus...invadunt. Liv. xxi. 60. ipse dux cum principibus capiuntur.

3. **De actionibus Ciceronis]** "Of the actions, i. e. conduct of Cicero." *Actiones* in the plur. is rare in this sense. Comp. Cic. *de Off*. ii. 1. actiones suas scriptis mandare. It is generally used technically of legal proceedings. It was the policy of the conspirators to pretend that Cicero had got up a false rumour of a plot in order to drive innocent men away from the city. Comp. Appian, *Bell. Civ*. ii. 3. Λεύκιον δὲ Βηστίαν τὸν δήμαρχον ἐκκλησίαν εὐθὺς ὑπὸ κήρυξι συνάγειν, καὶ κατηγορεῖν τοῦ Κικέρωνος, ὡς ἀεὶ δειλοῦ καὶ πολεμοποιοῦ, καὶ τὴν πόλιν ἐν οὐδενὶ δεινῷ διαταράσσοντος.

4. **Optimo consuli]** It seems that M. Brutus in writing an account of these transactions used this same expression, *optimus consul*, with reference to Cicero's part in them. Cicero in a letter to Atticus, xii. 21, complains of the account as calculated to exalt Cato's conduct in comparison with his own, and refers to this phrase as disparaging. Hic autem se etiam tribuere multum mihi putat, quod scripserit optimum consulem. It is probable, from the character of his mind, that Brutus was very cold and measured in his laudation of the consul, and in his mouth the word *optimus* might have a formal and pedantic sound. But I do not think Sallust meant anything depreciatory. *Optimus* was itself a hearty and genial word, and occurs in the most complimentary descriptions. Juvenal, x. 331. optimus hic et formosissimus idem Gentis patriciae. Cicero himself uses it of Pansa; consul fortissimus atque optimus. *Philipp*. vii. 2.

5. **Eo signo proxima nocte]** "The night after that signal should be given." There is no need to insert *dato*, as in some MSS. and editt. Plutarch says that the night fixed was one of the Saturnalia, which commenced with the 17th of December. The tribunes were to enter upon their office the 10th of that month. But Cicero's vigilance anticipated this design. He got the conspirators executed December 5.

6. **Cetera multitudo coniurationis]** "All the rest of the conspirators." *Exsequeretur* in the sing. (the reading of the MSS.) refers to *quisque*, not to *multitudo*. Comp. Cic. *de Off*. i. 41. et vero etiam poetae suum quisque opus a vulgo considerari vult.

7. **Duodecim simul]** Plutarch doubtless exaggerates when he says that the conspirators assigned a hundred different places to be fired at the same time.

8. **Filii familiarum**] Catilina's adherents were mostly young men. Cicero calls them, libidinosa et delicata juventus (*ad Att.* i. 19); sanguinaria juventus (*ad Att.* ii. 7). Comp. *in Catil.* ii. 3. hos quos volitare in foro, quos stare ad curiam, quos etiam in senatum venire, qui nitent unguentis, qui fulgent purpura. Of the proscriptions of the second triumvirate Velleius remarks: Id tamen notandum, fuisse in proscriptos uxorum fidem summam, libertorum mediam, servorum aliquam, filiorum nullam. ii. 67. Appian, however, affirms that many Roman matrons helped Catiline with money in the hope that he would exterminate their husbands. *Bell. Civ.* ii. 2.

9. **Dies prolatando**] "By putting off the days fixed for the enterprise." Tac. *Ann.* vi. 42. diem ex die prolatare. *Prolatare*, an intensive form, from *proferre*, *prolatum*.

CHAPTER XLIV.

1. **Ceteros conveniunt**] "Have an interview with the others."

2. **Postulant jusjurandum**] "Demand a written form of oath."

3. **Signatum**] "With the seals of the parties affixed."

4. **Aliter**] i. q. *alioquin*, "unless they did so."

5. **Crotoniensem**] "A citizen of Crotona," in Bruttium.

6. **Quis sim**] Some MSS. read *qui sim*. *Quis sim*, means, "who I am;" *qui sim*, "what sort of person I am." So Cic. *in Caec. Div.* 12. qui sis et quid facere possis, considera. Liv. i. 41. qui sis, non unde natus sis, reputa.

7. **Etiam ab infimis**] This was a covert suggestion to arm slaves, which was too atrocious a design to be committed to writing, though recommended, as we see immediately afterwards, orally. Comp. the same letter recited, with some variation, by Cicero, *in Catil.* iii. 5. Probably neither author cared to quote with perfect accuracy. No reliance whatever can be placed on Sallust saying just above, quarum exemplum infra scriptum.

8. **Quo consilio servitia repudiet?**] "What would be the sense of rejecting the employment of slaves?"

CHAPTER XLV.

1. **L. Valerio Flacco**]. The same whom Cicero defended upon a charge of malversation in the province of Asia.

NOTES. 105

2. C. Pomptinius] Or *Pomtinus*. His family were probably of Suessa Pometia, in Latium, whence the *paludes Pomptinae* derived their name. This Pomptinius succeeded Murena in Transalpine Gaul, and effected the final pacification of the Allobroges, over whom he triumphed, A. U. 700, for his victory, A. U. 693.

3. In ponte Mulvio] The Mulvian, or Milvian bridge (perhaps, from M. Aemilius Scaurus, who is said to have built it), crossed the Tiber on the Flaminian way, two miles north of Rome. The great battle between Constantine and Maxentius, A.D. 312, took its name from this bridge. It is now called Ponte Molle: some part of the structure is supposed to be original. A bridge would be a convenient spot for intercepting travellers. At such a point it was more difficult to escape. Being narrow, and generally with a considerable elevation, carriages would slacken their pace at them. Beggars and loiterers infested them, and waylayers might keep a look out from them without exciting suspicion.

4. Homines militares] "Being men of military science."

5. Praesidiis collocatis] Comp. Cicero's description *in Catil.* iii. 2. illi...cum advesperasceret occulte ad pontem Mulvium pervenerunt, atque ibi in proximis villis ita bipartito fuerunt, ut Tiberis inter eos et pons interesset, etc.

6. Pontem obsidunt] "Occupy the bridge." *Obsident*, the reading of some MSS. and Edd. would mean, "besiege," "beleaguer."

7. Utrimque] "On either side of the bridge;" the ambush being laid, as Cicero describes, on both sides.

8. Cito cognito consilio] "quickly apprehending the device."

9. Multa...obtestatus] "Urging Pomptinius with many arguments."

10. Dedit] Probably the pres. from *dedo*, "gives himself up:" *dedo* implies more entire submission than the simple *do*. Comp. Cic. *de Off.* i. 21. qui excellenti ingenio doctrinae se dediderunt.

CHAPTER XLVI.

1. Sibi oneri, etc.] "Would bring a burden of odium upon himself."

2. Perdendae reipublicae, etc.] "Would conduce to the destruction of the commonwealth."

3. **Tarracinensem**] "Of Tarracina," or Anxur on the coast of Latium, now Terracina.

4. **Manu tenens**] "Leading by the hand;" as a mark of honour.

5. **In aedem Concordiae**] The foundations of this temple are still visible at the foot of the Capitoline hill, facing the forum. It was built by Camillus, and commemorated the restoration of concord between the senate and people. Plutarch, *Camill.* 42. It was reconstructed by Tiberius and his mother Livia A. U. 765, perhaps after some intermediate restoration or repair by L. Opimius, cons. A. U. 633. Plut. *C. Gracch.* 17. The first and last of these occasions are mentioned by Ovid, *Fast.* 1. 644.

> Furius antiquum, populi superator Etrusci,
> Voverat, et voti solverat ante fidem.
> Causa quod a patribus sumptis secesserat armis
> Vulgus, et ipsa suas Roma timebat opes.
> Causa recens melior: passos Germania crines
> Porrigit auspiciis, dux venerande, tuis.

6. **Magna frequentia**] "At a full meeting." The senate at this time amounted nominally to six hundred members; but the vacancies caused by death had not been regularly supplied by the censors. Four hundred and fifteen members divided at a full meeting. Cic. *ad Att.* i. 14. Comp. Cic. *post Red. in Sen.* 10. Allowance must be made for the number of senators engaged in the provincial administration. When Cicero, *Philipp.* ii. 8, praises his own speeches, in hac cella Concordiae, he refers to the temple itself, not to an inner shrine, which could not have held any such meeting.

CHAPTER XLVII.

1. **Alia**] "Other than the truth;" so the phrase, *in alia omnia abire*, "to run off to matters others than those in hand, not pertinent to the affair."

2. **Fide publica**] (Scil. *data*) "on the public faith being pledged for his safety." Comp. *Catil.* 48. se indicaturum si fides publica data esset. *Jugur.* 32, 35.

3. **Nihil amplius scire quam legatos**] "That he knew no more of the secrets of the plot than the Allobroges," who as foreigners could not be supposed intimate with its secret objects and ramifications: in short, he professed to be an instrument of the conspirators, but not an associate. He had only heard the names of a few individuals among them. Kritz explains it otherwise; se praeterquam quod legatos sciat conjurationis participes esse nullam plane ex conjuratis nosse: and adds, *nihil* de personis dictum non insolens est.

4. **Ex libris Sibyllinis**] Certain volumes so called, containing predictions regarding the destinies of the republic, were kept in custody of special officers called Quindecimvirs, and formed an important engine of state. Many other vaticinations, pretending to the authority of the Sibyls, were current among the citizens, and it is to some of these probably that Lentulus referred. The emperor Augustus found these impostures such a nuisance to the government that he caused a pretended authentic compilation to be made, and gave all the rest he could collect to the flames.

5. **Cinnam**] L. Cornelius Cinna, a leader of the popular party during the absence of Sulla in the east (A.U. 666—669). He was consul A.U. 667, when he impeached Sulla, and recalled Marius from exile. Being driven out of Rome by his colleague Octavius, he returned with a military force, took the city, and exacted a proscription of the aristocratic party. He was eventually killed in a mutiny of his own soldiers whom he was leading against Sulla.

6. **Ab incenso Capitolio**] i. e. from the year 671, when the Capitol was destroyed in the wars of Marius and Sulla. It was again burnt in the contest of the Vitellian and Flavian soldiers, A.D. 70, and once more by accident in the reign of Domitian. Lactantius says that, up to his time, in the fourth century, it had been frequently destroyed by lightning, iii. 17.

7. **Cognovissent**] "Recognised:" the proper word in such cases. Comp. Cic. *in Catil.* iii. 5. Statilius cognovit signum et manum suam.

8. **In liberis custodiis**] "In free custody." Persons of distinction were often placed under the care of the magistrates in their houses, instead of being consigned to the prison. Comp. Tac. *Ann.* vi. 3. Gallio retrahitur in urbem custoditurque domibus magistratuum. Cic. *Brut.* 96. quoniam eloquentiae quasi tutores relicti sumus, domi teneamus eam septam liberali custodia.

9. **P. Lentulo Spintheri**] Consul A.U. 697. *Spinther* means, a bracelet. Gr. σφιγκτήρ. Lentulus is said to have derived his surname from his similarity to a certain actor of the day so called.

10. **Q. Cornificio**] A colleague of Cicero's in the augurship. Cic. *ad Div.* xii. 17.

11. **C. Caesari**] Caius Julius Caesar.

12. **Gabinius**] This obscure personage is not to be confounded with Aulus Gabinius, an adherent of Pompey, in whose interest he proposed the *Lex Gabinia*, for giving him

the conduct of the war against the pirates, and *imperium* throughout all the coasts of the Mediterranean and fifty miles inland, A.U. 688.

13. M. Crasso] M. Licinius Crassus the triumvir.

CHAPTER XLVIII.

1. Conjuratione patefacta] The affair was revealed to the people by Cicero in a speech (his third Catilinarian oration) which he delivered in the forum on the 3rd of December (= Feb. 5. B.C. 62), after the examination of the Allobroges before the senate. Cic. *ad Att.* ii. 1. quo die Allobroges involgarunt.

2. Gaudium atque laetitiam] The second is a stronger word than the first. Comp. Cic. *Tusc. Disp.* iv. 6. quum ratione animus movetur placide atque constanter, tum illud gaudium dicitur; quum autem inaniter et effuse animus exsultat, tum illa laetitia gestiens vel nimia dici potest. The grammarian Nonius says: gaudium in sapiente et in rebus bonis semper est, laetitia etiam in malis esse potest. But such delicate distinctions are not much observed. Comp. c. 61. *in fin.*

3. Quippe cui, etc.] The lower orders contemplated the plunder of the city with little alarm, inasmuch as they had no possessions but what they carried in their hands or wore on their backs: their tools and clothes.

4. Ne eum Lentulus...deprehensi terrerent] "Not to be alarmed at the arrest of Lentulus," &c.

5. Obnoxii] "Under private obligations to Crassus:" persons whom he had assisted with loans.

6. Uti referatur] Scil. *ad senatum.* They insisted that the question of Crassus's complicity should be referred to a vote of the senate, that is, to their own decision, and not left to be dealt with by the consuls.

7. Potestatem] "Leave to make disclosures."

8. Appellato] *Appellare a nominare* ita diversum est, ut hoc sit aliquem per nomen quod ejus proprium est, designare; illud, proprie aliquem voce compellare. Dietsch.

9. Immissum] "Instigated;" i.e. sent against a person with a bad purpose; used of informers, false witnesses, hired assassins, &c.

10. More suo] Connect with *susc. mal. patr.* Comp. Cic. *de Off.* i. 30, for the artifice of Crassus in pleading for profligate characters: alii qui quidvis perpetiantur, cuivis deserviant, dum quod velint consequantur, ut Sullam et M. Crassum videbamus. See also Cic. *Parad.* 6. Comp. for a more favourable representation of Crassus's proceedings, Plutarch, *Crass.* 3.

11. Praedicantem] "Openly affirming." Comp. *Jugur.* 14. uti praedicantem audiveram patrem meum.

12. Contumeliam...impositam] "Insult cast upon him." So *imponere injurias, labem, pudorem,* &c.

CHAPTER XLIX.

1. C. Piso] C. Calpurnius Piso, consul 687, proconsul of the further Gaul 688; defended by Cicero when accused of extortion in his province. He is to be distinguished from L. Calpurnius Piso Caesoninus, consul A. U. 696, and father-in-law of Caesar, a great enemy of Cicero. Also from M. Pupius Piso, and Cn. Calpurnius Piso, contemporary nobles. See above, note on ch. 18.

2. Neque precibus, etc.] "Neither by entreaty, nor by the offer of political favour and support, nor by direct bribery." The *gratia* or "support" of the Optimates was of the utmost consequence to Cicero at this juncture, as was afterwards shown when they declined the task of defending his action against the Catilinarians. Comp. *Jugur.* 13. ut ex maxima invidia in gratiam et favorem nobilitatis Jugurtha veniret.

3. Falso] Sallust affirms on his own authority that Caesar was not concerned in the conspiracy, while he insinuates the guilt of Crassus. It is probable that both were equally aware of the machinations in progress, and disposed to regard with satisfaction a movement which would harass, if not overthrow, the government of the oligarchy. But it is not likely that either of them was directly implicated. Caesar was named as an accomplice the following year by L. Vettius, a man of bad character, whose accusation would have been treated with contempt, but that, being thrown into prison on another account about the same time, he was found dead in his bed, which gave occasion to odious suspicions.

4. Transpadani] An inhabitant of the part of the Cisalpine province beyond the Po. Caesar was patron of this people, and as such had impeached Piso.

5. Ex petitione pontificatus] Catulus had offered himself as a candidate for the high-priesthood in the year 691, but was opposed, much to his mortification, by Caesar, then comparatively young and little known. He offered contemptuously to buy off Caesar's competition by assisting to pay his debts; but Caesar refused, and declared that he would plunge still more deeply in debt, if necessary, to gain the election: πλείω προσδανεισάμενος ἔφη διαγωνιεῖσθαι. Plutarch, *in Caes.* 7. The people, who had the appointment, elected their favourite.

6. **Adolescentulo**] Caesar at this time was 37: see note on ch. 38.

7. **Res autem opportuna videbatur**] "The charge seemed well timed," i. e. likely from the circumstances of the case to obtain credit.

8. **Privatim egregia liberalitate publice maximis muneribus**] Comp. *Catil.* 54. Caesar, beneficiis atque munificentia magnus habebatur...mansuetudine et misericordia...dando, sublevando, ignoscendo...miseris perfugium...facilitas: in all which respects he is contrasted with Cato. Caesar's public munificence had been displayed in the shows of his aedileship.

9. **Grandem pecuniam debebat**] Caesar is said by Plutarch to have owed thirteen hundred talents (= £251,875) before he obtained any public employment. When he was about to enter upon his propraetorship in Spain, A.U. 693, he is reported to have said that he wanted one hundred million of sesterces (= £807,291) to be "worth nothing." Crassus on this occasion lent him the sum necessary to defray his outfit, and satisfy his most pressing creditors. But money was at all times freely lent him by the wealthy men of his party, who expected to be amply repaid on his advancement to the highest offices.

10. **Impellere nequeunt**] Caesar engaged Cicero to come forward and declare that he had been actually the first to reveal the existence of the plot to him; and the senate decreed that the reward assigned to Curius should be taken from him, and handed over to the prior informant. Suet. *Jul.* 17.

11. **Ementiendo**] "By falsely proclaiming." *Ementiri* is to utter falsehoods audaciously and openly. Comp. Liv. i. 8; ix. 18; xxv. 3.

12. **Invidiam conflaverant**] "Had raised a prejudice or hostile spirit." See note on ch. 14.

13. **Nobilitate**] Rather read *mobilitate*, which is supported by several MSS.

14. **Clarius esset**] This refers to the clause following: "they brandished their swords to display their zeal more conspicuously." For the circumstance comp. Plutarch, *Caes.* 8, who affirms that these knights looked to Cicero for a signal to

massacre Caesar, which he withheld. He wonders, indeed, why, if this were true, Cicero did not mention it in the history of his consulship. This outrage, however, caused great indignation among the people, who on a subsequent occasion, when Caesar defended himself in the senate, and was ill received there, surrounded the curia with loud outcries, and insisted on his being dismissed in safety.

CHAPTER L.

1. **Liberti**] "The freedmen of Lentulus:" *liberti* used in relation to their masters, *libertini* in relation to free-born citizens, i. e. *ingenui*.

2. **Duces multitudinum**] "The leaders of mobs." At this period public affairs were often interrupted by mob violence, and some party chiefs hired the known leaders of the rabble to engage their followers to excite disturbances.

3. **Familiam**] "His domestic slaves."

4. **Dispositis praesidiis**] Cicero speaks contemptuously of the failure of these attempts at exciting a commotion (*in Catil.* iv. 8). Appian, *Bell. Civ.* ii. 5, says that a tumult was created, but easily put down by the consul's precautions.

5. **Convocato senatu**] This meeting took place Dec. 5 = Feb. 7, B.C. 62.

6. **Contra rempublicam fecisse**] Upon the occasion of Cicero's second Catilinarian oration (Nov. 9), the senate had declared Catilina and Manlius public enemies. See above, *Catil.* 36. The other conspirators, on being convicted of correspondence with them, fell under the same sentence.

7. **D. Junius Silanus**] He succeeded to the consulship in the following year, with Murena. He was married to Cato's half sister, Servilia. The *consul designatus*, elected but not yet entered upon his office, was usually asked his opinion first by the actual consul. Comp. Tac. *Ann.* iii. 22. Tiberius exemit Drusum, consulem designatum, dicendae primo loco sententiae. Appian, *Bell. Civ.* ii. 5.

8. **Supplicium**] "Capital punishment." Appian, ii. 5. τοὺς ἄνδρας ἐσχάτῃ κολάσει μετιέναι.

9. **Pedibus...iturum**] "He would take his station by the side of Tib. Nero," i. e. divide with him. The phrase expresses implicitness of assent. Some verbo assentiebantur (see c. 52) or gave their own opinions in favour of a motion, others simply followed their leader on a division.

10. Referendum censuerat] He had proposed that the question of punishment should stand over for the present, probably till the issue of the contest with Catilina; the culprits being kept in custody during the interval: *praesidiis additis,* "guards placed over them."

11. Ubi ad eum ventum] There was much irregularity in the order in which opinions were demanded in the senate. The consul (or praetor in his absence) who summoned the meeting, called upon all the members separately to declare their sentiments, which they did either in a speech, or by merely assenting to the opinion of some preceding speaker; in which case they rose from their place, and went over to him. At the conclusion of the debate, the groups thus assembled were counted. Comp. Plin. *Ep.* viii. 14. 19. lex apertè jubet dirimi debere sententias occidentis et relegantis, cum ita discessionem fieri jubet; qui haec sentitis in hanc partem, qui alia omnia in illam partem ite, qua sentitis...i.e. in eam in qua sedet qui censuit relegandos. The consul usually called first upon one of the consuls designate, next upon the consulars, the praetors, and other high magistrates. But he was not bound to any particular order; and in the present case we find Catulus, a consular, speaking after Caesar, who was praetor-designate. But whatever order the consul assigned at the commencement of his term of office, he was expected to maintain throughout. Caesar's violating this usage, in his own consulship, was remarked upon. See Suet. *Jul.* 21. post novam affinitatem, Pompeium primum rogare sententiam coepit, cum Crassum soleret; essetque consuetudo, ut quem ordinem interrogandi sententias consul kalendis Januariis instituisset, cum toto anno conservaret. On this occasion it seems that Crassus was not present, otherwise Sallust, or Cicero himself, would undoubtedly have recorded his opinion. He was indignant, perhaps, at the suspicion of complicity cast upon him. Many of the senators abstained from attending, from various motives. Comp. Cic. *in Catil.* iv. 5; *ad Att.* xii. 21.

CHAPTER LI.

1. Omnes homines] The beginning of the speech is supposed to be imitated from Demosthenes, (περὶ τῶν ἐν Χερσονήσῳ πραγμάτων) ἔδει μὲν, ὦ ἄνδρες Ἀθηναῖοι, τοὺς λέγοντας ἅπαντας ἐν ὑμῖν μήτε πρὸς ἔχθραν ποιεῖσθαι λόγον μηδένα, μήτε πρὸς χάριν.

2. Usui] i.e. *utilitati.* Comp. Cic. *pro Leg. Manil.* 20. majores nostros semper in pace consuetudini, in bello utilitati paruisse. Comp. Nepos, *Alcib.* 4. plus irae suae quam utilitati communi paruisse.

3. **Valet**] Scil. *animus*.

4. **Recte atque ordine**] A familiar idiom. Comp. Liv. xxiv. 31; xxviii. 39; xxx. 17.

5. **Bello Macedonico**] Perses, or Perseus, the last of the kings of Macedonia, was subdued by L. Aemilius Paullus at the battle of Pydna, A.U. 586, B.C. 168. Perses is the form of the name adopted by Cicero and Sallust, Perseus by Livy, Pliny, Justin, and Eutropius.

6. **Rhodiorum civitas**] The state of Rhodes became famous as the greatest maritime power of the eastern Mediterranean, after the fall of Athens in the fourth century B.C. It had proved itself a faithful ally of the Romans in the war with Antiochus, king of Syria (B.C. 190), and had received from them the countries of Lycia and Caria. In the Macedonian war it inclined to the other side, or, at least, trimmed between the two. Comp. Vell. i. 9. dubia fide speculati fortunam proniores regis partibus fuisse visi sunt.

7. **Impunitos**] The Romans did not turn their arms upon them, and overthrow their commonwealth: they contented themselves with taking from them their possessions in Lycia and Caria. See Liv. xlv. 25. Comp. also A. Gellius, vii. 3.

8. **Per inducias**] "In time of truce."

9. **Per occasionem**] "When opportunity offered."

10. **Talia fecere**] "Did the like," "retaliated."

11. **In illis**] "In their case." Comp. *Catil.* 9. in amicis fideles; and examples there given.

12. **Hoc idem**] "This, which is a similar case to the foregoing."

13. **Novum consilium**] "A new course of proceeding," unusual, novel; i.e. the proposition of Silanus for inflicting death on the conspirators, which the senate had no right to do. No Roman citizen could, in strict law, be condemned to death, except by a vote of the people. On the other hand, the senate by the appointment of a dictator, or by investing the consuls with summary powers, by a senatus-consultum ultimum, i.e. caveant consules ne respublica aliquid detrimenti capiat, claimed the right of suspending the ordinary operation of the laws. The people always regarded these stretches of prerogative as illegal encroachments, and in the sequel declared, at the instigation of the tribune Clodius, that Cicero had committed a judicial murder in executing the conspirators by virtue of a decree of the senate.

14. **Omnium ingenia exsuperat]** "Transcends the imaginations of all."

15. **Composite]** "In studied and elaborate orations." So *composito:* Virgil, *Aen.* ii. 129. Composito rumpit vocem et me destinat arae.

16. **Magnifice]** "In glowing colours;" expressive of some enhancement of the subject. Comp. Liv. xxi. 41. non vereor ne quis me hoc vestri adhortandi causa magnifice loqui existimet, ipsum aliter animo affectum esse. Sallust may have had in his mind the highly wrought description of the licence of war in Homer, *Iliad*, ix. 591:

καί οἱ κατέλεξεν ἅπαντα
κήδε', ὅσ' ἀνθρώποισι πέλει τῶν ἄστυ ἁλώῃ,
ἄνδρας μὲν κτείνουσι, πόλιν δέ τε πῦρ ἀμαθύνει,
τέκνα δέ τ' ἄλλοι ἄγουσι βαθυζώνους τε γυναῖκας·
τοῦ δ' ὠρίνετο θυμὸς ἀκούοντος κακὰ ἔργα.

17. **Sed alia aliis licentia est]** Scil. *irascendi*, or *iracundia delinquendi*, "some men have more licence to give way to anger than others."

18. **Eos mores, eam modestiam]** Comp. *Catil.* 7. eas divitias, eam bonam famam putabant. Tac. *Hist.* iv. 42. ea principis aetas, ea moderatio. In such cases *hic* is more usual than *is.* *Jugur.* 85. hae sunt meae imagines, haec nobilitas. Lucan, ii. 380. hi mores, haec duri immota Catonis Secta fuit. Virg. *Aen.* vi. 129. Hoc opus hic labor est.

19. **Aut metus, aut injuria]** "You were impelled to propose capital punishment, either by excessive alarm (which there was no occasion for), or by a sense of the atrocity of the crime (in respect to which even capital punishment is quite inadequate.)" *Novum poenae genus*, is *per euphemismum* for *death*, which the Romans never named if they could avoid it. Hence the phrases *supplicium* for "capital punishment," *in hostium numero habere*, for "to put to the sword."

20. **Possumus equidem dicere]** "We may surely say." The common opinion, adopted among the Romans themselves, that *equidem* is a contraction of *ego quidem*, is refuted by the grammarian Priscian. Sciendum tamen quod quidam *equidem* conjunctionem compositam esse existimant ab *ego* et *quidem;* sed errant. Simplex enim est. Et hoc maxime ex ipsa constructione orationis possumus intelligere. Nam *equidem facio, equidem facis, equidem facit* dicimus. He goes on to prove the same from the combination of *ego* and *equidem*, citing from this chapter of the *Catilina, Equidem ego sic existimo.* Bentley maintained, however, that the use of *equidem* was confined at least to the first person singular down to the time of Nero: but

this may be shewn to be erroneous from various passages in Plautus and Terence. *Equidem* then is best explained as a stronger form of *quidem*, the *e* being an intensive particle, as in *edurus, egelidus*, or *enim, ecastor*. (Handii *Tursellinus*, ii. 423.) If we consider the *e* to be a long syllable, *equidem* must be scanned *ēqu'em*, as we find the *d* of *quidem, modo, idem*, &c. frequently dropped by Plautus and Terence. (Donaldson's *Varronianus*, p. 280, 1 ed. See Bentley on Ter. *Andr.* i. 3. 20.) Accordingly read in Pers. i. 10. per me equ'em sint omnia protinus alba ; or per me qu'em. Lucan, viii. 824. Haud equ'em immerito......Cautum ; Virg. *Geor.* i. 415. Haud equ'em, credo, quia sit divinitus illis. But it is not likely that this vulgar contraction would be admitted in heroic poetry ; and it is better to consider the *e* short, as in *enim*. The various constructions in which *equidem* occurs may be seen in the following instances taken from good and early authors :

Sallust, *Catil.* 52.
> Equidem nos amisimus.

Varro, *de R. R.* i. 5.
> Equidem innumerabiles mihi videntur.

Cic. *Tusc.* v. 35.
> Vestrae equidem coenae jucundae sunt.

Virgil, *Aen.* x. 29.
> Equidem, credo, mea vulnera restant.

Plaut. *Epid.* iv. 2. 33.
> Adolescentem equidem dicebant emissae.

——— *Pers.* 2. 3.
> Equidem si scis.

Terent. *Eunuch.* v. 4. 34.
> Atque equidem orante ut ne id faceret Thaide.

Lucret. iii. 1091.
> Certe equidem finis vitae mortalibus instat.

Sallust, *Catil.* 53.
> Scitis equidem milites.

——— *Jugur.* 10.
> Equidem ego vobis regnum trado.

21. **Ultra neque curae neque gaudio locum esse**] A remarkable avowal of materialism in the Chief Pontiff of the national religion. That such an avowal was really made appears from Cicero's reference to it in *Catil.* iv. 4, alter intelligit mortem a Dis immortalibus non esse supplicii causa

constitutam, sed aut necessitatem naturae aut laborum ac miseriarum quietem esse. Cicero himself only ventures, in opposition to this opinion, to allude to the belief of the ancients as a convenient check to crime: itaque ut aliqua in vita formido improbis esset posita, apud inferos ejusmodi quaedam illi antiqui supplicia impiis constituta esse voluerunt.

22. **Lex Porcia**] The Porcian law, proposed by P. Porcius Laeca, a tribune of the plebs, A.U. 454. See Liv. x. 9. Porcia lex sola pro tergo civium lata videtur, quod gravi poena, si quis verberasset necassetve civem Romanum, sanxit. A citizen brought on a capital charge before the people might decline a trial by withdrawing into banishment.

23. **Aliae leges**] The lex Sempronia of C. Gracchus also forbade the magistrate pronouncing a capital sentence against a citizen without first obtaining the sanction of the people.

24. **Qui convenit**] *Qui* the old ablat. for *quo*.

25. **At enim**] A formula for meeting a supposed objection. "But some one will say."

26. **Tempus, dies, etc.**] Scil. *reprehendent:* in answer to the foregoing question.

27. **In alios**] *In aliis*, the reading of one MS., seems preferable. Comp. above *in illis*, and *Catil*. 9. *in amicis*, etc.

28. **Triginta viros**] Commonly called the thirty tyrants; an oligarchical administration imposed upon Athens by the Spartans at the end of the Peloponnesian war, B.C. 404. Xenophon, *Hellen*. ii. 3. 2.

29. **Ea**] Scil. *facta*. Laetari with the accus. Comp. *Jugur*. 14. laetandum magis puto quam dolendum casum tuum. Cic. *ad Div*. vii. 1. utrumque laetor.

30. **Damasippus**] L. Junius Brutus Damasippus, an adherent of the Marian faction, put to death by Sulla, A.U. 672, after he had murdered many distinguished senators. See Vell. ii. 26; Appian, *Bell. Civ*. i. 88. 93.

31. **Trahebantur**] "Were dragged to execution."

32. **Item**] i. q. *pariter*.

33. **Ab Samnitibus**] A warlike people inhabiting the mountainous country in the centre of southern Italy. Niebuhr has remarked that while the Latin names of domestic animals, agricultural implements, &c. are mostly adopted from the civilized Greeks, those of weapons, &c. are taken from the language of some indigenous warlike race. This, however, is not strictly the case. Comp. ensis, ἔγχος; gladius, κλάδος; scutum, σκῦτος; galea, γαλῆ; hasta, ἵστημι; etc.

NOTES. 117

34. **Insignia magistratuum**] Such, perhaps, as the trabea, or white robe bordered or striped with purple, worn by the consuls and other magistrates; the curule chair, the fasces, and the lictors.

35. **Bonis**] Scil. *institutis*. The dative of the thing, instead of the person, which is more usual with *invidere*.

36. **Graeciae morem**] The Romans were proud of the mildness of their laws in regard to their own citizens, which they considered the mark of a free and liberal constitution, and Caesar throughout his career was sparing of their blood. But it was a bold thing to insinuate, as this passage seems to imply, that it was from the Greeks that the Romans adopted the punishment of death by flogging, of which there is no trace in the laws of Draco or of Solon. At Athens citizens were liable to capital punishment, which was frequently inflicted on slight grounds, though the mode of death, by administering a draught of hemlock, was studiously mild.

37. **Circumveniri**] "Were oppressed by civil arts." Comp. c. 31. circumventus ab inimicis praeceps agor.

38. **Aliaeque leges**] *Leges* is omitted by some MSS., but the repetition seems to be studied, in order to enforce upon the audience the contrast between law and illegal violence.

39. **Publicandas**] i.e. to be made *publici juris*, to be transferred to the public treasury.

40. **Per municipia**] Comp. Cicero, *in Catil.* iv. 4. adjungit gravem poenam municipibus si quis eorum vincula ruperit; horribiles custodias circumdat, etc. It appears that the Roman government allowed so much independence to the municipal administrations, that they might have refused to undertake the confinement of these prisoners. Cicero says: municipiis dispertiri jubet. Habere videtur ista res iniquitatem, si imperare velis; difficultatem, si rogas.

41. **Cum populo agat**] "Transact business with the people," i.e. appeal to the people.

CHAPTER LII.

1. **Verbo...varie**] "With a single word," signifying their agreement with one of the previous speakers, but *varie*, i.e. "giving their reasons accordingly."

2. **M. Porcius Cato**] The Porcian was a plebeian gens, but of ancient nobility. Cato the censor was great grandfather of the Cato here mentioned, who is distinguished from him by

the surname of *Uticensis*, from the place of his death. He was born, A.U. 659, B.C. 95. Accordingly, he was at this time 32 years of age. He had not yet served any high office, and was only beginning to become known in the political world. The uncompromising opinions he expressed on this occasion marked him out as a leader for the nobles, who were dissatisfied with Pompeius and Crassus, and disdained Cicero for his obscure origin.

3. **Orationem habuit**] Cicero characterizes Cato's speech on this occasion in his pleading for Sestius, c. 28. consule me, quum esset designatus tribunus plebis, obtulit in discrimen vitam suam; dixit eam sententiam, cujus invidiam capitis periculo sibi praestandam videbat; dixit vehementer, egit acriter, ea quae sensit prae se tulit; dux, auctor, actor illarum rerum fuit. Comp. Vell. ii. 35. The beginning of this speech may be compared with that of the third Olynthiac of Demosthenes.

The conciseness of Sallust's style is observable in his use of the neut. adject. for substantives; e. g. alieni appetens, sui profusus for alienarum, suarum rerum. This is particularly noticeable in the use of the words *bonum, malum, commodum, certum, aequum, honestum*, and others. Dietsch.

4. **Aris atque focis**] The best opinion seems to be that both these words refer to the citizens' private dwellings; the *ara* being the altar of the *Penates*, in the central court of the house (impluvium), the *focus* the hearth in the hall (atrium) around which the little images of the *Lares* were ranged. See Ernesti *in Clav. Cicer.* v. *Ara*.

5. **Cavere ab illis, quam**] *Magis* is omitted by the best critics on the authority of many MSS. So in cc. 8, 9, 48.

6. **Cujuscumque modi sunt**] The indic. mood implying the certainty in the mind of the speaker of there being such things. Comp. below, cujus haec cumque modi videntur. Cic. *de Off.* i. 25. utilitatem civium tueantur, ut quaecunque agunt, ad rem publicam referant. Tac. *Ann.* i. 42. quicquid istuc sceleris imminet.

7. **Capessite rem publicam**] "Take public affairs in hand."

8. **In dubio**] i.e. *in periculo*. Comp. Ovid, *Amor.* ii. 13. 2. In dubio vitae nostra Corinna jacet.

9. **In hoc ordine**] "In this assembly," i.e. before the senatorial order.

10. **Haud facile, etc.**] "I am not wont easily to forgive

NOTES. 119

other men's evil passions their misdeeds:" *condonare*, to forgive, i.e. to give up, as a thing in which we have no concern.

11. **Opulentia negligentiam tolerabat**] "The resources of the state enabled it to bear the loss inflicted by your carelessness."

12. **Nostra, an nobiscum una**, etc.] "Whether they shall continue ours, or become our enemies', together with ourselves."

13. **Hic mihi quisquam**] "Here some one, I suppose," (with irony) "speaks to me of mildness and pitifulness." Comp. Cic. *Phil.* viii. 4. hic mihi Fufius pacis commoda commemorat. Some editions make the sentence interrogative.

14. **Vera rerum vocabula amisimus**] Comp. Thucyd. ii. 82. τὴν εἰωθυῖαν ἀξίωσιν ὀνομάτων ἀντήλλαξαν κ.τ.λ.

15. **Eo respublica in extremo sita est**] "To such an extremity is the state reduced."

16. **In furibus**] "In the case of plunderers." For the ablat. see above, cc. 9, 51, &c.

17. **Ne**] i.q. *dummodo ne*, "as long as they do not." Comp. Liv. xxxvi. 1. permissum ut auxilia ab sociis, ne supra quinque millium numerum, acciperet.

18. **Illi**] (With emphasis and indignation.) This reading, supported by several MSS. is preferable to *illis*, which must be referred grammatically to *fures aerarii;* but such is certainly not the writer's meaning. The critics who read *illis* generally understand it of the conspirators, who could only be referred to by the word *his*, δεικτικῶς.

19. **Credo, falsa**] This is the order of all the MSS. inverted by Cortius, as unusual where *credo* is introduced ironically: "deeming false, forsooth." But compare Hor. *Sat.* ii. 2. 90. credo, hac mente (for h. m. c.). Cic. *in Catil.* i. 2. si te interfici jussero, credo, erit verendum mihi.

20. **Diverso itinere malos a bonis**] "The bad in a contrary direction from the good:" scil. *diverso a bonis.* Comp. Caes. *B. C.* i. 69. erat iter a proposito diversum; contrariamque in partem iri videbatur. *B. G.* vi. 25. diversis ab flumine regionibus. Stat. *Theb.* vii. 706. quantum diversus ab illo.

21. **Habere**] i.q. tenere. Comp. Virg. *Aen.* vi. 434. Proxima deinde tenent moesti loca.

22. **Videlicet**] Ironical. There is irony also in *timens*, as if any suggestion of *fear* on Caesar's part must have been a

pretence, insinuating that he was on a perfect understanding with the conspirators.

23. **A popularibus conjurationis**] "By the associates of the cabal." Comp. above, c. 24. quod factum populares conjurationis concusserat: *populares*, fig. persons of the same class, prop. of the same nation.

24. **Aderunt**] "Will attack you." Comp. *Jugur.* 50. Numidae infensi adesse atque instare. Liv. xxii. 32. Hannibali diversis locis opportuni aderant, carpentes agmen.

25. **Quae nobis nulla sunt**] "Which are lost and gone for us:" an antique idiom. Comp. Plaut. *Casin.* ii. 4. 26. si id factum est, ecce me nullum senem. Ter. *Phorm.* i. 4. 1. nullus es, Geta, "you are lost, done for."

26. **Neque delicto neque lubidini obnoxios**] "Biassed neither by conscious guilt, nor by passion."

27. **Possidet**] "Enjoys:" *possidere*, not to possess as one's own property, but to have the usufruct of a thing.

Ambitio is always used by Sallust in its secondary sense, as the immoderate or illegitimate pursuit of honours. Dietsch.

28. **In vacuam rempublicam**] "Upon the unprotected commonwealth."

29. **Supra caput**] A phrase implying imminent, impending danger. Comp. Liv. iii. 17. quum hostes supra caput sint.

30. **Vos cunctamini, etc.**] "Are you even now deliberating?"

31. **Deprehensis**] "Caught and convicted." Comp. c. 46. in maximo scelere tantis civibus deprehensis. *Jugur.* 35. ipse deprehensus indicium profitetur: the dative, as *Catil.* 53. idem fit ceteris. *Jugur.* 85. faciunt idem majoribus suis.

32. **Misereamini censeo**] "Have compassion, I advise you," (ironically).

33. **Nae**] Or *ne*, "yes," *val.* Comp. *Jugur.* 15. nae ille graves poenas reddet; 85. nae illi falsi sunt. Cic. *in Catil.* ii. 3. nae illi vehementer errant.

34. **Scilicet res ipsa, etc.**] "In good sooth the affair is a perilous one; but you, for your part, have no fear, as you say: yes indeed, but you do fear, and most exceedingly."

35. **Prospera omnia cedunt**] "Everything ends well."

36. **T. Manlius Torquatus**] For the story of Manlius, who, as imperator, caused his son to be put to death by

military execution for engaging in combat contrary to orders, see Liv. viii. 7. Sallust and Dion Hal. refer this event to a Gallic war; but other writers to a war with the Latins. Sallust's error arose probably from his confounding this occasion with that on which Manlius won the collar (torquis) from the Gaulish champion.

37. **Nisi iterum**] "Unless this is now the second time," referring probably to the former abortive conspiracy of Catiline. See c. 18.

38. **Si quidquam unquam pensi fuisset**] "If they had ever reflected at all."

39. **Peccato locus**] "If this were an occasion on which you might err with impunity."

40. **Faucibus urget**] "Has seized you by the throat;" as a robber or beast of prey. Comp. Cic. *pro Cluent.* 31: cum faucibus premeretur. Val. Max. v. 3. 3. faucibus apprehensam rempublicam strangulari passus. Plaut. *Cas.* v. 3. 4. manifesto faucibus teneor.

41. **Manifestis**] Comp. *Jugur.* 35. manifestus tanti sceleris. Plaut. *Truc.* i. 2. 30. manifestam mendacii, and above, c. 41, note 6.

42. **More majorum**] i. e. to be strangled in prison: the ancient mode of execution in use before the abolition of capital punishment by the lex Sempronia. When it was proposed, in the reign of Nero, that Antistius should be executed *more majorum*, it was urged that the sentence should be commuted to banishment: for, carnificem et laqueum pridem abolita. Tac. *Ann.* xiv. 48.

CHAPTER LIII.

1. **Adsedit**] "Took his seat;" in which sense the present *adsido* is used, not *adsideo*. Comp. Plaut. *Bacch.* iii. 3. 28. Adsido, accurrunt servi, soccos detrahunt. Cic. *Acad.* i. 4. adsidamus si videtur. Ter. *Heaut.* i. 1. 72. eo mulier adsidat.

2. **Ad caelum ferunt**] "Exalt to heaven." Comp. Virg. *Aen.* i. 260. sublimemque feres ad sidera caeli Magnanimum Aenean. Fero may stand alone in the same sense: *Aen.* vi. 823. utcunque ferent ea facta minores.

3. **Clarus atque magnus**] Comp. Tac. *Agric.* 18. clarus ac magnus haberi Agricola. Lucan, ix. 202. clarum et venerabile nomen.

4. **Sicuti ille censuerat**] The decree is said to have been made in accordance with Cato's opinion, not as if he had been

the only speaker on that side, but because his speech was the most effective, and had evidently carried the point. See Cicero to Atticus, xii. 21. cur ego in sententiam Catonis? quia verbis luculentioribus et pluribus eandem rem comprehenderat. He insists that Cato's merit lay in recommending his own (i. e. Cicero's) policy, whereas M. Brutus, in writing a panegyric on his uncle Cato, had made it appear as if the capital punishment had been Cato's original suggestion. Much weight cannot be given to Brutus's authority on this point, but it is in some degree corroborated by the silence of Sallust regarding the part which Cicero claimed in the business.

5. **Forte lubuit attendere]** "It has chanced that I have chosen to turn my attention to the inquiry," &c.

6. **Contendisse...toleravisse]** Scil. *pop. Romanum.*

7. **Ante Romanos]** "To have surpassed the R." Comp. for this use of the prep. Tac. *Hist.* iv. 55. Classicus nobilitate ante alios. *Ann.* i. 27. Lentulus ante alios aetate et gloria belli. And see note 3 on *Jugur.* 15.

8. **Multa agitanti]** "On much reflection."

9. **Rursus]** i. q. *contra.* Comp. Tac. *Ann.* i. 80. neque enim eminentes virtutes sectabatur, et rursus vitia oderat. Cic. *De Fin.* iii. 10. neque in bonis numerata sit, neque rursus in malis.

10. **Sustentabat]** "Endured," "bore up under:" as *sustinuisset,* supra. Both words are of frequent occurrence in Sallust. (*Catil.* i. 14. *Jugur.* 56, 97, 109.)

11. **Effeta aetate parentum]** *Aetate* is introduced on the conjecture of Dietsch: "as when parents have grown old and exhausted." For *effeta aetas,* comp. Virg. *Aen.* vii. 440:

> Sed te victa situ verique effeta senectus.

The readings of the MSS. *effeta parente, effetae parentum,* cannot be explained satisfactorily.

CHAPTER LIV.

1. **Genus, aetas...aequalia]** Cato was of a plebeian, Caesar of a patrician family; both however ennobled by public honours. Cato was thirty-three, Caesar thirty-eight years of age. Of Caesar's eloquence Quintilian says, *Inst. Orat.* x. 1. 114. C. vero Caesar si foro tantum vacasset, non alius ex nostris contra Ciceronem nominaretur.

2. **Alia alii]** Scil. *gloria. Alii* for *alteri,* although of two only, to correspond with the preceding *alia.* Comp. Liv. i. 25. duo Romani super alium alius, vulneratis tribus Albanis, exspirantes corruerunt.

NOTES.

3. **Dono dignum**] "Fitting to give," i. e. consistent with proper principles.

4. **Novum bellum**] "A fresh war," the conduct of which he might have for his own. Pompey had monopolized the conduct of the last great war in the East.

5. **Cum innocente**] "With the pure and incorrupt." So *innocentia* is opposed to *avaritia* in c. 12, and *Jugur.* 46.

6. **Esse quam videri bonus**] This may be taken from Aeschylus (*Sept. c. Theb.* 589.) οὐ γὰρ δοκεῖν δίκαιος ἀλλ' εἶναι θέλει. The idea, however, is common. Comp. Cic. *De Amic.* virtute ipsa non tam multi praediti esse quam videri volunt. Martial, viii. 38. Refert sis bonus an velis videri. Vell. ii. 35, speaking also of Cato, nunquam recte fecit ut facere videretur, sed quia aliter facere non poterat. For Cato's character, see particularly the fine panegyric in Lucan, ii. 380 foll.

CHAPTER LV.

1. **Noctem antecapere**] "To anticipate nightfall."

2. **Triumviros**] Scil. *capitales*: magistrates who had the charge of the prisons and of public executions. Hence triumvirale supplicium. Tac. *Ann.* v. 9.

3. **Praesidiis**] Juvenal, viii. 238. galeatum ponit ubique Praesidium attonitis.

4. **Quod Tullianum appellatur**] The Carcer, a public prison, under the eastern side of the Capitoline hill, was built by Ancus, and enlarged by Servius Tullius. Varro, *de L. L.* iv. 32. carcer a coercendo, quod exire prohibentur: in hoc pars quae sub terra Tullianum, quod additum a Tullio rege. Comp. Liv. xxiv. 22. This place now exists, and is used as a chapel to a church built over it, in honour of the supposed imprisonment there of St Peter. Formerly criminals were let down into it by a hole in the chamber above. Quod is made to agree with Tullianum, by prolepsis or anticipation, rather than with carcer. The neuter *Tullianum* may depend on *robur*, "a prison," understood.

5. **Ascenderis**] Some editions read *escenderis*, with the same sense, but with no authority. Certain MSS. give *descenderis*, which would imply descent within the walls of the *carcer* to the chamber called the *Tullianum* on the left hand, the entrance to which was reached by twelve steps. But the phrase *ubi ascenderis*, which has most authority, seems to imply some common passengers' route, and refers, probably, to the ascent of the street in which the *carcer* stood from the forum, and this agrees with the existing localities.

6. **Camera, lapideis fornicibus vincta**] "A ceiling vaulted with stone arches."

7. **Vindices**] Not the triumvirs themselves, but the *carnifices*, common executioners, under their orders.

8. **Laqueo gulam fregere**] Either by stopping the windpipe or breaking the neck. Hor. *Epod.* 3. Parentis olim si quis impia manu Senile guttur fregerit.

CHAPTER LVI.

1. **Instituit**] "Makes two skeleton legions." He had not men enough to form two legions complete, but he created the regular number of cohorts, maniples and centuries for each, appointed officers, and filled up the ranks as fast as new recruits arrived. Caesar seems, on the contrary, on a similar occasion to have reduced the number of his cohorts. *Bell. Civ.* iii. 93. quartae aciei, quam instituerat sex cohortium numero, signum dedit. The full complement of the legion was ten cohorts.

2. **Numero hominum**] With their complement of men. This is not superfluous, though *expleverat* follows, inasmuch as the writer wishes to mark that the *number* was complete, but they were incompletely *armed*.

3. **In Galliam versus**] For this construction compare Caesar, *Bell. Gall.* vi. 33, vii. 8; *Jugur.* 58. fugam ad se versum fieri.

4. **Cujus**] Supply, *rei* or *generis*. Comp. Liv. xlii. 8. bonaque ut iis, quicquid ejus recuperari possit, reddantur. Compare Plaut. *Bacch.* iv. 4. 74. Quae imperavisti, imperatum bene bonis, factum illico est.

5. **Alienum suis rationibus**] "Inconsistent with his policy."

CHAPTER LVII.

1. **In agrum Pistoriensem**] "The territory of Pistoria," modern Pistoia, in Etruria. Catiline had fixed his quarters at Faesulae. Coins have been found buried there, with dates reaching to this year, and no later, evidently to escape the search of his pillaging bands. Pistoria lay north-west of Faesulae, among the Apennines, on the road to Gaul. The direct road to the Cisalpine province lay to the north, through Bononia, but Celer occupied this. Besides, Catiline wanted to get to the Allobroges in the Transalpine.

NOTES.

2. Ex difficultate rerum] "From the difficult circumstances he was in;" i. q. *propter difficultatem.*

3. Consedit] i. e. *castra posuit.* Comp. Caes. *B. G.* i. 21. *Consido* is the form of the present, *consedi* of the praeterite or past time. Virg. *Aen.* xi. extr. Considunt castris ante urbem. Ovid. *Metam.* xiii. 1. Consedere duces. Comp. note 1, c. 53, *adsedit.*

4. In fuga] i. e. *fugientem.*

CHAPTER LVIII.

1. Natura aut moribus] "Natural or acquired."

2. Unus ab urbe, alter a Gallia] "One on the side of the city, the other on the side of Gaul."

3. Si maxime] "However much;" i. q. *etiam si maxime.*

4. Commeatus abunde] Scil. *erunt.* Comp. c. 21. quibus mala abunde omnia erant. *Jugur.* 87. Romanos laxius licentiusque futuros. Hor. *Sat.* ii. 2. 106. recte tibi semper erunt res. So the adverbs *impune, adversus,* are joined with the verb subst.

5. Supervacaneum] "Superfluous," "a work of supererogation;" i. e. they already possess all the things that we are compelled to fight for, life, liberty, &c., and it is a mere matter of choice with them to fight for the ascendancy of the nobles.

6. Habetur] See note on c. 1. "The possession of boldness is as good as a rampart."

7. Queat] Dietsch observes that this word, rarely used by other good writers, occurs six times in Sallust. See *Jugur.* 10, 44, 58, 97 bis.

CHAPTER LIX.

1. Signa canere jubet] "Orders the trumpets to sound." Understand *signa* however as the object, subaud. *tubicines* the subject, as in *Jugur.* 29. Marius jubet tubicines simul omnes signa canere. This subject and object are rarely expressed together. We have Liv. xxiv. 46. cornicines canere jubent. Sall. *Fr. Hist.* i. 38. cornicines occinuerunt. But it is more common to meet with the phrase in the text. Comp. Liv. i. 1; xxiv. 15; xxvii. 47. Some critics take *signa* as the subject, in which case the idiom is identical with the English given above.

2. Omnium equis] Comp. Caes. *Bell. Gall.* i. 25. Caesar primum suo deinde omnium e conspectu remotis equis, ut aequato omnium periculo spem fugae tolleret.

3. **Ipse pedes**] "Himself on foot;" as a foot-soldier. Comp. Senec. *Ep.* 104. per medias Africae solitudines pedes duxit exercitum. Lucan, ix. 587. praecedit anheli Militis ora pedes.

4. **Rupes aspera**] Sub. *erat*. The MSS. read *rupe*, which can only be explained, aspera (loca) ab dextra rupe, and may be pronounced inadmissible.

5. **Reliqua signa**] "The rest of his forces." Every maniple had its own standard.

6. **Evocatos**] Veterans discharged or entitled to their discharge, but continuing to serve, or returning to service, with higher pay and peculiar privileges.

7. **Faesulanum quemdam**] Plutarch gives him the name of Furius.

8. **Curare**] "To command;" a proper military term. Comp. *Jugur.* 46, 57, and elsewhere. Tacitus sometimes adds the object. *Annal.* i. 31. inferiorem exercitum A. Caecina curabat.

9. **Libertis et colonis**] "His own freedmen and the Sullan veterans settled in colonies:" a chosen band of men attached to his person.

10. **Propter aquilam**] "Beside his eagle." A silver eagle, belonging to one of the legions of Marius, which Catiline kept as a sort of amulet. See Cic. *in Catil.* i. 9.

11. **Pedibus aeger**] Antonius is surmised to have feigned sickness, to escape the necessity of fighting with Catiline, in whose designs he may have been partly implicated. See Dion, xxxvii. 39.

12. **M. Petreio**] The same who was joined in command with Afranius, as a legatus of Pompey in Spain, and was there defeated by Caesar, A.U. 705. He caused himself to be killed in single combat with Juba, king of Numidia, after the disastrous battle of Thapsus.

13. **Tumulti caussa**] *Tumultus*, a sudden occasion of peril from a foreign foe, when the ordinary rules of service are suspended, and the citizens generally liable to be called out for the defence of the state. A *tumultus* was usually proclaimed when the Gauls threatened an invasion, as was said to be the case now.

14. **Inermes**] "Without the regular arms of legionaries."

15. **Homo militaris**] "A man of military experience." Comp. the same phrase above, ch. 45.

16. **Tribunus**] Scil. *militum*. There were six of these to each legion. In early times they commanded the legion successively day by day, and even at this period a tribune might still be called by courtesy, the commander of a legion. Horace, at the age of 22, joined the army of M. Brutus in Greece, and was appointed a tribunus. He says of himself: Quod mihi pareret legio Romana tribuno. It is impossible that so young and obscure a man could have been actual commander of a legion.

17. **Praefectus**] The commander of the auxiliary horse, appointed by the imperator from among his Roman officers.

18. **Legatus**] The consul's or imperator's lieutenant, generally in command of a detachment.

19. **Praetor**] i. q. *imperator*. Qui praeit exercitui.

20. **Plerosque ipsos**] "Most of them personally."

CHAPTER LX.

1. **Ferentarii**] 1. Men who brought supplies of missiles to the armed combatants. 2. The bowmen and slingers on the wings. 3. Any light-armed irregulars.

2. **Cum infestis signis**] "With opposing standards." Caes. *B. G.* vii. 51. legiones infestis contra hostes signis constiterunt. Lucan, i. 6. infestis obvia signis Signa.

3. **Pila omittunt**] So in Caes. *Bell. Gall.* i. 52, vii. 88. nostri omissis pilis gladio rem gerunt. Comp. Lucan, vii. 490:

Odiis solus civilibus ensis
Sufficit, et dextras Romana in viscera ducit.

And again, viii. 385:

Ensis habet vires et gens quaecunque virorum est
Bella gerit gladiis.

4. **Veterani**] i. e. the soldiers of the republic, referring to the *veteranae cohortes* just mentioned.

5. **Magna vi tendere**] "To exert himself vigorously." Comp. Virg. *Aen.* xii. 553. vasto certamine tendunt. Liv. xxxii. 32. quod summa vi ut tenderet mandaverat.

6. **Cohortem praetoriam**] The imperator's body-guard.

7. **In primis pugnantes cadunt**] "Foremost fighting fall," or, "are among the first to fall." The first seems the preferable interpretation. Comp. Tyrtaeus, *fragm.* i. 1. τεθνάμεναι γὰρ καλὸν ἐνὶ προμάχοισι πεσόντα. ii. 11. ἰθὺς δ' εἰς προμάχους ἀσπίδ' ἀνὴρ ἐχέτω. The expression comes originally from Homer, *Il.* xix. ult. ἐν πρώτοις ἰάχων ἔχε μούνυχας ἵππους.

CHAPTER LXI.

1. **Tum vero**] For this redundant use of the conjunction, comp. Liv. xxii. 11. ita rebus divinis peractis, tum de bello dictator retulit. xxvi. 31. reductis in curiam legatis tum consul, etc. See a nearly similar construction above, c. 51. postquam respublica adolevit...tum lex Porcia, etc.

2. **Medios**] "In the centre." See the last chapter: in medios hostes inducit.

3. **Disjecerat**] "Had broken, routed, dispersed." Virg. Aen. v. Disjice compositam pacem.

4. **Paullo diversius**] "Somewhat more scattered;" subaud. *quidem*.

5. **Etiam**] i. q. *adhuc*. Comp. Ter. *Andr.* i. 1. 89. non satis pernosti me etiam. Virg. *Aen.* vi. 485. etiam currus etiam arma tenentem.

6. **Vivus**] "While living ;" i. q. *vivens*. Comp. Virg. *Aen.* vi. 653 :

> Quae gratia currûm
> Armorumque fuit vivis.

7. **Civis ingenuus**] A free citizen born of free citizens.

8. **Ita...juxta**] "So equally unsparing had they all been both of their own and their opponents' lives."

9. **Laetitia**] For a distinction between "laetitia" and "gaudium" see note on ch. 48. "Moeror" may differ from "luctus" as sorrow from mourning, the one the inward feeling, the other the outward sign of grief. Here luctus is plural, answering to gaudia. Comp. Lucan, vii. 705 :

> lacrimas luctusque remitte.

December, 1887.

A Catalogue

OF

Educational Books

PUBLISHED BY

Macmillan & Co.

BEDFORD STREET, STRAND, LONDON.

20.12.87.

CONTENTS.

CLASSICS— PAGE
    Elementary Classics 3
    Classical Series 7
    Classical Library, (1) Text, (2) Translations . . . 12
    Grammar, Composition, and Philology . . . 17
    Antiquities, Ancient History, and Philosophy . . 22

MATHEMATICS—
    Arithmetic and Mensuration 24
    Algebra 26
    Euclid, and Elementary Geometry 28
    Trigonometry 29
    Higher Mathematics 30

SCIENCE—
    Natural Philosophy 37
    Astronomy 43
    Chemistry 43
    Biology 45
    Medicine 49
    Anthropology 50
    Physical Geography and Geology 50
    Agriculture 52
    Political Economy 52
    Mental and Moral Philosophy 53

HISTORY AND GEOGRAPHY 55, 79

MODERN LANGUAGES AND LITERATURE—
    English 59
    French 65
    German 68
    Modern Greek 70
    Italian 70
    Spanish 70

DOMESTIC ECONOMY 71

ART AND KINDRED SUBJECTS 71

WORKS ON TEACHING 72

DIVINITY 73

29 AND 30, BEDFORD STREET, COVENT GARDEN,
LONDON, W.C., *December*, 1887.

CLASSICS.

ELEMENTARY CLASSICS.

18mo, Eighteenpence each.

THIS SERIES FALLS INTO TWO CLASSES—

(1) First Reading Books for Beginners, provided not only with **Introductions and Notes**, but with **Vocabularies**, and in some cases with **Exercises** based upon the Text.

(2) Stepping-stones to the study of particular authors, intended for more advanced students who are beginning to read such authors as Terence, Plato, the Attic Dramatists, and the harder parts of Cicero, Horace, Virgil, and Thucydides.

These are provided with Introductions and Notes, **but no Vocabulary.** The Publishers have been led to provide the more strictly Elementary Books with Vocabularies by the representations of many teachers, who hold that beginners do not understand the use of a Dictionary, and of others who, in the case of middle-class schools where the cost of books is a serious consideration, advocate the Vocabulary system on grounds of economy. It is hoped that the two parts of the Series, fitting into one another, may together fulfil all the requirements of Elementary and Preparatory Schools, and the Lower Forms of Public Schools.

The following Elementary Books, with Introductions, Notes, and Vocabularies, and in some cases with Exercises, are either ready or in preparation:—

Aeschylus.—PROMETHEUS VINCTUS. Edited by Rev. H. M. STEPHENSON, M.A.

Arrian.—THE EXPEDITION OF ALEXANDER. Selections adapted for the use of Beginners, and edited, with Introduction, Notes, Vocabulary, and Exercises, by JOHN BOND, M.A., and A. S. WALPOLE, M.A. [*In preparation.*

Cæsar.—THE HELVETIAN WAR. Being Selections from Book I. of the "De Bello Gallico." Adapted for the use of Beginners. With Notes, Exercises, and Vocabulary, by W. WELCH, M.A., and C. G. DUFFIELD, M.A.

THE INVASION OF BRITAIN. Being Selections from Books IV. and V. of the "De Bello Gallico." Adapted for the use of Beginners. With Notes, Vocabulary, and Exercises, by W. WELCH, M.A., and C. G. DUFFIELD, M.A.

THE GALLIC WAR. BOOK I. Edited by A. S. WALPOLE, M.A.

THE GALLIC WAR. BOOKS II. AND III. Edited by the Rev. W. G. RUTHERFORD, M.A., LL.D., Head-Master of Westminster School.

THE GALLIC WAR. BOOK IV. Edited by CLEMENT BRYANS, M.A., Assistant-Master at Dulwich College.

THE GALLIC WAR. SCENES FROM BOOKS V. AND VI. Edited by C. COLBECK, M.A., Assistant-Master at Harrow; formerly Fellow of Trinity College, Cambridge.

THE GALLIC WAR. BOOKS V. AND VI. (separately). By the same Editor. Book V. *ready.* Book VI. *in preparation.*

THE GALLIC WAR. BOOK VII. Edited by JOHN BOND, M.A., and A. S. WALPOLE, M.A.

Cicero.—DE SENECTUTE. Edited by E. S. SHUCKBURGH, M.A., late Fellow of Emmanuel College, Cambridge.

DE AMICITIA. By the same Editor.

STORIES OF ROMAN HISTORY. Adapted for the Use of Beginners. With Notes, Vocabulary, and Exercises, by the Rev. G. E. JEANS, M.A., Fellow of Hertford College, Oxford, and A. V. JONES, M.A., Assistant-Masters at Haileybury College.

Eutropius.—Adapted for the Use of Beginners. With Notes, Vocabulary, and Exercises, by WILLIAM WELCH, M.A., and C. G. DUFFIELD, M.A., Assistant-Masters at Surrey County School, Cranleigh.

Homer.—ILIAD. BOOK I. Edited by Rev. JOHN BOND, M.A., and A. S. WALPOLE, M.A.

ELEMENTARY CLASSICS. 5

Homer.—ILIAD. BOOK XVIII. THE ARMS OF ACHILLES.
Edited by S. R. JAMES, M.A., Assistant-Master at Eton College.
ODYSSEY. BOOK I. Edited by Rev. JOHN BOND, M.A. and A. S. WALPOLE, M.A.

Horace.—ODES. BOOKS I.—IV. Edited by T. E. PAGE, M.A., late Fellow of St. John's College, Cambridge; Assistant-Master at the Charterhouse. Each 1s. 6d.

Livy.—BOOK I. Edited by H. M. STEPHENSON, M.A., Head Master of St. Peter's School, York.
THE HANNIBALIAN WAR. Being part of the XXI. AND XXII. BOOKS OF LIVY, adapted for the use of beginners, by G. C. MACAULAY, M.A., late Fellow of Trinity College, Cambridge.
THE SIEGE OF SYRACUSE. Being part of the XXIV. AND XXV. BOOKS OF LIVY, adapted for the use of beginners. With Notes, Vocabulary, and Exercises, by GEORGE RICHARDS, M.A., and A. S. WALPOLE, M.A.
LEGENDS OF EARLY ROME. Adapted for the use of beginners. With Notes, Exercises, and Vocabulary, by HERBERT WILKINSON, M.A. [*In preparation.*

Lucian.—EXTRACTS FROM LUCIAN. Edited, with Notes, Exercises, and Vocabulary, by Rev. JOHN BOND, M.A., and A. S. WALPOLE, M.A.

Nepos.—SELECTIONS ILLUSTRATIVE OF GREEK AND ROMAN HISTORY. Edited for the use of beginners with Notes, Vocabulary and Exercises, by G. S. FARNELL, M.A.

Ovid.—SELECTIONS. Edited by E. S. SHUCKBURGH, M.A. late Fellow and Assistant-Tutor of Emmanuel College, Cambridge.
EASY SELECTIONS FROM OVID IN ELEGIAC VERSE. Arranged for the use of Beginners with Notes, Vocabulary, and Exercises, by HERBERT WILKINSON, M.A.
STORIES FROM THE METAMORPHOSES. Edited for the Use of Schools. With Notes, Exercises, and Vocabulary. By J. BOND, M.A., and A. S. WALPOLE, M.A.

Phædrus.—SELECT FABLES. Adapted for the Use of Beginners. With Notes, Exercises, and Vocabularies, by A. S. WALPOLE, M.A.

Thucydides.—THE RISE OF THE ATHENIAN EMPIRE. BOOK I. CC. LXXXIX. — CXVII. AND CXXVIII. — CXXXVIII. Edited with Notes, Vocabulary and Exercises, by F. H. COLSON, M.A., Senior Classical Master at Bradford Grammar School; Fellow of St. John's College, Cambridge.

Virgil.—ÆNEID. BOOK I. Edited by A. S. WALPOLE, M.A.
ÆNEID. BOOK IV. Edited by Rev. H. M. STEPHENSON, M.A. [*In preparation.*

Virgil.—ÆNEID. BOOK V. Edited by Rev. A. CALVERT, M.A., late Fellow of St. John's College, Cambridge.
ÆNEID. BOOK VI. Edited by T. E. PAGE, M.A.
[*In preparation.*
ÆNEID. BOOK IX. Edited by Rev. H. M. STEPHENSON, M.A. [*In the press.*
GEORGICS. BOOK I. Edited by C. BRYANS, M.A.
[*In preparation.*
SELECTIONS. Edited by E. S. SHUCKBURGH, M.A.

Xenophon.—ANABASIS. BOOK I. Edited by A. S. WALPOLE, M.A.
SELECTIONS FROM ANABASIS. BOOK I. Edited for the use of Beginners, with Notes, Vocabulary, and Exercises, by E. A. WELLS, M.A., Assistant Master in Durham School.
SELECTIONS FROM ANABASIS. BOOK IV. Edited for the use of Beginners, with Notes, Vocabulary, and Exercises, by Rev. E. D. STONE, M.A., formerly Assistant-Master at Eton.
[*In preparation.*
SELECTIONS FROM THE CYROPÆDIA. Edited, with Notes, Vocabulary, and Exercises, by A. H. COOKE, M.A., Fellow and Lecturer of King's College, Cambridge.

The following more advanced Books, with Introductions and Notes, **but no Vocabulary,** are either ready, or in preparation:—

Cicero.—SELECT LETTERS. Edited by Rev. G. E. JEANS, M.A., Fellow of Hertford College, Oxford, and Assistant-Master at Haileybury College.

Euripides.—HECUBA. Edited by Rev. JOHN BOND, M.A. and A. S. WALPOLE, M.A.

Herodotus.—SELECTIONS FROM BOOKS VII. AND VIII., THE EXPEDITION OF XERXES. Edited by A. H. COOKE, M.A., Fellow and Lecturer of King's College, Cambridge.

Horace. — SELECTIONS FROM THE SATIRES AND EPISTLES. Edited by Rev. W. J. V. BAKER, M.A., Fellow of St. John's College, Cambridge.
SELECT EPODES AND ARS POETICA. Edited by H. A. DALTON, M.A., formerly Senior Student of Christchurch; Assistant-Master in Winchester College.

Plato.—EUTHYPHRO AND MENEXENUS. Edited by C. E. GRAVES, M.A., Classical Lecturer and late Fellow of St. John's College, Cambridge.

Terence.—SCENES FROM THE ANDRIA. Edited by F. W. CORNISH, M.A., Assistant-Master at Eton College.

The Greek Elegiac Poets.— FROM CALLINUS TO CALLIMACHUS. Selected and Edited by Rev. HERBERT KYNASTON, D.D., Principal of Cheltenham College, and formerly Fellow of St. John's College, Cambridge.

Thucydides.—BOOK IV. CHS. I.—XLI. THE CAPTURE OF SPHACTERIA. Edited by C. E. GRAVES, M.A.

Virgil.—GEORGICS. BOOK II. Edited by Rev. J. H. SKRINE, M.A., late Fellow of Merton College, Oxford; Assistant-Master at Uppingham.

* *Other Volumes to follow.*

CLASSICAL SERIES FOR COLLEGES AND SCHOOLS.

Fcap. 8vo.

Being select portions of Greek and Latin authors, edited with Introductions and Notes, for the use of Middle and Upper forms of Schools, or of candidates for Public Examinations at the Universities and elsewhere.

Attic Orators.—Selections from ANTIPHON, ANDOKIDES, LYSIAS, ISOKRATES, AND ISAEOS. Edited by R. C. JEBB, M.A., LL.D., Litt.D., Professor of Greek in the University of Glasgow. [*New Edition in the press.*

Æschines.— IN CTESIPHONTEM. Edited by Rev. T. GWATKIN, M.A., late Fellow of St. John's College, Cambridge.
[*In the press.*

Æschylus. — PERSÆ. Edited by A. O. PRICKARD, M.A. Fellow and Tutor of New College, Oxford. With Map. 3s. 6d.

Andocides.—DE MYSTERIIS. Edited by W. J. HICKIE, M.A., formerly Assistant-Master in Denstone College. 2s. 6d.

Cæsar.—THE GALLIC WAR. Edited, after Kraner, by Rev. JOHN BOND, M.A., and A. S. WALPOLE, M.A. With Maps. 6s.

Catullus.—SELECT POEMS. Edited by F. P. SIMPSON, B.A., late Scholar of Balliol College, Oxford. New and Revised Edition. 5s. The Text of this Edition is carefully adapted to School use.

Cicero.—THE CATILINE ORATIONS. From the German of KARL HALM. Edited, with Additions, by A. S. WILKINS M.A., LL.D., Professor of Latin at the Owens College, Manchester, Examiner of Classics to the University of London. New Edition. 3s. 6d.

Cicero.—PRO LEGE MANILIA. Edited, after HALM, by Professor A. S. WILKINS, M.A., LL.D. 2s. 6d.

THE SECOND PHILIPPIC ORATION. From the German of KARL HALM. Edited, with Corrections and Additions, by JOHN E. B. MAYOR, Professor of Latin in the University of Cambridge, and Fellow of St. John's College. New Edition, revised. 5s.

PRO ROSCIO AMERINO. Edited, after HALM, by E. H. DONKIN, M.A., late Scholar of Lincoln College, Oxford; Assistant-Master at Sherborne School. 4s. 6d.

PRO P. SESTIO. Edited by Rev. H. A. HOLDEN, M.A., LL.D., late Fellow of Trinity College, Cambridge; and late Classical Examiner to the University of London. 5s.

Demosthenes.—DE CORONA. Edited by B. DRAKE, M.A. late Fellow of King's College, Cambridge. New and revised Edition. 4s. 6d.

ADVERSUS LEPTINEM. Edited by Rev. J. R. KING, M.A. Fellow and Tutor of Oriel College, Oxford. 4s. 6d.

THE FIRST PHILIPPIC. Edited, after C. REHDANTZ, by Rev. T. GWATKIN, M.A., late Fellow of St. John's College, Cambridge. 2s. 6d.

IN MIDIAM. Edited by Prof. A. S. WILKINS, LL.D., and HERMAN HAGER, Ph.D., of the Owens College, Manchester.
[*In preparation.*

Euripides.—HIPPOLYTUS. Edited by J. P. MAHAFFY, M.A., Fellow and Pofessor of Ancient History in Trinity College, Dublin, and J. B. BURY, Fellow of Trinity College, Dublin. 3s. 6d.

MEDEA. Edited by A. W. VERRALL, M.A., Fellow and Lecturer of Trinity College, Cambridge. 3s. 6d.

IPHIGENIA IN TAURIS. Edited by E. B. ENGLAND, M.A., Lecturer at the Owens College, Manchester. 4s. 6d.

Herodotus.—BOOKS V. AND VI. Edited by J. STRACHAN, M.A., Professor of Greek in the Owens College, Manchester.
[*In preparation.*

BOOKS VII. AND VIII. Edited by Miss A. RAMSAY.
[*In preparation.*

Homer.—ILIAD. BOOKS I., IX., XI., XVI.—XXIV. THE STORY OF ACHILLES. Edited by the late J. H. PRATT, M.A., and WALTER LEAF, M.A., Fellows of Trinity College, Cambridge. 6s.

ODYSSEY. BOOK IX. Edited by Prof. JOHN E. B. MAYOR. 2s. 6d.

ODYSSEY. BOOKS XXI.—XXIV. THE TRIUMPH OF ODYSSEUS. Edited by S. G. HAMILTON, B.A., Fellow of Hertford College, Oxford. 3s. 6d.

CLASSICAL SERIES.

Horace.—THE ODES. Edited by T. E. PAGE, M.A., formerly Fellow of St. John's College, Cambridge; Assistant-Master at the Charterhouse. 6s. (BOOKS I., II., III., and IV. separately, 2s. each.)
    THE SATIRES. Edited by ARTHUR PALMER, M.A., Fellow of Trinity College, Dublin; Professor of Latin in the University of Dublin. 6s.
    THE EPISTLES AND ARS POETICA. Edited by A. S. WILKINS, M.A., LL.D., Professor of Latin in Owens College, Manchester; Examiner in Classics to the University of London. 6s.

Isaeos.—THE ORATIONS. Edited by WILLIAM RIDGEWAY, M.A., Fellow of Caius College, Cambridge; and Professor of Greek in the University of Cork. [*In preparation.*

Juvenal. THIRTEEN SATIRES. Edited, for the Use of Schools, by E. G. HARDY, M.A., late Fellow of Jesus College, Oxford. 5s.
    The Text of this Edition is carefully adapted to School use.
    SELECT SATIRES. Edited by Professor JOHN E. B. MAYOR. X. AND XI. 3s. 6d. XII.—XVI. 4s. 6d.

Livy.—BOOKS II. AND III. Edited by Rev. H. M. STEPHENSON, M.A. 5s.
    BOOKS XXI. AND XXII. Edited by the Rev. W. W. CAPES, M.A. Maps. 5s.
    BOOKS XXIII. AND XXIV. Edited by G. C. MACAULAY, M.A. With Maps. 5s.
    THE LAST TWO KINGS OF MACEDON. EXTRACTS FROM THE FOURTH AND FIFTH DECADES OF LIVY. Selected and Edited, with Introduction and Notes, by F. H. RAWLINS, M.A., Fellow of King's College, Cambridge; and Assistant-Master at Eton. With Maps. 3s. 6d.

Lucretius. BOOKS I.—III. Edited by J. H. WARBURTON LEE, M.A., late Scholar of Corpus Christi College, Oxford, and Assistant-Master at Rossall. 4s. 6d.

Lysias.—SELECT ORATIONS. Edited by E. S. SHUCKBURGH, M.A., late Assistant-Master at Eton College, formerly Fellow and Assistant-Tutor of Emmanuel College, Cambridge. New Edition, revised. 6s.

Martial. — SELECT EPIGRAMS. Edited by Rev. H. M. STEPHENSON, M.A. New Edition, Revised and Enlarged. 6s. 6d.

Ovid.—FASTI. Edited by G. H. HALLAM, M.A., Fellow of St. John's College, Cambridge, and Assistant-Master at Harrow. With Maps. 5s.

Ovid.—HEROIDUM EPISTULÆ XIII. Edited by E. S. SHUCKBURGH, M.A. 4s. 6d.
   METAMORPHOSES. BOOKS XIII. AND XIV. Edited by C. SIMMONS, M.A. 4s. 6d.

Plato.—MENO. Edited by E. S. THOMPSON, M.A., Fellow of Christ's College, Cambridge. [*In preparation.*
   APOLOGY AND CRITO. Edited by F. J. H. JENKINSON, M.A., Fellow of Trinity College, Cambridge. [*In preparation.*
   THE REPUBLIC. BOOKS I.—V. Edited by T. H. WARREN, M.A., President of Magdalen College, Oxford. [*In the press.*

Plautus.—MILES GLORIOSUS. Edited by R. Y. TYRRELL, M.A., Fellow of Trinity College, and Regius Professor of Greek in the University of Dublin. Second Edition Revised. 5s.
   AMPHITRUO. Edited by ARTHUR PALMER, M.A., Fellow of Trinity College and Regius Professor of Latin in the University of Dublin. [*In preparation.*
   CAPTIVI. Edited by A. RHYS SMITH, late Junior Student of Christ Church, Oxford. [*In preparation.*

Pliny.—LETTERS. BOOK III. Edited by Professor JOHN E. B. MAYOR. With Life of Pliny by G. H. RENDALL, M.A. 5s.
   LETTERS. BOOKS I. and II. Edited by J. COWAN, B.A., Assistant-Master in the Grammar School, Manchester.
   [*In preparation.*

Plutarch.—LIFE OF THEMISTOKLES. Edited by Rev. H. A. HOLDEN, M.A., LL.D. 5s.

Polybius.—HISTORY OF THE ACHÆAN LEAGUE. Being Parts of Books II., III., and IV. Edited by W. W. CAPES. M.A. [*In the press.*

Propertius.—SELECT POEMS. Edited by Professor J. P. POSTGATE, M.A., Fellow of Trinity College, Cambridge. Second Edition, revised. 6s.

Sallust.—CATILINA AND JUGURTHA. Edited by C. MERIVALE, D.D., Dean of Ely. New Edition, carefully revised and enlarged, 4s. 6d. Or separately, 2s. 6d. each.
   BELLUM CATULINAE. Edited by A. M. COOK, M.A., Assistant Master at St. Paul's School. 4s. 6d.
   JUGURTHA. By the same Editor. [*In preparation.*

Sophocles.—ANTIGONE. Edited by Rev. JOHN BOND, M.A., and A. S. WALPOLE, M.A. [*In preparation.*

Tacitus.—AGRICOLA AND GERMANIA. Edited by A. J. CHURCH, M.A., and W. J. BRODRIBB, M.A., Translators of Tacitus. New Edition, 3s. 6d. Or separately, 2s. each.

Tacitus.—THE ANNALS. BOOK VI. By the same Editors. 2s. 6d.
  THE HISTORIES. BOOKS I. AND II. Edited by A. D. GODLEY. M.A. 5s.
  THE ANNALS. BOOKS I. AND II. Edited by J. S. REID, M.L., Litt.D. [*In preparation.*

Terence.—HAUTON TIMORUMENOS. Edited by E. S. SHUCKBURGH, M.A. 3s. With Translation, 4s. 6d.
  PHORMIO. Edited by Rev. JOHN BOND, M.A., and A. S. WALPOLE, M.A. 4s. 6d.

Thucydides. BOOK IV. Edited by C. E. GRAVES, M.A., Classical Lecturer, and late Fellow of St. John's College, Cambridge. 5s.
  BOOKS I. II. III. AND V. By the same Editor. To be published separately. [*In preparation. (Book V. in the press.*)
  BOOKS VI. AND VII. THE SICILIAN EXPEDITION. Edited by the Rev. PERCIVAL FROST, M.A., late Fellow of St. John's College, Cambridge. New Edition, revised and enlarged, with Map. 5s.

Tibullus.—SELECT POEMS. Edited by Professor J. P. POSTGATE, M.A. [*In preparation.*

Virgil.—ÆNEID. BOOKS II. AND III. THE NARRATIVE OF ÆNEAS. Edited by E. W. HOWSON, M.A., Fellow of King's College, Cambridge, and Assistant-Master at Harrow. 3s.

Xenophon.—HELLENICA, BOOKS I. AND II. Edited by H. HAILSTONE, B.A., late Scholar of Peterhouse, Cambridge. With Map. 4s. 6d.
  CYROPÆDIA. BOOKS VII. AND VIII. Edited by ALFRED GOODWIN, M.A., Professor of Greek in University College, London. 5s.
  MEMORABILIA SOCRATIS. Edited by A. R. CLUER, B.A., Balliol College, Oxford. 6s.
  THE ANABASIS. BOOKS I.—IV. Edited by Professors W. W. GOODWIN and J. W. WHITE. Adapted to Goodwin's Greek Grammar. With a Map. 5s.
  HIERO. Edited by Rev. H. A. HOLDEN, M.A., LL.D. 3s. 6d.
  OECONOMICUS. By the same Editor. With Introduction, Explanatory Notes, Critical Appendix, and Lexicon. 6s.

*** *Other Volumes will follow.*

CLASSICAL LIBRARY.

(1) **Texts**, Edited with **Introductions and Notes**, for the use of Advanced Students. (2) **Commentaries and Translations.**

Æschylus.—THE EUMENIDES. The Greek Text, with Introduction, English Notes, and Verse Translation. By BERNARD DRAKE, M.A., late Fellow of King's College, Cambridge. 8vo. 5s.

AGAMEMNON, CHOEPHOROE, AND EUMENIDES. Edited, with Introduction and Notes, by A. O. PRICKARD, M.A., Fellow and Tutor of New College, Oxford. 8vo.
[*In preparation.*

AGAMEMNO. Emendavit DAVID S. MARGOLIOUTH, Coll. Nov. Oxon. Soc. Demy 8vo. 2s. 6d.

THE "SEVEN AGAINST THEBES." Edited, with Introduction, Commentary, and Translation, by A. W. VERRALL, M.A., Fellow of Trinity College, Cambridge. 8vo. 7s. 6d.

Antoninus, Marcus Aurelius.—BOOK IV. OF THE MEDITATIONS. The Text Revised, with Translation and Notes, by HASTINGS CROSSLEY, M.A., Professor of Greek in Queen's College, Belfast. 8vo. 6s.

Aristotle.—THE METAPHYSICS. BOOK I. Translated by a Cambridge Graduate. 8vo. 5s. [*Book II. in preparation.*

THE POLITICS. Edited, after SUSEMIHL, by R. D. HICKS, M.A., Fellow of Trinity College, Cambridge. 8vo.
[*In the press.*

THE POLITICS. Translated by Rev. J. E. C. WELLDON, M.A., Fellow of King's College, Cambridge, and Head-Master of Harrow School. Crown 8vo. 10s. 6d.

THE RHETORIC. Translated, with an Analysis and Critical Notes, by the same. Crown 8vo. 7s. 6d.

THE ETHICS. Translated, with an Analysis and Critical Notes, by the same. Crown 8vo. [*In preparation.*

AN INTRODUCTION TO ARISTOTLE'S RHETORIC. With Analysis, Notes, and Appendices. By E. M. COPE, Fellow and Tutor of Trinity College, Cambridge. 8vo. 14s.

THE SOPHISTICI ELENCHI. With Translation and Notes by E. POSTE, M.A., Fellow of Oriel College, Oxford. 8vo. 8s. 6d.

Aristophanes.—THE BIRDS. Translated into English Verse, with Introduction, Notes, and Appendices, by B. H. KENNEDY, D.D., Regius Professor of Greek in the University of Cambridge. Crown 8vo. 6s. Help Notes to the same, for the use of Students, 1s. 6d.

Attic Orators.—FROM ANTIPHON TO ISAEOS. By R. C. JEBB, M.A., LL.D., Professor of Greek in the University of Glasgow. 2 vols. 8vo. 25s.

Babrius.—Edited, with Introductory Dissertations, Critical Notes, Commentary and Lexicon. By Rev. W. GUNION RUTHERFORD, M.A., LL.D., Head-Master of Westminster School. 8vo. 12s. 6d.

Cicero.—THE ACADEMICA. The Text revised and explained by J. S. REID, M.L., Litt.D., Fellow of Caius College, Cambridge. 8vo. 15s.
THE ACADEMICS. Translated by J. S. REID, M.L. 8vo. 5s. 6d.
SELECT LETTERS. After the Edition of ALBERT WATSON, M.A. Translated by G. E. JEANS, M.A., Fellow of Hertford College, Oxford, and late Assistant-Master at Haileybury. 8vo. 10s. 6d.

Ctesias.—THE FRAGMENTS OF CTESIAS. Edited, with Introduction and Notes, by J. E. GILMORE, M.A. 8vo. (Classical Library.) [*In the press.*
(See also *Classical Series*.)

Euripides.—MEDEA. Edited, with Introduction and Notes, by A. W. VERRALL, M.A., Fellow and Lecturer of Trinity College, Cambridge. 8vo. 7s. 6d.
IPHIGENIA IN AULIS. Edited, with Introduction and Notes, by E. B. ENGLAND, M.A., Lecturer in the Owens College, Manchester. 8vo. [*In preparation.*
INTRODUCTION TO THE STUDY OF EURIPIDES. By Professor J. P. MAHAFFY. Fcap. 8vo. 1s. 6d. (*Classical Writers Series*.)
(See also *Classical Series*.)

Herodotus.—BOOKS I.—III. THE ANCIENT EMPIRES OF THE EAST. Edited, with Notes, Introductions, and Appendices, by A. H. SAYCE, Deputy-Professor of Comparative Philology, Oxford; Honorary LL.D., Dublin. Demy 8vo. 16s.
BOOKS IV.—IX. Edited by REGINALD W. MACAN, M.A., Lecturer in Ancient History at Brasenose College, Oxford. 8vo. [*In preparation.*

Homer.—THE ILIAD. Edited, with Introduction and Notes, by WALTER LEAF, M.A., late Fellow of Trinity College, Cambridge. 8vo. Vol. I. Books I.—XII. 14s. [Vol. II. *in the press.*
THE ILIAD. Translated into English Prose. By ANDREW LANG, M.A., WALTER LEAF, M.A., and ERNEST MYERS, M.A. Crown 8vo. 12s. 6d.
THE ODYSSEY. Done into English by S. H. BUTCHER, M.A., Professor of Greek in the University of Edinburgh, and ANDREW LANG, M.A., late Fellow of Merton College, Oxford. Seventh and Cheaper Edition, revised and corrected. Crown 8vo. 4s. 6d.

Homer.—INTRODUCTION TO THE STUDY OF HOMER. By the Right Hon. W. E. GLADSTONE, M.P. 18mo. 1s. (*Literature Primers.*)

HOMERIC DICTIONARY. For Use in Schools and Colleges. Translated from the German of Dr. G. AUTENRIETH, with Additions and Corrections, by R. P. KEEP, Ph.D. With numerous Illustrations. Crown 8vo. 6s.

(See also *Classical Series*.)

Horace.—THE WORKS OF HORACE RENDERED INTO ENGLISH PROSE. With Introductions, Running Analysis, Notes, &c. By J. LONSDALE, M.A., and S. LEE, M.A. (*Globe Edition.*) 3s. 6d.

STUDIES, LITERARY AND HISTORICAL, IN THE ODES OF HORACE. By A. W. VERRALL, Fellow of Trinity College, Cambridge. Demy 8vo. 8s. 6d.

(See also *Classical Series*.)

Juvenal.—THIRTEEN SATIRES OF JUVENAL. With a Commentary. By JOHN E. B. MAYOR, M.A., Professor of Latin in the University of Cambridge. Crown 8vo.

⁎ Vol. I. Fourth Edition, Revised and Enlarged. 10s. 6d. Vol. II. Second Edition. 10s. 6d.

⁎ The new matter consists of an Introduction (pp. 1—53), Additional Notes (pp. 333—466) and Index (pp. 467—526). It is also issued separately, as a Supplement to the previous edition, at 5s.

THIRTEEN SATIRES. Translated into English after the Text of J. E. B. MAYOR by ALEXANDER LEEPER, M.A., Warden of Trinity College, in the University of Melbourne. Crown 8vo. 3s. 6d.

(See also *Classical Series*.)

Livy.—BOOKS I.—IV. Translated by Rev. H. M. STEPHENSON, M.A., Head-Master of St. Peter's School, York. [*In preparation.*

BOOKS XXI.—XXV. Translated by ALFRED JOHN CHURCH, M.A., of Lincoln College, Oxford, Professor of Latin, University College, London, and WILLIAM JACKSON BRODRIBB, M.A., late Fellow of St. John's College, Cambridge. Cr. 8vo. 7s. 6d.

INTRODUCTION TO THE STUDY OF LIVY. By Rev. W. W. CAPES, Reader in Ancient History at Oxford. Fcap. 8vo. 1s. 6d. (*Classical Writers Series.*)

(See also *Classical Series*.)

Martial.—BOOKS I. AND II. OF THE EPIGRAMS. Edited, with Introduction and Notes, by Professor J. E. B. MAYOR, M.A. 8vo. [*In the press.*

(See also *Classical Series*.)

CLASSICAL LIBRARY. 15

Pausanias.—DESCRIPTION OF GREECE. Translated by J. G. FRAZER, M.A., Fellow of Trinity College, Cambridge.
[*In preparation.*

Phrynichus.—THE NEW PHRYNICHUS; being a Revised Text of the Ecloga of the Grammarian Phrynichus. With Introduction and Commentary by Rev. W. GUNION RUTHERFORD, M.A., LL.D., Head-Master of Westminster School. 8vo. 18s.

Pindar.—THE EXTANT ODES OF PINDAR. Translated into English, with an Introduction and short Notes, by ERNEST MYERS, M.A., late Fellow of Wadham College, Oxford. Second Edition. Crown 8vo. 5s.

THE OLYMPIAN AND PYTHIAN ODES. Edited, with an Introductory Essay, Notes, and Indexes, by BASIL GILDERSLEEVE, Professor of Greek in the Johns Hopkins University, Baltimore. Crown 8vo. 7s. 6d.

Plato.—PHÆDO. Edited, with Introduction, Notes, and Appendices, by R. D. ARCHER-HIND, M.A., Fellow of Trinity College, Cambridge. 8vo. 8s. 6d.

TIMÆUS.—Edited, with Introduction, Notes, and a Translation, by the same Editor. 8vo. [*In the press.*

PHÆDO. Edited, with Introduction and Notes, by W. D. GEDDES, LL.D., Principal of the University of Aberdeen. Second Edition. Demy 8vo. 8s. 6d.

PHILEBUS. Edited, with Introduction and Notes, by HENRY JACKSON, M.A., Fellow of Trinity College, Cambridge. 8vo.
[*In preparation.*

THE REPUBLIC.—Edited, with Introduction and Notes, by H. C. GOODHART, M.A., Fellow of Trinity College, Cambridge. 8vo. [*In preparation.*

THE REPUBLIC OF PLATO. Translated into English, with an Analysis and Notes, by J. LL. DAVIES, M.A., and D. J. VAUGHAN, M.A. 18mo. 4s. 6d.

EUTHYPHRO, APOLOGY, CRITO, AND PHÆDO. Translated by F. J. CHURCH. 18mo. 4s. 6d.

PHÆDRUS, LYSIS, AND PROTAGORAS. Translated by Rev. J. WRIGHT, M.A. [*New edition in preparation.*
(See also *Classical Series.*)

Plautus.—THE MOSTELLARIA OF PLAUTUS. With Notes, Prolegomena, and Excursus. By WILLIAM RAMSAY, M.A., formerly Professor of Humanity in the University of Glasgow. Edited by Professor GEORGE G. RAMSAY, M.A., of the University of Glasgow. 8vo. 14s.
(See also *Classical Series.*)

Polybius.—THE HISTORIES. Translated, with Introduction and Notes, by E. S. SHUCKBURGH, M.A. 8vo. [*In preparation.*

Sallust.—CATILINE AND JUGURTHA. Translated, with Introductory Essays, by A. W. POLLARD, B.A. Crown 8vo. 6s.

THE CATILINE (separately). Crown 8vo. 3s.

(See also *Classical Series*.)

Sophocles.—ŒDIPUS THE KING. Translated from the Greek of Sophocles into English Verse by E. D. A. MORSHEAD, M.A., late Fellow of New College, Oxford; Assistant Master at Winchester College. Fcap. 8vo. 3s. 6d.

Studia Scenica.—Part I., Section I. Introductory Study on the Text of the Greek Dramas. The Text of SOPHOCLES' TRACHINIAE, 1-300. By DAVID S. MARGOLIOUTH, Fellow of New College, Oxford. Demy 8vo. 2s. 6d.

Tacitus.—THE ANNALS. Edited, with Introductions and Notes, by G. O. HOLBROOKE, M.A., Professor of Latin in Trinity College, Hartford, U.S.A. With Maps. 8vo. 16s.

THE ANNALS. Translated by A. J. CHURCH, M.A., and W. J. BRODRIBB, M.A. With Notes and Maps. New Edition. Cr. 8vo. 7s. 6d.

THE HISTORIES. Edited, with Introduction and Notes, by Rev. W. A. SPOONER, M.A., Fellow of New College, and H. M. SPOONER, M.A., formerly Fellow of Magdalen College, Oxford. 8vo. [*In preparation.*

THE HISTORY. Translated by A. J. CHURCH, M.A., and W. J. BRODRIBB, M.A. With Notes and a Map. Crown 8vo. 6s.

THE AGRICOLA AND GERMANY, WITH THE DIALOGUE ON ORATORY. Translated by A. J. CHURCH, M.A., and W. J. BRODRIBB, M.A. With Notes and Maps. New and Revised Edition. Crown 8vo. 4s. 6d.

INTRODUCTION TO THE STUDY OF TACITUS. By A. J. CHURCH, M.A. and W. J. BRODRIBB, M.A. Fcap. 8vo. 1s. 6d. (*Classical Writers Series*.)

Theocritus, Bion, and Moschus. Rendered into English Prose, with Introductory Essay, by A. LANG, M.A. Crown 8vo. 6s.

Virgil.—THE WORKS OF VIRGIL RENDERED INTO ENGLISH PROSE, with Notes, Introductions, Running Analysis, and an Index, by JAMES LONSDALE, M.A., and SAMUEL LEE, M.A. New Edition. Globe 8vo. 3s. 6d.

THE ÆNEID. Translated by J. W. MACKAIL, M.A., Fellow of Balliol College, Oxford. Crown 8vo. 7s. 6d.

Xenophon.—COMPLETE WORKS. Translated, with Introduction and Essays, by H. G. DAKYNS, M.A., Assistant-Master in Clifton College. Four Volumes. Crown 8vo. [*In the press.*

GRAMMAR, COMPOSITION, & PHILOLOGY.

Belcher.—SHORT EXERCISES IN LATIN PROSE COMPOSITION AND EXAMINATION PAPERS IN LATIN GRAMMAR, to which is prefixed a Chapter on Analysis of Sentences. By the Rev. H. BELCHER, M.A., Rector of the High School, Dunedin, N.Z. New Edition. 18mo. 1s. 6d.
KEY TO THE ABOVE (for Teachers only). 3s. 6d.
SHORT EXERCISES IN LATIN PROSE COMPOSITION. Part II., On the Syntax of Sentences, with an Appendix, including EXERCISES IN LATIN IDIOMS, &c. 18mo. 2s.
KEY TO THE ABOVE (for Teachers only). 3s.

Blackie.—GREEK AND ENGLISH DIALOGUES FOR USE IN SCHOOLS AND COLLEGES. By JOHN STUART BLACKIE, Emeritus Professor of Greek in the University of Edinburgh. New Edition. Fcap. 8vo. 2s. 6d.

Bryans.—LATIN PROSE EXERCISES BASED UPON CAESAR'S GALLIC WAR. With a Classification of Cæsar's Chief Phrases and Grammatical Notes on Cæsar's Usages. By CLEMENT BRYANS, M.A., Assistant-Master in Dulwich College. Second Edition, Revised and Enlarged. Extra fcap. 8vo. 2s. 6d.
KEY TO THE ABOVE (for Teachers only). 3s. 6d.
GREEK PROSE EXERCISES based upon Thucydides. By the same Author. Extra fcap. 8vo. [*In preparation.*

Colson.—A FIRST GREEK READER. Stories and Legends from Greek Writers. By F. H. COLSON, M.A., Fellow of St. John's College, Cambridge, and Senior Classical Master at Bradford Grammar School. Globe 8vo. [*In the press.*

Eicke.—FIRST LESSONS IN LATIN. By K. M. EICKE, B.A., Assistant-Master in Oundle School. Globe 8vo. 2s.

England.—EXERCISES ON LATIN SYNTAX AND IDIOM. ARRANGED WITH REFERENCE TO ROBY'S SCHOOL LATIN GRAMMAR. By E. B. ENGLAND, M.A., Assistant Lecturer at the Owens College, Manchester. Crown 8vo. 2s. 6d. Key for Teachers only, 2s. 6d.

Goodwin.—Works by W. W. GOODWIN, LL.D., Professor of Greek in Harvard University, U.S.A.

Goodwin.—Works by W. W. GOODWIN LL.D., &c., *continued*—
SYNTAX OF THE MOODS AND TENSES OF THE GREEK VERB. New Edition, revised. Crown 8vo. 6s. 6d.
A GREEK GRAMMAR. New Edition, revised. Crown 8vo. 6s.
"It is the best Greek Grammar of its size in the English language."—ATHENÆUM.
A GREEK GRAMMAR FOR SCHOOLS. Crown 8vo. 3s. 6d.

Greenwood.—THE ELEMENTS OF GREEK GRAMMAR, including Accidence, Irregular Verbs, and Principles of Derivation and Composition; adapted to the System of Crude Forms. By J. G. GREENWOOD, Principal of Owens College, Manchester. New Edition. Crown 8vo. 5s. 6d.

Hadley and Allen.—A GREEK GRAMMAR FOR SCHOOLS AND COLLEGES. By JAMES HADLEY, late Professor in Yale College. Revised and in part Rewritten by FREDERIC DE FOREST ALLEN, Professor in Harvard College. Crown 8vo. 6s.

Hodgson.—MYTHOLOGY FOR LATIN VERSIFICATION. A brief Sketch of the Fables of the Ancients, prepared to be rendered into Latin Verse for Schools. By F. HODGSON, B.D., late Provost of Eton. New Edition, revised by F. C. HODGSON, M.A. 18mo. 3s.

Jackson.—FIRST STEPS TO GREEK PROSE COMPOSITION. By BLOMFIELD JACKSON, M.A., Assistant-Master in King's College School, London. New Edition, revised and enlarged. 18mo. 1s. 6d.
KEY TO FIRST STEPS (for Teachers only). 18mo. 3s. 6d.
SECOND STEPS TO GREEK PROSE COMPOSITION, with Miscellaneous Idioms, Aids to Accentuation, and Examination Papers in Greek Scholarship. 18mo. 2s. 6d.
KEY TO SECOND STEPS (for Teachers only). 18mo. 3s. 6d.

Kynaston.—EXERCISES IN THE COMPOSITION OF GREEK IAMBIC VERSE by Translations from English Dramatists. By Rev. H. KYNASTON, D.D., Principal of Cheltenham College. With Introduction, Vocabulary, &c. New Edition, revised and enlarged. Extra fcap. 8vo. 5s.
KEY TO THE SAME (for Teachers only). Extra fcap. 8vo. 4s. 6d.

Lupton.—AN INTRODUCTION TO LATIN ELEGIAC VERSE COMPOSITION. By J. H. LUPTON, M.A., Sur-Master of St. Paul's School, and formerly Fellow of St. John's College, Cambridge. Globe 8vo. 2s. 6d.
LATIN RENDERING OF THE EXERCISES IN PART II. (XXV.-C.). Globe 8vo. 3s. 6d.

CLASSICAL PUBLICATIONS.

Lupton.—Works by J. H. LUPTON, *continued*—
AN INTRODUCTION TO THE COMPOSITION OF LATIN LYRICS. Globe 8vo. [*In preparation.*

Mackie.—PARALLEL PASSAGES FOR TRANSLATION INTO GREEK AND ENGLISH. Carefully graduated for the use of Colleges and Schools. With Indexes. By Rev. ELLIS C. MACKIE, Classical Master at Heversham Grammar School. Globe 8vo. 4s. 6d.

Macmillan.—FIRST LATIN GRAMMAR. By M. C. MACMILLAN, M.A., late Scholar of Christ's College, Cambridge; sometime Assistant-Master in St. Paul's School. New Edition, enlarged. Fcap. 8vo. 1s. 6d.

Macmillan's Latin Course. FIRST YEAR. By A. M. COOK, M.A., Assistant-Master at St. Paul's School. New Edition, revised and enlarged. Globe 8vo. 3s. 6d.

*** *The Second Part is in preparation.*

Macmillan's Shorter Latin Course. By A. M. COOK, M.A., Assistant-Master at St. Paul's School. Being an abridgment of "Macmillan's Latin Course," First Year. Globe 8vo. 1s. 6d.

Marshall.—A TABLE OF IRREGULAR GREEK VERBS, classified according to the arrangement of Curtius's Greek Grammar. By J. M. MARSHALL, M.A., Head Master of the Grammar School, Durham. New Edition. 8vo. 1s.

Mayor (John E. B.)—FIRST GREEK READER. Edited after KARL HALM, with Corrections and large Additions by Professor JOHN E. B. MAYOR, M.A., Fellow of St. John's College, Cambridge. New Edition, revised. Fcap. 8vo. 4s. 6d.

Mayor (Joseph B.)—GREEK FOR BEGINNERS. By the Rev. J. B. MAYOR, M.A., Professor of Classical Literature in King's College, London. Part I., with Vocabulary, 1s. 6d. Parts II. and III., with Vocabulary and Index, 3s. 6d. Complete in one Vol. fcap. 8vo. 4s. 6d.

Nixon.—PARALLEL EXTRACTS, Arranged for Translation into English and Latin, with Notes on Idioms. By J. E. NIXON, M.A., Fellow and Classical Lecturer, King's College, Cambridge. Part I.—Historical and Epistolary. New Edition, revised and enlarged. Crown 8vo. 3s. 6d.
PROSE EXTRACTS, Arranged for Translation into English and Latin, with General and Special Prefaces on Style and Idiom. I. Oratorical. II. Historical. III. Philosophical and Miscellaneous. By the same Author. Crown 8vo. 3s. 6d.

*** *Translations of Select Passages supplied by Author only.*

Peile.—A PRIMER OF PHILOLOGY. By J. PEILE, M.A., Litt. D., Master of Christ's College, Cambridge. 18mo. 1s.

Postgate.—PASSAGES FOR TRANSLATION INTO LATIN PROSE. With Introduction and Notes, by J. P. POSTGATE, M.A. Crown 8vo. [*In the press.*

Postgate and Vince.—A DICTIONARY OF LATIN ETYMOLOGY. By J. P. POSTGATE, M.A., and C. A. VINCE, M.A. [*In preparation.*

Potts (A. W.)—Works by ALEXANDER W. POTTS, M.A., LL.D., late Fellow of St. John's College, Cambridge; Head Master of the Fettes College, Edinburgh.

HINTS TOWARDS LATIN PROSE COMPOSITION. New Edition. Extra fcap. 8vo. 3s.

PASSAGES FOR TRANSLATION INTO LATIN PROSE. Edited with Notes and References to the above. New Edition. Extra fcap. 8vo. 2s. 6d.

LATIN VERSIONS OF PASSAGES FOR TRANSLATION INTO LATIN PROSE (for Teachers only). 2s. 6d.

Reid.—A GRAMMAR OF TACITUS. By J. S. REID, M.L., Fellow of Caius College, Cambridge. [*In preparation.*

A GRAMMAR OF VERGIL. By the same Author. [*In preparation.*

*** *Similar Grammars to other Classical Authors will probably follow.*

Roby.—A GRAMMAR OF THE LATIN LANGUAGE, from Plautus to Suetonius. By H. J. ROBY, M.A., late Fellow of St. John's College, Cambridge. In Two Parts. Part I. Fifth Edition, containing:—Book I. Sounds. Book II. Inflexions. Book III. Word-formation. Appendices. Crown 8vo. 9s. Part II. Syntax, Prepositions, &c. Crown 8vo. 10s. 6d.

" Marked by the clear and practised insight of a master in his art. A book that would do honour to any country."—ATHENÆUM.

SCHOOL LATIN GRAMMAR. By the same Author. Crown 8vo. 5s.

Rush.—SYNTHETIC LATIN DELECTUS. A First Latin Construing Book arranged on the Principles of Grammatical Analysis. With Notes and Vocabulary. By E. RUSH, B.A. With Preface by the Rev. W. F. MOULTON, M.A., D.D. New and Enlarged Edition. Extra fcap. 8vo. 2s. 6d.

Rust.—FIRST STEPS TO LATIN PROSE COMPOSITION. By the Rev. G. RUST, M.A., of Pembroke College, Oxford, Master of the Lower School, King's College, London. New Edition. 18mo. 1s. 6d.

KEY TO THE ABOVE. By W. M. YATES, Assistant-Master in the High School, Sale. 18mo. 3s. 6d.

CLASSICAL PUBLICATIONS.

Rutherford.—Works by the Rev. W. GUNION RUTHERFORD, M.A., LL.D., Head-Master of Westminster School.
 A FIRST GREEK GRAMMAR. New Edition, enlarged. Extra fcap. 8vo. 1s. 6d.
 REX LEX. A Short Digest of the principal Relations between Latin, Greek, and Anglo-Saxon Sounds. 8vo. [*In preparation.*
 THE NEW PHRYNICHUS; being a Revised Text of the Ecloga of the Grammarian Phrynichus. With Introduction and Commentary. 8vo. 18s.

Simpson.—LATIN PROSE AFTER THE BEST AUTHORS. By F. P. SIMPSON, B.A., late Scholar of Balliol College, Oxford. Part I. CÆSARIAN PROSE. Extra fcap. 8vo. 2s. 6d.
 KEY TO THE ABOVE, for Teachers only. Extra fcap. 8vo. 5s.

Thring.—Works by the Rev. E. THRING, M.A., late Head-Master of Uppingham School.
 A LATIN GRADUAL. A First Latin Construing Book for Beginners. New Edition, enlarged, with Coloured Sentence Maps. Fcap. 8vo. 2s. 6d.
 A MANUAL OF MOOD CONSTRUCTIONS. Fcap. 8vo. 1s. 6d.

Welch and Duffield.—A FIRST LATIN ACCIDENCE, WITH EXERCISES. By WM. WELCH, M.A., and C. G. DUFFIELD, M.A., Editors of "Eutropius," &c. 18mo.
[*In preparation.*

White.—FIRST LESSONS IN GREEK. Adapted to GOODWIN'S GREEK GRAMMAR, and designed as an introduction to the ANABASIS OF XENOPHON. By JOHN WILLIAMS WHITE, Ph.D., Assistant-Professor of Greek in Harvard University. Crown 8vo. 4s. 6d.

Wilkins and Strachan.—PASSAGES FOR TRANSLATION FROM GREEK AND LATIN. Selected and Arranged by A. S. WILKINS, M.A., Professor of Latin, and J. STRACHAN, M.A., Professor of Greek, in the Owens College, Manchester.
[*In the press.*

Wright.—Works by J. WRIGHT, M.A., late Head Master of Sutton Coldfield School.
 A HELP TO LATIN GRAMMAR; or, The Form and Use of Words in Latin, with Progressive Exercises. Crown 8vo. 4s. 6d.
 THE SEVEN KINGS OF ROME. An Easy Narrative, abridged from the First Book of Livy by the omission of Difficult Passages; being a First Latin Reading Book, with Grammatical Notes and Vocabulary. New and revised Edition. Fcap. 8vo. 3s. 6d.

Wright.—FIRST LATIN STEPS; OR, AN INTRODUCTION BY A SERIES OF EXAMPLES TO THE STUDY OF THE LATIN LANGUAGE. Crown 8vo. 3s.
ATTIC PRIMER. Arranged for the Use of Beginners. Extra fcap. 8vo. 2s. 6d.
A COMPLETE LATIN COURSE, comprising Rules with Examples, Exercises, both Latin and English, on each Rule, and Vocabularies. Crown 8vo. 2s. 6d.

ANTIQUITIES, ANCIENT HISTORY, AND PHILOSOPHY.

Arnold.—Works by W. T. ARNOLD, M.A.
A HANDBOOK OF LATIN EPIGRAPHY. [*In preparation.*
THE ROMAN SYSTEM OF PROVINCIAL ADMINISTRATION TO THE ACCESSION OF CONSTANTINE THE GREAT. Crown 8vo. 6s.

Arnold (T.)—THE SECOND PUNIC WAR. Being Chapters on THE HISTORY OF ROME. By the late THOMAS ARNOLD, D.D., formerly Head Master of Rugby School, and Regius Professor of Modern History in the University of Oxford. Edited, with Notes, by W. T. ARNOLD, M.A. With 8 Maps. Crown 8vo. 8s. 6d.

Beesly.—STORIES FROM THE HISTORY OF ROME. By Mrs. BEESLY. Fcap. 8vo. 2s. 6d.

Classical Writers.—Edited by JOHN RICHARD GREEN, M.A., LL.D. Fcap. 8vo. 1s. 6d. each.
EURIPIDES. By Professor MAHAFFY.
MILTON. By the Rev. STOPFORD A. BROOKE, M.A.
LIVY. By the Rev. W. W. CAPES, M.A.
VIRGIL. By Professor NETTLESHIP, M.A.
SOPHOCLES. By Professor L. CAMPBELL, M.A.
DEMOSTHENES. By Professor S. H. BUTCHER, M.A.
TACITUS. By Professor A. J. CHURCH, M.A., and W. J. BRODRIBB, M.A.

Freeman.—Works by EDWARD A. FREEMAN, D.C.L., LL.D., Hon. Fellow of Trinity College, Oxford, Regius Professor of Modern History in the University of Oxford.
HISTORY OF ROME. (*Historical Course for Schools.*) 18mo. [*In preparation.*
A SCHOOL HISTORY OF ROME. Crown 8vo. [*In preparation.*
HISTORICAL ESSAYS. Second Series. [Greek and Roman History.] 8vo. 10s. 6d.

CLASSICAL PUBLICATIONS. 23

Fyffe.—A SCHOOL HISTORY OF GREECE. By C. A. FYFFE, M.A. Crown 8vo. [*In preparation.*

Geddes. — THE PROBLEM OF THE HOMERIC POEMS. By W. D. GEDDES, Principal of the University of Aberdeen. 8vo. 14*s.*

Gladstone.—Works by the Rt. Hon. W. E. GLADSTONE, M.P.
THE TIME AND PLACE OF HOMER. Crown 8vo. 6*s.* 6*d.*
A PRIMER OF HOMER. 18mo. 1*s.*

Gow.—SHORT PREFACES TO SCHOOL CLASSICS. By JAMES GOW, M.A., Litt.D., Head Master of the High School, Nottingham; formerly Fellow of Trinity College, Cambridge. With Illustrations. Crown 8vo. [*In the press.*

Jackson.—A MANUAL OF GREEK PHILOSOPHY. By HENRY JACKSON, M.A., Litt.D., Fellow and Prælector in Ancient Philosophy, Trinity College, Cambridge. [*In preparation.*

Jebb.—Works by R. C. JEBB, M.A., LL.D., Professor of Greek in the University of Glasgow.
THE ATTIC ORATORS FROM ANTIPHON TO ISAEOS. 2 vols. 8vo. 25*s.*
A PRIMER OF GREEK LITERATURE. 18mo. 1*s.*
(See also *Classical Series.*)

Kiepert.—MANUAL OF ANCIENT GEOGRAPHY, Translated from the German of Dr. HEINRICH KIEPERT. Crown 8vo. 5*s.*

Mahaffy.—Works by J. P. MAHAFFY, M.A., D.D., Fellow and Professor of Ancient History in Trinity College, Dublin, and Hon. Fellow of Queen's College, Oxford.
SOCIAL LIFE IN GREECE; from Homer to Menander. Fifth Edition, revised and enlarged. Crown 8vo. 9*s.*
GREEK LIFE AND THOUGHT; from the Age of Alexander to the Roman Conquest. Crown 8vo. 12*s.* 6*d.*
RAMBLES AND STUDIES IN GREECE. With Illustrations. Third Edition, Revised and Enlarged. With Map. Crown 8vo. 10*s.* 6*d.*
A PRIMER OF GREEK ANTIQUITIES. With Illustrations. 18mo. 1*s.*
EURIPIDES. 18mo. 1*s.* 6*d.* (*Classical Writers Series.*)

Mayor (J. E. B.)—BIBLIOGRAPHICAL CLUE TO LATIN LITERATURE. Edited after HÜBNER, with large Additions by Professor JOHN E. B. MAYOR. Crown 8vo. 10*s.* 6*d.*

Newton.—ESSAYS IN ART AND ARCHÆOLOGY. By Sir CHARLES NEWTON, K.C.B., D.C.L., Professor of Archæology in University College, London, and formerly Keeper of Greek and Roman Antiquities at the British Museum. 8vo. 12s. 6d.

Ramsay.—A SCHOOL HISTORY OF ROME. By G. G. RAMSAY, M.A., Professor of Humanity in the University of Glasgow. With Maps. Crown 8vo. [*In preparation.*

Sayce.—THE ANCIENT EMPIRES OF THE EAST. By A. H. SAYCE, Deputy-Professor of Comparative Philosophy, Oxford, Hon. LL.D. Dublin. Crown 8vo. 6s.

Stewart.—THE TALE OF TROY. Done into English by AUBREY STEWART, M.A., late Fellow of Trinity College, Cambridge. Globe 8vo. 3s. 6d.

Wilkins.—A PRIMER OF ROMAN ANTIQUITIES. By Professor WILKINS, M.A., LL.D. Illustrated. 18mo. 1s.
A PRIMER OF LATIN LITERATURE. By the same Author.
[*In preparation.*

MATHEMATICS.

(1) Arithmetic and Mensuration, (2) Algebra (3) Euclid and Elementary Geometry, (4) Trigonometry, (5) Higher Mathematics.

ARITHMETIC AND MENSURATION.

Aldis.—THE GREAT GIANT ARITHMOS. A most Elementary Arithmetic for Children. By MARY STEADMAN ALDIS. With Illustrations. Globe 8vo. 2s. 6d.

Brook-Smith (J.).—ARITHMETIC IN THEORY AND PRACTICE. By J. BROOK-SMITH, M.A., LL.B., St. John's College, Cambridge; Barrister-at-Law; one of the Masters of Cheltenham College. New Edition, revised. Crown 8vo. 4s. 6d.

Candler.—HELP TO ARITHMETIC. Designed for the use of Schools. By H. CANDLER, M.A., Mathematical Master of Uppingham School. Second Edition. Extra fcap. 8vo. 2s. 6d.

Dalton.—RULES AND EXAMPLES IN ARITHMETIC. By the Rev. T. DALTON, M.A., Assistant-Master in Eton College. New Edition. 18mo. 2s. 6d.
[*Answers to the Examples are appended.*

Goyen.—HIGHER ARITHMETIC AND ELEMENTARY MENSURATION. By P. Goyen, M.A., Inspector of Schools, Dunedin, N. Z. Globe 8vo. [*In the press.*

Lock.—ARITHMETIC FOR SCHOOLS. By Rev. J. B. Lock, M.A., Senior Fellow, Assistant Tutor, and Lecturer of Caius College, Teacher of Physics in the University of Cambridge, formerly Assistant-Master at Eton. With Answers and 1000 additional Examples for Exercise. Second Edition, revised. Globe 8vo. 4s. 6d. Or in Two Parts :—Part I. Up to and including Practice, with Answers. Globe 8vo. 2s. Part II. With Answers and 1000 additional Examples for Exercise. Globe 8vo. 3s. [*A Key is in the press.*

** *The complete book and both parts can also be obtained* without answers *at the same price, though in different binding. But the edition with answers* will always be supplied unless the other is specially asked for.

Pedley.—EXERCISES IN ARITHMETIC for the Use of Schools. Containing more than 7,000 original Examples. By S. Pedley, late of Tamworth Grammar School. Crown 8vo. 5s. Also in Two Parts 2s. 6d. each.

Smith.—Works by the Rev. Barnard Smith, M.A., late Rector of Glaston, Rutland, and Fellow and Senior Bursar of S. Peter's College, Cambridge.

ARITHMETIC AND ALGEBRA, in their Principles and Application; with numerous systematically arranged Examples taken from the Cambridge Examination Papers, with especial reference to the Ordinary Examination for the B.A. Degree. New Edition, carefully Revised. Crown 8vo. 10s. 6d.

ARITHMETIC FOR SCHOOLS. New Edition. Crown 8vo. 4s. 6d.

A KEY TO THE ARITHMETIC FOR SCHOOLS. New Edition. Crown 8vo. 8s. 6d.

EXERCISES IN ARITHMETIC. Crown 8vo, limp cloth, 2s. With Answers, 2s. 6d. Answers separately, 6d.

SCHOOL CLASS-BOOK OF ARITHMETIC. 18mo, cloth. 3s. Or sold separately, in Three Parts, 1s. each.

KEYS TO SCHOOL CLASS-BOOK OF ARITHMETIC. Parts I., II., and III., 2s. 6d. each.

SHILLING BOOK OF ARITHMETIC FOR NATIONAL AND ELEMENTARY SCHOOLS. 18mo, cloth. Or separately, Part I. 2d.; Part II. 3d.; Part III. 7d. Answers, 6d.

THE SAME, with Answers complete. 18mo, cloth. 1s. 6d.

KEY TO SHILLING BOOK OF ARITHMETIC. 18mo. 4s. 6d.

Smith.—EXAMINATION PAPERS IN ARITHMETIC. 18mo. 1s. 6d. The same, with Answers, 18mo, 2s. Answers, 6d.

KEY TO EXAMINATION PAPERS IN ARITHMETIC. 18mo. 4s. 6d.

THE METRIC SYSTEM OF ARITHMETIC, ITS PRINCIPLES AND APPLICATIONS, with numerous Examples, written expressly for Standard V. in National Schools. New Edition. 18mo, cloth, sewed. 3d.

A CHART OF THE METRIC SYSTEM, on a Sheet, size 42 in. by 34 in. on Roller, mounted and varnished. New Edition. Price 3s. 6d.

Also a Small Chart on a Card, price 1d.

EASY LESSONS IN ARITHMETIC, combining Exercises in Reading, Writing, Spelling, and Dictation. Part I. for Standard I. in National Schools. Crown 8vo. 9d.

EXAMINATION CARDS IN ARITHMETIC. (Dedicated to Lord Sandon.) With Answers and Hints.
Standards I. and II. in box, 1s. Standards III., IV., and V., in boxes, 1s. each. Standard VI. in Two Parts, in boxes, 1s. each.

A and B papers, of nearly the same difficulty, are given so as to prevent copying, and the colours of the A and B papers differ in each Standard, and from those of every other Standard, so that a master or mistress can see at a glance whether the children have the proper papers.

Todhunter.—MENSURATION FOR BEGINNERS. By I. TODHUNTER, M.A., F.R.S., D.Sc., late of St. John's College, Cambridge. With Examples. New Edition. 18mo. 2s. 6d.

KEY TO MENSURATION FOR BEGINNERS. By the Rev. FR. LAWRENCE MCCARTHY, Professor of Mathematics in St. Peter's College, Agra. Crown 8vo. 7s. 6d.

ALGEBRA.

Dalton.—RULES AND EXAMPLES IN ALGEBRA. By the Rev. T. DALTON, M.A., Assistant-Master of Eton College. Part I. New Edition. 18mo. 2s. Part II. 18mo. 2s. 6d.

⁎ A Key to Part I. for Teachers only, 7s. 6d.

Hall and Knight.—ELEMENTARY ALGEBRA FOR SCHOOLS. By H. S. HALL, M.A., formerly Scholar of Christ's College, Cambridge, Master of the Military and Engineering Side, Clifton College ; and S. R. KNIGHT, B.A., formerly Scholar of Trinity College, Cambridge, late Assistant-Master at Marlborough College. Third Edition, Revised and Corrected. Globe 8vo, bound in maroon coloured cloth, 3s. 6d. ; with Answers, bound in green coloured cloth, 4s. 6d.

Hall and Knight.—Works by Messrs. HALL and KNIGHT, *continued—*
ALGEBRAICAL EXERCISES AND EXAMINATION PAPERS. To accompany ELEMENTARY ALGEBRA. Second Edition, revised. Globe 8vo. 2s. 6d.
HIGHER ALGEBRA. A Sequel to "ELEMENTARY ALGEBRA FOR SCHOOLS." Crown 8vo. 7s. 6d.

Jones and Cheyne.—ALGEBRAICAL EXERCISES. Progressively Arranged. By the Rev. C. A. JONES, M.A., and C. H. CHEYNE, M.A., F.R.A.S., Mathematical Masters of Westminster School. New Edition. 18mo. 2s. 6d.
SOLUTIONS AND HINTS FOR THE SOLUTION OF SOME OF THE EXAMPLES IN THE ALGEBRAICAL EXERCISES OF MESSRS. JONES AND CHEYNE. By Rev. W. FAILES, M.A., Mathematical Master at Westminster School, late Scholar of Trinity College, Cambridge. Crown 8vo. 7s. 6d.

Smith (Barnard).—ARITHMETIC AND ALGEBRA, in their Principles and Application; with numerous systematically arranged Examples taken from the Cambridge Examination Papers, with especial reference to the Ordinary Examination for the B.A. Degree. By the Rev. BARNARD SMITH, M.A., late Rector of Glaston, Rutland, and Fellow and Senior Bursar of St. Peter's College, Cambridge. New Edition, carefully Revised. Crown 8vo. 10s. 6d.

Smith (Charles).—Works by CHARLES SMITH, M.A., Fellow and Tutor of Sidney Sussex College, Cambridge.
ELEMENTARY ALGEBRA. Globe 8vo. 4s. 6d.
In this work the author has endeavoured to explain the principles of Algebra in as simple a manner as possible for the benefit of beginners, bestowing great care upon the explanations and proofs of the fundamental operations and rules.
ALGEBRA FOR SCHOOLS AND COLLEGES. Crown 8vo.
[*In the press.*

Todhunter.—Works by I. TODHUNTER, M.A., F.R.S., D.Sc., late of St. John's College, Cambridge.
"Mr. Todhunter is chiefly known to Students of Mathematics as the author of a series of admirable mathematical text-books, which possess the rare qualities of being clear in style and absolutely free from mistakes, typographical or other."—SATURDAY REVIEW
ALGEBRA FOR BEGINNERS. With numerous Examples. New Edition. 18mo. 2s. 6d.
KEY TO ALGEBRA FOR BEGINNERS. Crown 8vo. 6s. 6d.
ALGEBRA. For the Use of Colleges and Schools. New Edition. Crown 8vo. 7s. 6d.
KEY TO ALGEBRA FOR THE USE OF COLLEGES AND SCHOOLS. Crown 8vo. 10s. 6d.

EUCLID, & ELEMENTARY GEOMETRY.

Constable.—GEOMETRICAL EXERCISES FOR BEGINNERS. By SAMUEL CONSTABLE. Crown 8vo. 3s. 6d.

Cuthbertson.—EUCLIDIAN GEOMETRY. By FRANCIS CUTHBERTSON, M.A., LL.D., Head Mathematical Master of the City of London School. Extra fcap. 8vo. 4s. 6d.

Dodgson.—Works by CHARLES L. DODGSON, M.A., Student and late Mathematical Lecturer of Christ Church, Oxford.
    EUCLID. BOOKS I. AND II. Fourth Edition, with words substituted for the Algebraical Symbols used in the First Edition. Crown 8vo. 2s.
    ⁎ The text of this Edition has been ascertained, by counting the words, to be less than *five-sevenths* of that contained in the ordinary editions.
    EUCLID AND HIS MODERN RIVALS. Second Edition. Crown 8vo. 6s.

Eagles.—CONSTRUCTIVE GEOMETRY OF PLANE CURVES. By T. H. EAGLES, M.A., Instructor in Geometrical Drawing, and Lecturer in Architecture at the Royal Indian Engineering College, Cooper's Hill. With numerous Examples. Crown 8vo. 12s.

Hall and Stevens.—A TEXT BOOK OF EUCLID'S ELEMENTS. Including alternative Proofs, together with additional Theorems and Exercises, classified and arranged. By H. S. HALL, M.A., formerly Scholar of Christ's College, Cambridge, and F. H. STEVENS, M.A., formerly Scholar of Queen's College, Oxford: Masters of the Military and Engineering Side, Clifton College. Globe 8vo. Part I., containing Books I. and II. 2s.
                                                        [*Part II. in preparation.*

Halsted.—THE ELEMENTS OF GEOMETRY. By GEORGE BRUCE HALSTED, Professor of Pure and Applied Mathematics in the University of Texas. 8vo. 12s. 6d.

Kitchener.—A GEOMETRICAL NOTE-BOOK, containing Easy Problems in Geometrical Drawing preparatory to the Study of Geometry. For the Use of Schools. By F. E. KITCHENER, M.A., Head-Master of the Grammar School, Newcastle, Staffordshire. New Edition. 4to. 2s.

Mault.—NATURAL GEOMETRY: an Introduction to the Logical Study of Mathematics. For Schools and Technical Classes. With Explanatory Models, based upon the Tachymetrical works of Ed. Lagout. By A. MAULT. 18mo. 1s.
    Models to Illustrate the above, in Box, 12s. 6d.

MATHEMATICS.

Millar.—ELEMENTS OF DESCRIPTIVE GEOMETRY. By J. B. MILLAR, M.E., Civil Engineer, Lecturer on Engineering in the Victoria University, Manchester. Second Edition. Cr. 8vo. 6s.

Snowball.—THE ELEMENTS OF PLANE AND SPHERICAL TRIGONOMETRY. By J. C. SNOWBALL, M.A. Fourteenth Edition. Crown 8vo. 7s. 6d.

Syllabus of Plane Geometry (corresponding to Euclid, Books I.—VI.). Prepared by the Association for the Improvement of Geometrical Teaching. New Edition. Crown 8vo. 1s.

Todhunter.—THE ELEMENTS OF EUCLID. For the Use of Colleges and Schools. By I. TODHUNTER, M.A., F.R.S., D.Sc., of St. John's College, Cambridge. New Edition. 18mo. 3s 6d.
KEY TO EXERCISES IN EUCLID. Crown 8vo. 6s. 6d.

Wilson (J. M.).—ELEMENTARY GEOMETRY. BOOKS I.—V. Containing the Subjects of Euclid's first Six Books. Following the Syllabus of the Geometrical Association. By the Rev. J. M. WILSON, M.A., Head Master of Clifton College. New Edition. Extra fcap. 8vo. 4s. 6d.

TRIGONOMETRY.

Beasley.—AN ELEMENTARY TREATISE ON PLANE TRIGONOMETRY. With Examples. By R. D. BEASLEY, M.A. Ninth Edition, revised and enlarged. Crown 8vo. 3s. 6d.

Lock.—Works by Rev. J. B. LOCK, M.A., Senior Fellow, Assistant Tutor and Lecturer of Caius College, Teacher of Physics in the University of Cambridge; formerly Assistant-Master at Eton.
TRIGONOMETRY FOR BEGINNERS, as far as the Solution of Triangles. Globe 8vo. 2s. 6d.
ELEMENTARY TRIGONOMETRY. Fifth Edition (in this edition the chapter on logarithms has been carefully revised). Globe 8vo. 4s. 6d. [*A Key is in the press.*
Mr. E. J. ROUTH, D.Sc., F.R.S., writes:—"It is an able treatise. It takes the difficulties of the subject one at a time, and so leads the young student easily along."
HIGHER TRIGONOMETRY. Fifth Globe 8vo. 4s. 6d.
Both Parts complete in One Volume. Globe 8vo. 7s. 6d.
(See also under *Arithmetic* and *Higher Mathematics*.)

M'Clelland and Preston.—A TREATISE ON SPHERICAL TRIGONOMETRY. With numerous Examples. By WILLIAM J. M'CLELLAND, Sch.B.A., Principal of the Incorporated Society's School, Santry, Dublin, and THOMAS PRESTON, Sch.B.A. In Two Parts. Crown 8vo. Part I. To the End of Solution of Triangles, 4s. 6d. Part II., 5s.

Todhunter.—Works by I. TODHUNTER, M.A., F.R.S., D.Sc., late of St. John's College, Cambridge.
TRIGONOMETRY FOR BEGINNERS. With numerous Examples. New Edition. 18mo. 2s. 6d.

Todhunter.—KEY TO TRIGONOMETRY FOR BEGINNERS. Crown 8vo. 8s. 6d.
    PLANE TRIGONOMETRY. For Schools and Colleges. New Edition. Crown 8vo. 5s.
    KEY TO PLANE TRIGONOMETRY. Crown 8vo. 10s. 6d.
    A TREATISE ON SPHERICAL TRIGONOMETRY. New Edition, enlarged. Crown 8vo. 4s. 6d.
    (See also under *Arithmetic and Mensuration*, *Algebra*, and *Higher Mathematics*.)

HIGHER MATHEMATICS.

Airy.—Works by Sir G. B. AIRY, K.C.B., formerly Astronomer-Royal.
    ELEMENTARY TREATISE ON PARTIAL DIFFERENTIAL EQUATIONS. Designed for the Use of Students in the Universities. With Diagrams. Second Edition. Crown 8vo. 5s. 6d.
    ON THE ALGEBRAICAL AND NUMERICAL THEORY OF ERRORS OF OBSERVATIONS AND THE COMBINATION OF OBSERVATIONS. Second Edition, revised. Crown 8vo. 6s. 6d.

Alexander (T.).—ELEMENTARY APPLIED MECHANICS. Being the simpler and more practical Cases of Stress and Strain wrought out individually from first principles by means of Elementary Mathematics. By T. ALEXANDER, C.E., Professor of Civil Engineering in the Imperial College of Engineering, Tokei, Japan. Part I. Crown 8vo. 4s. 6d.

Alexander and Thomson.—ELEMENTARY APPLIED MECHANICS. By THOMAS ALEXANDER, C.E., Professor of Engineering in the Imperial College of Engineering, Tokei, Japan; and ARTHUR WATSON THOMSON, C.E., B.SC., Professor of Engineering at the Royal College, Cirencester. Part II. TRANSVERSE STRESS. Crown 8vo. 10s. 6d.

Boole.—THE CALCULUS OF FINITE DIFFERENCES. By G. BOOLE, D.C.L., F.R.S., late Professor of Mathematics in the Queen's University, Ireland. Third Edition, revised by J. F. MOULTON. Crown 8vo. 10s. 6d.

Cambridge Senate-House Problems and Riders, with Solutions:—
    1875—PROBLEMS AND RIDERS. By A. G. GREENHILL, M.A. Crown 8vo. 8s. 6d.
    1878—SOLUTIONS OF SENATE-HOUSE PROBLEMS. By the Mathematical Moderators and Examiners. Edited by J. W. L. GLAISHER, M.A., Fellow of Trinity College, Cambridge. 12s.

Carll.—A TREATISE ON THE CALCULUS OF VARIATIONS. Arranged with the purpose of Introducing, as well as Illustrating, its Principles to the Reader by means of Problems, and Designed to present in all Important Particulars a Complete View of the Present State of the Science. By LEWIS BUFFETT CARLL, A.M. Demy 8vo. 21s.

Cheyne.—AN ELEMENTARY TREATISE ON THE PLANETARY THEORY. By C. H. H. CHEYNE, M.A., F.R.A.S. With a Collection of Problems. Third Edition. Edited by Rev. A. FREEMAN, M.A., F.R.A.S. Crown 8vo. 7s. 6d.

Christie.—A COLLECTION OF ELEMENTARY TEST-QUESTIONS IN PURE AND MIXED MATHEMATICS; with Answers and Appendices on Synthetic Division, and on the Solution of Numerical Equations by Horner's Method. By JAMES R. CHRISTIE, F.R.S., Royal Military Academy, Woolwich. Crown 8vo. 8s. 6d.

Clausius.—MECHANICAL THEORY OF HEAT. By R. CLAUSIUS. Translated by WALTER R. BROWNE, M.A., late Fellow of Trinity College, Cambridge. Crown 8vo. 10s. 6d.

Clifford.—THE ELEMENTS OF DYNAMIC. An Introduction to the Study of Motion and Rest in Solid and Fluid Bodies. By W. K. CLIFFORD, F.R.S., late Professor of Applied Mathematics and Mechanics at University College, London. Part I.—KINEMATIC. Crown 8vo. Books I—III. 7s. 6d.; Book IV. and Appendix 6s.

Cockshott and Walters.—GEOMETRICAL CONICS. An Elementary Treatise. Drawn up in accordance with the Syllabus issued by the Society for the Improvement of Geometrical Teaching. By A. COCKSHOTT, M.A., formerly Fellow and Assistant-Tutor of Trinity College, Cambridge, and Assistant-Master at Eton; and Rev. F. B. WALTERS, M.A., Fellow of Queens' College, Cambridge, and Principal of King William's College, Isle of Man. With Diagrams. Crown 8vo.
[*In the press.*

Cotterill.—APPLIED MECHANICS: an Elementary General Introduction to the Theory of Structures and Machines. By JAMES H. COTTERILL, F.R.S., Associate Member of the Council of the Institution of Naval Architects, Associate Member of the Institution of Civil Engineers, Professor of Applied Mechanics in the Royal Naval College, Greenwich. Medium 8vo. 18s.

Day (R. E.)—ELECTRIC LIGHT ARITHMETIC. By R. E. DAY, M.A., Evening Lecturer in Experimental Physics at King's College, London. Pott 8vo. 2s.

Drew.—GEOMETRICAL TREATISE ON CONIC SECTIONS. By W. H. DREW, M.A., St. John's College, Cambridge. New Edition, enlarged. Crown 8vo. 5s.

Dyer.—EXERCISES IN ANALYTICAL GEOMETRY. Compiled and arranged by J. M. Dyer, M.A., Senior Mathematical Master in the Classical Department of Cheltenham College. With Illustrations. Crown 8vo. 4s. 6d.

Eagles.—CONSTRUCTIVE GEOMETRY OF PLANE CURVES. By T. H. Eagles, M.A., Instructor in Geometrical Drawing, and Lecturer in Architecture at the Royal Indian Engineering College, Cooper's Hill. With numerous Examples. Crown 8vo. 12s.

Edgar (J. H.) and Pritchard (G. S.).—NOTE-BOOK ON PRACTICAL SOLID OR DESCRIPTIVE GEOMETRY. Containing Problems with help for Solutions. By J. H. Edgar, M.A., Lecturer on Mechanical Drawing at the Royal School of Mines, and G. S. Pritchard. Fourth Edition, revised by Arthur Meeze. Globe 8vo. 4s. 6d.

Edwards.—THE DIFFERENTIAL CALCULUS. With Applications and numerous Examples. An Elementary Treatise by Joseph Edwards, M.A., formerly Fellow of Sidney Sussex College, Cambridge. Crown 8vo. 10s. 6d.

Ferrers.—Works by the Rev. N. M. Ferrers, M.A., Master of Gonville and Caius College, Cambridge.
  AN ELEMENTARY TREATISE ON TRILINEAR CO-ORDINATES, the Method of Reciprocal Polars, and the Theory of Projectors. New Edition, revised. Crown 8vo. 6s. 6d.
  AN ELEMENTARY TREATISE ON SPHERICAL HARMONICS, AND SUBJECTS CONNECTED WITH THEM. Crown 8vo. 7s. 6d.

Forsyth.—A TREATISE ON DIFFERENTIAL EQUATIONS. By Andrew Russell Forsyth, M.A., F.R.S., Fellow and Assistant Tutor of Trinity College, Cambridge. 8vo. 14s.

Frost.—Works by Percival Frost, M.A., D.Sc., formerly Fellow of St. John's College, Cambridge; Mathematical Lecturer at King's College.
  AN ELEMENTARY TREATISE ON CURVE TRACING. By Percival Frost, M.A. 8vo. 12s.
  SOLID GEOMETRY. Third Edition. Demy 8vo. 16s.
  HINTS FOR THE SOLUTION OF PROBLEMS in the Third Edition of SOLID GEOMETRY. 8vo. 8s. 6d.

Greaves.—A TREATISE ON ELEMENTARY STATICS. By John Greaves, M.A., Fellow and Mathematical Lecturer of Christ's College, Cambridge. Crown 8vo. 6s. 6d.
  STATICS FOR BEGINNERS. By the Same Author.
  [*In preparation.*

MATHEMATICS.

Greenhill.—DIFFERENTIAL AND INTEGRAL CALCULUS. With Applications. By A. G. GREENHILL, M.A., Professor of Mathematics to the Senior Class of Artillery Officers, Woolwich, and Examiner in Mathematics to the University of London. Crown 8vo. 7s. 6d.

Hemming.—AN ELEMENTARY TREATISE ON THE DIFFERENTIAL AND INTEGRAL CALCULUS, for the Use of Colleges and Schools. By G. W. HEMMING, M.A., Fellow of St. John's College, Cambridge. Second Edition, with Corrections and Additions. 8vo. 9s.

Ibbetson.—THE MATHEMATICAL THEORY OF PERFECTLY ELASTIC SOLIDS, with a short account of Viscous Fluids. An Elementary Treatise. By WILLIAM JOHN IBBETSON, M.A., Fellow of the Royal Astronomical Society, and of the Cambridge Philosophical Society, Member of the London Mathematical Society, late Senior Scholar of Clare College, Cambridge. 8vo. 21s.

Jellett (John H.).—A TREATISE ON THE THEORY OF FRICTION. By JOHN H. JELLETT, B.D., Provost of Trinity College, Dublin; President of the Royal Irish Academy. 8vo. 8s. 6d.

Johnson.—Works by WILLIAM WOOLSEY JOHNSON, Professor of Mathematics at the U.S. Naval Academy, Annapolis, Maryland.
INTEGRAL CALCULUS, an Elementary Treatise on the; Founded on the Method of Rates or Fluxions. Demy 8vo. 8s.
CURVE TRACING IN CARTESIAN CO-ORDINATES. Crown 8vo. 4s. 6d.

Jones.—EXAMPLES IN PHYSICS. By D. E. JONES, B.Sc., Lecturer in Physics in University College, Aberystwyth. Fcap. 8vo. [*In the press.*

Kelland and Tait.—INTRODUCTION TO QUATERNIONS, with numerous examples. By P. KELLAND, M.A., F.R.S., and P. G. TAIT, M.A., Professors in the Department of Mathematics in the University of Edinburgh. Second Edition. Crown 8vo. 7s. 6d.

Kempe.—HOW TO DRAW A STRAIGHT LINE: a Lecture on Linkages. By A. B. KEMPE. With Illustrations. Crown 8vo. 1s. 6d. (*Nature Series.*)

Kennedy.—THE MECHANICS OF MACHINERY. By A. B. W. KENNEDY, F.R.S., M.Inst.C.E., Professor of Engineering and Mechanical Technology in University College, London. With Illustrations. Crown 8vo. 12s. 6d.

Knox.—DIFFERENTIAL CALCULUS FOR BEGINNERS. By ALEXANDER KNOX. Fcap. 8vo. 3s. 6d.

d

Lock.—Works by the Rev. J. B. Lock, M.A., Author of "Trigonometry," "Arithmetic for Schools," &c., and Teacher of Physics in the University of Cambridge.
HIGHER TRIGONOMETRY. Fifth Edition. Globe 8vo. 4s. 6d.
DYNAMICS FOR BEGINNERS. Globe 8vo. 3s. 6d.
STATICS FOR BEGINNERS. Globe 8vo. [*In the press.*
(See also under *Arithmetic* and *Trigonometry*.)

Lupton.—CHEMICAL ARITHMETIC. With 1,200 Examples. By Sydney Lupton, M.A., F.C.S., F.I.C., formerly Assistant Master in Harrow School. Second Edition. Fcap. 8vo. 4s. 6d.

Macfarlane.—PHYSICAL ARITHMETIC. By Alexander Macfarlane, M.A., D.Sc., F.R.S.E., Examiner in Mathematics to the University of Edinburgh. Crown 8vo. 7s. 6d.

MacGregor.—KINEMATICS AND DYNAMICS. An Elementary Treatise. By James Gordon MacGregor, M.A., D.Sc., Fellow of the Royal Societies of Edinburgh and of Canada, Munro Professor of Physics in Dalhousie College, Halifax, Nova Scotia. With Illustrations. Crown 8vo. 10s. 6d.

Merriman.—A TEXT BOOK OF THE METHOD OF LEAST SQUARES. By Mansfield Merriman, Professor of Civil Engineering at Lehigh University, Member of the American Philosophical Society, American Association for the Advancement of Science, &c. Demy 8vo. 8s. 6d.

Millar.—ELEMENTS OF DESCRIPTIVE GEOMETRY. By J. B. Millar, C.E., Assistant Lecturer in Engineering in Owens College, Manchester. Crown 8vo. 6s.

Milne.—WEEKLY PROBLEM PAPERS. With Notes intended for the use of students preparing for Mathematical Scholarships, and for the Junior Members of the Universities who are reading for Mathematical Honours. By the Rev. John J. Milne, M.A., formerly Second Master of Heversham Grammar School. Pott 8vo. 4s. 6d.
SOLUTIONS TO WEEKLY PROBLEM PAPERS. By the same Author. Crown 8vo. 10s. 6d.
COMPANION TO "WEEKLY PROBLEM PAPERS." By the same Author. Crown 8vo. [*Nearly ready.*

Muir.—A TREATISE ON THE THEORY OF DETERMINANTS. With graduated sets of Examples. For use in Colleges and Schools. By Thos. Muir, M.A., F.R.S.E., Mathematical Master in the High School of Glasgow. Crown 8vo. 7s. 6d.

Parkinson.—AN ELEMENTARY TREATISE ON MECHANICS. For the Use of the Junior Classes at the University and the Higher Classes in Schools. By S. Parkinson, D.D., F.R.S., Tutor and Prælector of St. John's College, Cambridge. With a Collection of Examples. Sixth Edition, revised. Crown 8vo. 9s. 6d.

MATHEMATICS.

Pirie.—LESSONS ON RIGID DYNAMICS. By the Rev. G. PIRIE, M.A., late Fellow and Tutor of Queen's College, Cambridge; Professor of Mathematics in the University of Aberdeen. Crown 8vo. 6s.

Puckle.—AN ELEMENTARY TREATISE ON CONIC SECTIONS AND ALGEBRAIC GEOMETRY. With Numerous Examples and Hints for their Solution; especially designed for the Use of Beginners. By G. H. PUCKLE, M.A. Fifth Edition, revised and enlarged. Crown 8vo. 7s. 6d.

Reuleaux.—THE KINEMATICS OF MACHINERY. Outlines of a Theory of Machines. By Professor F. REULEAUX. Translated and Edited by Professor A. B. W. KENNEDY, F.R.S., C.E. With 450 Illustrations. Medium 8vo. 21s.

Rice and Johnson.—DIFFERENTIAL CALCULUS, an Elementary Treatise on the; Founded on the Method of Rates or Fluxions. By JOHN MINOT RICE, Professor of Mathematics in the United States Navy, and WILLIAM WOOLSEY JOHNSON, Professor of Mathematics at the United States Naval Academy. Third Edition, Revised and Corrected. Demy 8vo. 16s. Abridged Edition, 8s.

Robinson.—TREATISE ON MARINE SURVEYING. Prepared for the use of younger Naval Officers. With Questions for Examinations and Exercises principally from the Papers of the Royal Naval College. With the results. By Rev. JOHN L. ROBINSON, Chaplain and Instructor in the Royal Naval College, Greenwich. With Illustrations. Crown 8vo. 7s. 6d.

CONTENTS.—Symbols used in Charts and Surveying—The Construction and Use of Scales—Laying off Angles—Fixing Positions by Angles—Charts and Chart-Drawing—Instruments and Observing—Base Lines—Triangulation—Levelling—Tides and Tidal Observations—Soundings—Chronometers—Meridian Distances—Method of Plotting a Survey—Miscellaneous Exercises—Index.

Routh.—Works by EDWARD JOHN ROUTH, D.Sc., LL.D., F.R.S., Fellow of the University of London, Hon. Fellow of St. Peter's College, Cambridge.
A TREATISE ON THE DYNAMICS OF THE SYSTEM OF RIGID BODIES. With numerous Examples. Fourth and enlarged Edition. Two Vols. 8vo. Vol. I.—Elementary Parts. 14s. Vol. II.—The Advanced Parts. 14s.
STABILITY OF A GIVEN STATE OF MOTION, PARTICULARLY STEADY MOTION. Adams' Prize Essay for 1877. 8vo. 8s. 6d.

Smith (C.).—Works by CHARLES SMITH, M.A., Fellow and Tutor of Sidney Sussex College, Cambridge.
CONIC SECTIONS. Fourth Edition. Crown 8vo. 7s. 6d.
AN ELEMENTARY TREATISE ON SOLID GEOMETRY. Second Edition. Crown 8vo. 9s. 6d. (See also under *Algebra*.)

d 2

Tait and Steele.—A TREATISE ON DYNAMICS OF A PARTICLE. With numerous Examples. By Professor TAIT and Mr. STEELE. Fifth Edition, revised. Crown 8vo. 12s.

Thomson.—Works by J. J. THOMSON, Fellow of Trinity College, Cambridge, and Professor of Experimental Physics in the University.
A TREATISE ON THE MOTION OF VORTEX RINGS. An Essay to which the Adams Prize was adjudged in 1882 in the University of Cambridge. With Diagrams. 8vo. 6s.
APPLICATIONS OF DYNAMICS TO PHYSICS AND CHEMISTRY. Crown 8vo. [*In the press.*

Todhunter.—Works by I. TODHUNTER, M.A., F.R.S., D.Sc., late of St. John's College, Cambridge.
"Mr. Todhunter is chiefly known to students of Mathematics as the author of a series of admirable mathematical text-books, which possess the rare qualities of being clear in style and absolutely free from mistakes, typographical and other."—SATURDAY REVIEW.

MECHANICS FOR BEGINNERS. With numerous Examples. New Edition. 18mo. 4s. 6d.
KEY TO MECHANICS FOR BEGINNERS. Crown 8vo. 6s. 6d.
AN ELEMENTARY TREATISE ON THE THEORY OF EQUATIONS. New Edition, revised. Crown 8vo. 7s. 6d.
PLANE CO-ORDINATE GEOMETRY, as applied to the Straight Line and the Conic Sections. With numerous Examples. New Edition, revised and enlarged. Crown 8vo. 7s. 6d.
KEY TO PLANE CO-ORDINATE GEOMETRY. By C. W. BOURNE, M.A. Head Master of the College, Inverness. Crown 8vo. 10s. 6d.
A TREATISE ON THE DIFFERENTIAL CALCULUS. With numerous Examples. New Edition. Crown 8vo. 10s. 6d.
A KEY. By H. ST. J. HUNTER, M.A. [*In the press.*
A TREATISE ON THE INTEGRAL CALCULUS AND ITS APPLICATIONS. With numerous Examples. New Edition, revised and enlarged. Crown 8vo. 10s. 6d.
EXAMPLES OF ANALYTICAL GEOMETRY OF THREE DIMENSIONS. New Edition, revised. Crown 8vo. 4s.
A TREATISE ON ANALYTICAL STATICS. With numerous Examples. Fifth Edition. Edited by Professor J. D. EVERETT, F.R.S. Crown 8vo. 10s. 6d.
A HISTORY OF THE MATHEMATICAL THEORY OF PROBABILITY, from the time of Pascal to that of Laplace. 8vo. 18s.
A HISTORY OF THE MATHEMATICAL THEORIES OF ATTRACTION, AND THE FIGURE OF THE EARTH, from the time of Newton to that of Laplace. 2 vols. 8vo. 24s.
AN ELEMENTARY TREATISE ON LAPLACE'S, LAMÉ'S, AND BESSEL'S FUNCTIONS. Crown 8vo. 10s. 6d.

(See also under *Arithmetic and Mensuration, Algebra,* and *Trigonometry.*)

Wilson (J. M.).—SOLID GEOMETRY AND CONIC SECTIONS. With Appendices on Transversals and Harmonic Division. For the Use of Schools. By Rev. J. M. WILSON, M.A. Head Master of Clifton College. New Edition. Extra fcap. 8vo. 3s. 6d.

Woolwich Mathematical Papers, for Admission into the Royal Military Academy, Woolwich, 1880—1884 inclusive. Crown 8vo. 3s. 6d.

Wolstenholme.—MATHEMATICAL PROBLEMS, on Subjects included in the First and Second Divisions of the Schedule of subjects for the Cambridge Mathematical Tripos Examination. Devised and arranged by JOSEPH WOLSTENHOLME, D Sc., late Fellow of Christ's College, sometime Fellow of St. John's College, and Professor of Mathematics in the Royal Indian Engineering College. New Edition, greatly enlarged. 8vo. 18s.

EXAMPLES FOR PRACTICE IN THE USE OF SEVEN-FIGURE LOGARITHMS. By the same Author. [*In preparation.*

SCIENCE.

(1) Natural Philosophy, (2) Astronomy, (3) Chemistry, (4) Biology, (5) Medicine, (6) Anthropology, (7) Physical Geography and Geology, (8) Agriculture.

NATURAL PHILOSOPHY.

Airy.—Works by Sir G. B. AIRY, K.C.B., formerly Astronomer-Royal.
  ON SOUND AND ATMOSPHERIC VIBRATIONS. With the Mathematical Elements of Music. Designed for the Use of Students in the University. Second Edition, revised and enlarged. Crown 8vo 9s.
  A TREATISE ON MAGNETISM. Designed for the Use of Students in the University. Crown 8vo. 9s. 6d.
  GRAVITATION : an Elementary Explanation of the Principal Perturbations in the Solar System. Second Edition. Crown 8vo. 7s. 6d.

Alexander (T.).—ELEMENTARY APPLIED MECHANICS. Being the simpler and more practical Cases of Stress and Strain wrought out individually from first principles by means of Elementary Mathematics. By T. ALEXANDER, C.E., Professor of Civil Engineering in the Imperial College of Engineering, Tokei, Japan. Crown 8vo. Part I. 4s. 6d.

Alexander — Thomson. — ELEMENTARY APPLIED MECHANICS. By THOMAS ALEXANDER, C.E., Professor of Engineering in the Imperial College of Engineering, Tokei, Japan; and ARTHUR WATSON THOMSON, C.E., B.Sc., Professor of Engineering at the Royal College, Cirencester. Part II. TRANSVERSE STRESS; upwards of 150 Diagrams, and 200 Examples carefully worked out. Crown 8vo. 10s. 6d.

Ball (R. S.). — EXPERIMENTAL MECHANICS. A Course of Lectures delivered at the Royal College of Science for Ireland. By Sir R. S. BALL, M.A., Astronomer Royal for Ireland. Cr. 8vo. *[New and Cheaper Edition in the press.*

Bottomley. — FOUR-FIGURE MATHEMATICAL TABLES. Comprising Logarithmic and Trigonometrical Tables, and Tables of Squares, Square Roots, and Reciprocals. By J. T. BOTTOMLEY, M.A., F.R.S.E., F.C.S., Lecturer in Natural Philosophy in the University of Glasgow. 8vo. 2s. 6d.

Chisholm. — THE SCIENCE OF WEIGHING AND MEASURING, AND THE STANDARDS OF MEASURE AND WEIGHT. By H. W. CHISHOLM, Warden of the Standards. With numerous Illustrations. Crown 8vo. 4s. 6d. (*Nature Series*).

Clausius. — MECHANICAL THEORY OF HEAT. By R. CLAUSIUS. Translated by WALTER R. BROWNE, M.A., late Fellow of Trinity College, Cambridge. Crown 8vo. 10s. 6d.

Cotterill. — APPLIED MECHANICS: an Elementary General Introduction to the Theory of Structures and Machines. By JAMES H. COTTERILL, F.R.S., Associate Member of the Council of the Institution of Naval Architects, Associate Member of the Institution of Civil Engineers, Professor of Applied Mechanics in the Royal Naval College, Greenwich. Medium 8vo. 18s.

Cumming. — AN INTRODUCTION TO THE THEORY OF ELECTRICITY. By LINNÆUS CUMMING, M.A., one of the Masters of Rugby School. With Illustrations. Crown 8vo. 8s. 6d.

Daniell. — A TEXT-BOOK OF THE PRINCIPLES OF PHYSICS. By ALFRED DANIELL, M.A., LL.B., D.Sc., F.R.S.E., late Lecturer on Physics in the School of Medicine, Edinburgh. With Illustrations. Second Edition. Revised and Enlarged. Medium 8vo. 21s.

Day. — ELECTRIC LIGHT ARITHMETIC. By R. E. DAY, M.A., Evening Lecturer in Experimental Physics at King's College, London. Pott 8vo. 2s.

Everett. — UNITS AND PHYSICAL CONSTANTS. By J. D. EVERETT, M.A., D.C.L., F.R.S., F.R.S.E., Professor of Natural Philosophy, Queen's College, Belfast. Second Edition. Extra fcap. 8vo. 5s.

SCIENCE.

Gray.—ABSOLUTE MEASUREMENTS IN ELECTRICITY AND MAGNETISM. By ANDREW GRAY, M.A., F.R.S.E., Professor of Physics in the University College of North Wales. Two Vols. Crown 8vo. [*New Edition in the press.*

Greaves.—STATICS FOR BEGINNERS. By JOHN GREAVES, M.A., Fellow and Mathematical Lecturer of Christ's College, Cambridge. [*In preparation.*

Grove.—A DICTIONARY OF MUSIC AND MUSICIANS. (A.D. 1450—1886). By Eminent Writers, English and Foreign. Edited by Sir GEORGE GROVE, D.C.L., Director of the Royal College of Music, &c. Demy 8vo.
Vols. I., II., and III. Price 21s. each.
Vol. I. A to IMPROMPTU. Vol. II. IMPROPERIA to PLAIN SONG. Vol. III. PLANCHE TO SUMER IS ICUMEN IN. Demy 8vo. cloth, with Illustrations in Music Type and Woodcut. Also published in Parts. Parts I. to XIV., Parts XIX—XXII., price 3s. 6d. each. Parts XV., XVI., price 7s. Parts XVII., XVIII., price 7s.

*** (Part XXII.) just published, completes the DICTIONARY OF MUSIC AND MUSICIANS as originally contemplated. But an Appendix and a full general Index are in the press.

"Dr. Grove's Dictionary will be a boon to every intelligent lover of music."—SATURDAY REVIEW.

Huxley.—INTRODUCTORY PRIMER OF SCIENCE. By T. H. HUXLEY, F.R.S., &c. 18mo. 1s.

Ibbetson.—THE MATHEMATICAL THEORY OF PERFECTLY ELASTIC SOLIDS, with a Short Account of Viscous Fluids. An Elementary Treatise. By WILLIAM JOHN IBBETSON, B.A., F.R.A.S., Senior Scholar of Clare College, Cambridge. 8vo. Price 21s.

Jones.—EXAMPLES IN PHYSICS. By D. E. JONES, B.Sc. Lecturer in Physics in University College, Aberystwyth. Fcap. 8vo. [*In the press.*

Kempe.—HOW TO DRAW A STRAIGHT LINE; a Lecture on Linkages. By A. B. KEMPE. With Illustrations. Crown 8vo. 1s. 6d. (*Nature Series.*)

Kennedy.—THE MECHANICS OF MACHINERY. By A. B. W. KENNEDY, F.R.S., M.Inst.C.E., Professor of Engineering and Mechanical Technology in University College, London. With numerous Illustrations. Crown 8vo. 12s. 6d.

Lang.—EXPERIMENTAL PHYSICS. By P. R. SCOTT LANG, M.A., Professor of Mathematics in the University of St. Andrews. With Illustrations. Crown 8vo.
[*In the press.*

Lock.—Works by Rev. J. B. LOCK, M.A.; Senior Fellow, Assistant Tutor, and Lecturer in Mathematics and Physics, of Gonville and Caius College, Teacher of Physics in the University of Cambridge, &c.
DYNAMICS FOR BEGINNERS. Globe 8vo. 3s. 6d.
STATICS FOR BEGINNERS. Globe 8vo. [*In preparation.*

Lupton.—NUMERICAL TABLES AND CONSTANTS IN ELEMENTARY SCIENCE. By SYDNEY LUPTON, M.A,. F.C.S., F.I.C., Assistant Master at Harrow School. Extra fcap. 8vo. 2s. 6d.

Macfarlane.—PHYSICAL ARITHMETIC. By ALEXANDER MACFARLANE, D.Sc., Examiner in Mathematics in the University of Edinburgh. Crown 8vo. 7s. 6d.

Macgregor.—KINEMATICS AND DYNAMICS. An Elementary Treatise. By JAMES GORDON MACGREGOR, M.A., D. Sc., Fellow of the Royal Societies of Edinburgh and of Canada, Munro Professor of Physics in Dalhousie College, Halifax, Nova Scotia. With Illustrations. Crown 8vo. 10s. 6d.

Mayer.—SOUND: a Series of Simple, Entertaining, and Inexpensive Experiments in the Phenomena of Sound, for the Use of Students of every age. By A. M. MAYER, Professor of Physics in the Stevens Institute of Technology, &c. With numerous Illustrations. Crown 8vo. 2s. 6d. (*Nature Series.*)

Mayer and Barnard.—LIGHT: a Series of Simple, Entertaining, and Inexpensive Experiments in the Phenomena of Light, for the Use of Students of every age. By A. M. MAYER and C. BARNARD. With numerous Illustrations. Crown 8vo. 2s. 6d. (*Nature Series.*)

Newton.—PRINCIPIA. Edited by Professor Sir W. THOMSON and Professor BLACKBURNE. 4to, cloth. 31s. 6d.
THE FIRST THREE SECTIONS OF NEWTON'S PRINCIPIA. With Notes and Illustrations. Also a Collection of Problems, principally intended as Examples of Newton's Methods. By PERCIVAL FROST, M.A. Third Edition. 8vo. 12s.

Parkinson.—A TREATISE ON OPTICS. By S. PARKINSON, D.D., F.R.S., Tutor and Prælector of St. John's College, Cambridge. Fourth Edition, revised and enlarged. Crown 8vo. 10s. 6d.

Perry.—STEAM. AN ELEMENTARY TREATISE. By JOHN PERRY, C.E., Whitworth Scholar, Fellow of the Chemical Society, Professor of Mechanical Engineering and Applied Mechanics at the Technical College, Finsbury. With numerous Woodcuts and Numerical Examples and Exercises. 18mo. 4s. 6d.

Ramsay.—EXPERIMENTAL PROOFS OF CHEMICAL EVERLRY FOR BEGINNERS. By WILLIAM RAMSAY, Ph.D., Natural if Chemistry in University College, Bristol. Pott 8vo. Extra fcap. 8vo.

Rayleigh.—THE THEORY OF SOUND. By Lord Rayleigh, M.A., F.R.S., formerly Fellow of Trinity College, Cambridge, 8vo. Vol. I. 12s. 6d. Vol. II. 12s. 6d. [*Vol. III. in the press.*

Reuleaux.—THE KINEMATICS OF MACHINERY. Outlines of a Theory of Machines. By Professor F. Reuleaux. Translated and Edited by Professor A. B. W. Kennedy, F.R.S., C.E. With 450 Illustrations. Medium 8vo. 21s.

Roscoe and Schuster.—SPECTRUM ANALYSIS. Lectures delivered in 1868 before the Society of Apothecaries of London. By Sir Henry E. Roscoe, LL.D., F.R.S., formerly Professor of Chemistry in the Owens College, Victoria University, Manchester. Fourth Edition, revised and considerably enlarged by the Author and by Arthur Schuster, F.R.S., Ph.D., Professor of Applied Mathematics in the Owens College, Victoria University. With Appendices, numerous Illustrations, and Plates. Medium 8vo. 21s.

Shann.—AN ELEMENTARY TREATISE ON HEAT, IN RELATION TO STEAM AND THE STEAM-ENGINE. By G. Shann, M.A. With Illustrations. Crown 8vo. 4s. 6d.

Spottiswoode.—POLARISATION OF LIGHT. By the late W. Spottiswoode, F.R.S. With many Illustrations. New Edition. Crown 8vo. 3s. 6d. (*Nature Series.*)

Stewart (Balfour).—Works by Balfour Stewart, F.R.S., Professor of Natural Philosophy in the Owens College, Victoria University, Manchester.
PRIMER OF PHYSICS. With numerous Illustrations. New Edition, with Questions. 18mo. 1s. (*Science Primers.*)
LESSONS IN ELEMENTARY PHYSICS. With numerous Illustrations and Chromolitho of the Spectra of the Sun, Stars, and Nebulæ. New Edition. Fcap. 8vo. 4s. 6d.
QUESTIONS ON BALFOUR STEWART'S ELEMENTARY LESSONS IN PHYSICS. By Prof. Thomas H. Core, Owens College, Manchester. Fcap. 8vo. 2s.

Stewart and Gee.—ELEMENTARY PRACTICAL PHYSICS, LESSONS IN. By Professor Balfour Stewart, M.A., LL.D., F.R.S., and W. W. Haldane Gee, B.Sc. Crown 8vo.
Vol. I.—GENERAL PHYSICAL PROCESSES. 6s.
Vol. II.—ELECTRICITY AND MAGNETISM. 7s. 6d.
Vol. III.—OPTICS, HEAT, AND SOUND. [*In the press.*
A SCHOOL COURSE OF PRACTICAL PHYSICS. By the same Authors.
Part I.—ELECTRICITY AND MAGNETISM. [*In the press.*

Stokes.—ON LIGHT. Being the Burnett Lectures, delivered in Aberdeen in 1883, 1884-1885. By GEORGE GABRIEL STOKES, M.A., P.R.S., &c., Fellow of Pembroke College, and Lucasian Professor of Mathematics in the University of Cambridge. First Course: ON THE NATURE OF LIGHT.—Second Course: ON LIGHT AS A MEANS OF INVESTIGATION.—Third Course: ON THE BENEFICIAL EFFECTS OF LIGHT. Crown 8vo. 2s. 6d. each. Also complete in one volume. 7s. 6d.

Stone.—AN ELEMENTARY TREATISE ON SOUND. By W. H. STONE, M.D. With Illustrations. 18mo. 3s. 6d.

Tait.—HEAT. By P. G. TAIT, M.A., Sec. R.S.E., formerly Fellow of St. Peter's College, Cambridge, Professor of Natural Philosophy in the University of Edinburgh. Crown 8vo. 6s.

Thompson.—ELEMENTARY LESSONS IN ELECTRICITY AND MAGNETISM. By SILVANUS P. THOMPSON, Principal and Professor of Physics in the Technical College, Finsbury. With Illustrations. New Edition, Revised. Twenty-Eighth Thousand. Fcap. 8vo. 4s. 6d.

Thomson, Sir W.—ELECTROSTATICS AND MAGNETISM, REPRINTS OF PAPERS ON. By Sir WILLIAM THOMSON, D.C.L., LL.D., F.R.S., F.R.S.E., Fellow of St. Peter's College, Cambridge, and Professor of Natural Philosophy in the University of Glasgow. Second Edition. Medium 8vo. 18s.

Thomson, J. J.—THE MOTION OF VORTEX RINGS, A TREATISE ON. An Essay to which the Adams Prize was adjudged in 1882 in the University of Cambridge. By J. J. THOMSON, Fellow of Trinity College, Cambridge, and Professor of Experimental Physics in the University. With Diagrams. 8vo. 6s.
APPLICATIONS OF DYNAMICS TO PHYSICS AND CHEMISTRY. By the same Author. Crown 8vo.
[*In the press.*

Todhunter.—NATURAL PHILOSOPHY FOR BEGINNERS. By I. TODHUNTER, M.A., F.R.S., D.Sc.
Part I. The Properties of Solid and Fluid Bodies. 18mo. 3s. 6d.
Part II. Sound, Light, and Heat. 18mo. 3s. 6d.

Turner.—HEAT AND ELECTRICITY, A COLLECTION OF EXAMPLES ON. By H. H. TURNER, B.A., Fellow of Trinity College, Cambridge. Crown 8vo. 2s. 6d.

Wright (Lewis).—LIGHT; A COURSE OF EXPERIMENTAL OPTICS, CHIEFLY WITH THE LANTERN. By LEWIS WRIGHT. With nearly 200 Engravings and Coloured Plates. Crown 8vo. 7s. 6d.

ASTRONOMY.

Airy.—POPULAR ASTRONOMY. With Illustrations by Sir G. B. AIRY, K.C.B., formerly Astronomer-Royal. New Edition. 18mo. 4s. 6d.

Forbes.—TRANSIT OF VENUS. By G. FORBES, M.A., Professor of Natural Philosophy in the Andersonian University, Glasgow. Illustrated. Crown 8vo. 3s. 6d. (*Nature Series.*)

Godfray.—Works by HUGH GODFRAY, M.A., Mathematical Lecturer at Pembroke College, Cambridge.
A TREATISE ON ASTRONOMY, for the Use of Colleges and Schools. Fourth Edition. 8vo. 12s. 6d.
AN ELEMENTARY TREATISE ON THE LUNAR THEORY, with a Brief Sketch of the Problem up to the time of Newton. Second Edition, revised. Crown 8vo. 5s. 6d.

Lockyer.—Works by J. NORMAN LOCKYER, F.R.S.
PRIMER OF ASTRONOMY. With numerous Illustrations. New Edition. 18mo. 1s. (*Science Primers.*)
ELEMENTARY LESSONS IN ASTRONOMY. With Coloured Diagram of the Spectra of the Sun, Stars, and Nebulæ, and numerous Illustrations. New Edition. Fcap. 8vo. 5s. 6d.
QUESTIONS ON LOCKYER'S ELEMENTARY LESSONS IN ASTRONOMY. For the Use of Schools. By JOHN FORBES-ROBERTSON. 18mo, cloth limp. 1s. 6d.
THE CHEMISTRY OF THE SUN. With Illustrations. 8vo. 14s.

Newcomb.—POPULAR ASTRONOMY. By S. NEWCOMB, LL.D., Professor U.S. Naval Observatory. With 112 Illustrations and 5 Maps of the Stars. Second Edition, revised. 8vo. 18s.
"It is unlike anything else of its kind, and will be of more use in circulating a knowledge of Astronomy than nine-tenths of the books which have appeared on the subject of late years."—SATURDAY REVIEW.

CHEMISTRY.

Armstrong.—A MANUAL OF INORGANIC CHEMISTRY. By HENRY ARMSTRONG, Ph.D., F.R.S., Professor of Chemistry in the City and Guilds of London Technical Institute. Crown 8vo. [*In preparation.*

Cohen.—THE OWENS COLLEGE COURSE OF PRACTICAL ORGANIC CHEMISTRY. By JULIUS B. COHEN, Ph.D., F.C.S., Assistant Lecturer on Chemistry in the Owens College, Manchester. With a Preface by SIR HENRY ROSCOE, F.R.S., and C. SCHORLEMMER, F.R.S. Fcap. 8vo. 2s. 6d.

Cooke.—ELEMENTS OF CHEMICAL PHYSICS. By JOSIAH P. COOKE, Junr., Erving Professor of Chemistry and Mineralogy in Harvard University. Fourth Edition. Royal 8vo. 21s.

Fleischer.—A SYSTEM OF VOLUMETRIC ANALYSIS. Translated, with Notes and Additions, from the Second German Edition by M. M. PATTISON MUIR, F.R.S.E. With Illustrations. Crown 8vo. 7s. 6d.

Frankland.—AGRICULTURAL CHEMICAL ANALYSIS, A Handbook of. By PERCY FARADAY FRANKLAND, Ph.D., B.Sc., F.C.S., Associate of the Royal School of Mines, and Demonstrator of Practical and Agricultural Chemistry in the Normal School of Science and Royal School of Mines, South Kensington Museum. Founded upon *Leitfaden für die Agriculture Chemiche Analyse*, von Dr. F. KROCKER. Crown 8vo. 7s. 6d.

Hartley.—A COURSE OF QUANTITATIVE ANALYSIS FOR STUDENTS. By W. N. HARTLEY, F.R.S., Professor of Chemistry in the Royal College of Science, Dublin. Illustrated. Fcap. 8vo. [*Just ready.*

Jones.—Works by FRANCIS JONES, F.R.S.E., F.C.S., Chemical Master in the Grammar School, Manchester.
  THE OWENS COLLEGE JUNIOR COURSE OF PRACTICAL CHEMISTRY. With Preface by Sir HENRY ROSCOE, F.R.S., and Illustrations. New Edition. 18mo. 2s. 6d.
  QUESTIONS ON CHEMISTRY. A Series of Problems and Exercises in Inorganic and Organic Chemistry. Fcap. 8vo. 3s.

Landauer.—BLOWPIPE ANALYSIS. By J. LANDAUER. Authorised English Edition by J. TAYLOR and W. E. KAY, of Owens College, Manchester. Extra fcap. 8vo. 4s. 6d.

Lupton.—CHEMICAL ARITHMETIC. With 1,200 Problems. By SYDNEY LUPTON, M.A., F.C.S., F.I.C., formerly Assistant-Master at Harrow. Second Edition, Revised and Abridged. Fcap. 8vo. 4s. 6d.

Muir.—PRACTICAL CHEMISTRY FOR MEDICAL STUDENTS. Specially arranged for the first M.B. Course. By M. M. PATTISON MUIR, F.R.S.E. Fcap. 8vo. 1s. 6d.

Muir and Wilson.—THE ELEMENTS OF THERMAL CHEMISTRY. By M. M. PATTISON MUIR, M.A., F.R.S.E., Fellow and Prælector of Chemistry in Gonville and Caius College, Cambridge; Assisted by DAVID MUIR WILSON. 8vo. 12s. 6d.

Remsen.—Works by IRA REMSEN, Professor of Chemistry in the Johns Hopkins University.
  COMPOUNDS OF CARBON; or, Organic Chemistry, an Introduction to the Study of. Crown 8vo. 6s. 6d.
  AN INTRODUCTION TO THE STUDY OF CHEMISTRY (INORGANIC CHEMISTRY). Crown 8vo. 6s. 6d.
  THE ELEMENTS OF CHEMISTRY. A Text Book for Beginners. By the same. Fcap. 8vo. [*In the press.*

SCIENCE. 45

Roscoe.—Works by Sir HENRY E. ROSCOE, F.R.S., formerly Professor of Chemistry in the Victoria University the Owens College, Manchester.
PRIMER OF CHEMISTRY. With numerous Illustrations. New Edition. With Questions. 18mo. 1s. (*Science Primers.*)
LESSONS IN ELEMENTARY CHEMISTRY, INORGANIC AND ORGANIC. With numerous Illustrations and Chromolitho of the Solar Spectrum, and of the Alkalies and Alkaline Earths. New Edition. Fcap. 8vo. 4s. 6d. (*See under* THORPE.)

Roscoe and Schorlemmer.—INORGANIC AND ORGANIC CHEMISTRY. A Complete Treatise on Inorganic and Organic Chemistry. By Sir HENRY E. ROSCOE, F.R.S., and Prof. C. SCHORLEMMER, F.R.S. With Illustrations. Medium 8vo.
Vols. I. and II.—INORGANIC CHEMISTRY.
Vol. I.—The Non-Metallic Elements. 21s. Vol. II. Part I.—Metals. 18s. Vol. II. Part II.—Metals. 18s.
Vol. III.—ORGANIC CHEMISTRY.
THE CHEMISTRY OF THE HYDROCARBONS and their Derivatives, or ORGANIC CHEMISTRY. With numerous Illustrations. Four Parts. Parts I. and II. 21s. each. Part III. 18s.
[*Part IV. in the press.*

Thorpe.—A SERIES OF CHEMICAL PROBLEMS, prepared with Special Reference to Sir H. E. Roscoe's Lessons in Elementary Chemistry, by T. E. THORPE, Ph.D., F.R.S., Professor of Chemistry in the Normal School of Science, South Kensington, adapted for the Preparation of Students for the Government, Science, and Society of Arts Examinations. With a Preface by Sir HENRY E. ROSCOE, F.R.S. New Edition, with Key. 18mo. 2s.

Thorpe and Rücker.—A TREATISE ON CHEMICAL PHYSICS. By T. E. THORPE, Ph.D., F.R.S. Professor of Chemistry in the Normal School of Science, and Professor A. W. RÜCKER. Illustrated. 8vo. [*In preparation.*

Wright.—METALS AND THEIR CHIEF INDUSTRIAL APPLICATIONS. By C. ALDER WRIGHT, D.Sc., &c., Lecturer on Chemistry in St. Mary's Hospital Medical School. Extra fcap. 8vo. 3s. 6d.

BIOLOGY.

Allen.—ON THE COLOUR OF FLOWERS, as Illustrated in the British Flora. By GRANT ALLEN. With Illustrations. Crown 8vo. 3s. 6d. (*Nature Series.*)

Balfour.—A TREATISE ON COMPARATIVE EMBRYOLOGY. By F. M. BALFOUR, M.A., F.R.S., Fellow and Lecturer of Trinity College, Cambridge. With Illustrations. Second Edition, reprinted without alteration from the First Edition. In 2 vols. 8vo. Vol. I. 18s. Vol. II. 21s.

Balfour and Ward.—A GENERAL TEXT BOOK OF BOTANY. By ISAAC BAYLEY BALFOUR, F.R.S., Professor of Botany in the University of Oxford, and H. MARSHALL WARD, Fellow of Christ's College, Cambridge, and Professor of Botany in the Royal Indian Engineering College, Cooper's Hill. 8vo.
[*In preparation.*

Bettany.—FIRST LESSONS IN PRACTICAL BOTANY. By G. T. BETTANY, M.A., F.L.S., formerly Lecturer in Botany at Guy's Hospital Medical School. 18mo. 1s.

Bower—Vines.—A COURSE OF PRACTICAL INSTRUCTION IN BOTANY. By F. O. BOWER, M.A., F.L.S., Professor of Botany in the University of Glasgow, and SYDNEY H. VINES, M.A., D.Sc., F.R.S., Fellow and Lecturer, Christ's College, Cambridge. With a Preface by W. T. THISELTON DYER, M.A., C.M.G., F.R.S., F.L.S., Director of the Royal Gardens, Kew. Crown 8vo.
Part I.—PHANEROGAMÆ—PTERIDOPHYTA. 6s. Part II.—BRYOPHYTA—THALLOPHYTA. 4s. 6d.

Darwin (Charles).—MEMORIAL NOTICES OF CHARLES DARWIN, F.R.S., &c. By THOMAS HENRY HUXLEY, F.R.S., G. J. ROMANES, F.R.S., ARCHIBALD GEIKIE, F.R.S., and W. T. THISELTON DYER, F.R.S. Reprinted from *Nature*. With a Portrait, engraved by C. H. JEENS. Crown 8vo. 2s. 6d. (*Nature Series.*)

Fearnley.—A MANUAL OF ELEMENTARY PRACTICAL HISTOLOGY. By WILLIAM FEARNLEY. With Illustrations. Crown 8vo. 7s. 6d.

Flower and Gadow.—AN INTRODUCTION TO THE OSTEOLOGY OF THE MAMMALIA. By WILLIAM HENRY FLOWER, LL.D., F.R.S., Director of the Natural History Departments of the British Museum, late Hunterian Professor of Comparative Anatomy and Physiology in the Royal College of Surgeons of England. With numerous Illustrations. Third Edition. Revised with the assistance of HANS GADOW, Ph.D., M.A., Lecturer on the Advanced Morphology of Vertebrates and Strickland Curator in the University of Cambridge. Crown 8vo. 10s. 6d.

Foster.—Works by MICHAEL FOSTER, M.D., Sec. R.S., Professor of Physiology in the University of Cambridge.
  PRIMER OF PHYSIOLOGY. With numerous Illustrations. New Edition. 18mo. 1s.
  A TEXT-BOOK OF PHYSIOLOGY. With Illustrations. Fourth Edition, revised. 8vo. 21s.

SCIENCE.

Foster and Balfour.—THE ELEMENTS OF EMBRYOLOGY. By MICHAEL FOSTER, M.A., M.D., LL.D., Sec. R.S., Professor of Physiology in the University of Cambridge, Fellow of Trinity College, Cambridge, and the late FRANCIS M. BALFOUR, M.A., LL.D., F.R.S., Fellow of Trinity College, Cambridge, and Professor of Animal Morphology in the University. Second Edition, revised. Edited by ADAM SEDGWICK, M.A., Fellow and Assistant Lecturer of Trinity College, Cambridge, and WALTER HEAPE, Demonstrator in the Morphological Laboratory of the University of Cambridge. With Illustrations. Crown 8vo. 10s. 6d.

Foster and Langley.—A COURSE OF ELEMENTARY PRACTICAL PHYSIOLOGY. By Prof. MICHAEL FOSTER, M.D., Sec. R.S., &c., and J. N. LANGLEY, M.A., F.R.S., Fellow of Trinity College, Cambridge. Fifth Edition. Crown 8vo. 7s. 6d.

Gamgee.—A TEXT-BOOK OF THE PHYSIOLOGICAL CHEMISTRY OF THE ANIMAL BODY. Including an Account of the Chemical Changes occurring in Disease. By A. GAMGEE, M.D., F.R.S., formerly Professor of Physiology in the Victoria University the Owens College, Manchester. 2 Vols. 8vo. With Illustrations. Vol. I. 18s. [*Vol. II. in the press.*

Gray.—STRUCTURAL BOTANY, OR ORGANOGRAPHY ON THE BASIS OF MORPHOLOGY. To which are added the principles of Taxonomy and Phytography, and a Glossary of Botanical Terms. By Professor ASA GRAY, LL.D. 8vo. 10s. 6d.

Hamilton.—A PRACTICAL TEXT-BOOK OF PATHOLOGY. By D. J. HAMILTON, Professor of Pathological Anatomy (Sir Erasmus Wilson Chair), University of Aberdeen. 8vo.
[*In the press.*

Hooker.—Works by Sir J. D. HOOKER, K.C.S.I., C.B., M.D., F.R.S., D.C.L.
PRIMER OF BOTANY. With numerous Illustrations. New Edition. 18mo. 1s. (*Science Primers.*)
THE STUDENT'S FLORA OF THE BRITISH ISLANDS. Third Edition, revised. Globe 8vo. 10s. 6d.

Howes.—AN ATLAS OF PRACTICAL ELEMENTARY BIOLOGY. By G. B. HOWES, Assistant Professor of Zoology, Normal School of Science and Royal School of Mines. With a Preface by THOMAS HENRY HUXLEY, F.R.S. Royal 4to. 14s.

Huxley.—Works by THOMAS HENRY HUXLEY, F.R.S.
INTRODUCTORY PRIMER OF SCIENCE. 18mo. 1s. (*Science Primers.*)
LESSONS IN ELEMENTARY PHYSIOLOGY. With numerous Illustrations. New Edition Revised. Fcap. 8vo. 4s. 6d.

Huxley.—QUESTIONS ON HUXLEY'S PHYSIOLOGY FOR SCHOOLS. By T. Alcock, M.D. New Edition. 18mo. 1s. 6d.

Huxley and Martin.—A COURSE OF PRACTICAL INSTRUCTION IN ELEMENTARY BIOLOGY. By Thomas Henry Huxley, F.R.S., assisted by H. N. Martin, M.B., D.Sc. New Edition, revised. Crown 8vo. 6s.

Kane.—EUROPEAN BUTTERFLIES, A HANDBOOK OF. By W. F. De Vismes Kane, M.A., M.R.I.A., Member of the Entomological Society of London, &c. With Copper Plate Illustrations. Crown 8vo. 10s. 6d.

A LIST OF EUROPEAN RHOPALOCERA WITH THEIR VARIETIES AND PRINCIPAL SYNONYMS. Reprinted from the *Handbook of European Butterflies*. Crown 8vo. 1s.

Klein.—MICRO-ORGANISMS AND DISEASE. An Introduction into the Study of Specific Micro-Organisms. By E. Klein, M.D., F.R.S., Lecturer on General Anatomy and Physiology in the Medical School of St. Bartholomew's Hospital, London. With 121 Illustrations. Third Edition, Revised. Crown 8vo. 6s.

THE BACTERIA IN ASIATIC CHOLERA. By the Same. Crown 8vo. [*In preparation*.

Lankester.—Works by Professor E. Ray Lankester, F.R.S.

A TEXT BOOK OF ZOOLOGY. 8vo. [*In preparation*.

DEGENERATION: A CHAPTER IN DARWINISM. Illustrated. Crown 8vo. 2s. 6d. (*Nature Series*.)

Lubbock.—Works by Sir John Lubbock, M.P., F.R.S., D.C.L.

THE ORIGIN AND METAMORPHOSES OF INSECTS. With numerous Illustrations. New Edition. Crown 8vo. 3s. 6d. (*Nature Series*.)

ON BRITISH WILD FLOWERS CONSIDERED IN RELATION TO INSECTS. With numerous Illustrations. New Edition. Crown 8vo. 4s. 6d. (*Nature Series*).

FLOWERS, FRUITS, AND LEAVES. With Illustrations. Crown 8vo. 4s. 6d. (*Nature Series*.)

M'Kendrick.—OUTLINES OF PHYSIOLOGY IN ITS RELATIONS TO MAN. By J. G. M'Kendrick, M.D., F.R.S.E. With Illustrations. Crown 8vo. 12s. 6d.

Martin and Moale.—ON THE DISSECTION OF VERTEBRATE ANIMALS. By Professor H. N. Martin and W. A. Moale. Crown 8vo. [*In preparation*.

Mivart.—Works by St. George Mivart, F.R.S., Lecturer on Comparative Anatomy at St. Mary's Hospital.

LESSONS IN ELEMENTARY ANATOMY. With upwards of 400 Illustrations. Fcap. 8vo. 6s. 6d.

THE COMMON FROG. With numerous Illustrations. Crown 8vo. 3s. 6d. (*Nature Series*.)

Müller.—THE FERTILISATION OF FLOWERS. By Professor HERMANN MÜLLER. Translated and Edited by D'ARCY W. THOMPSON, B.A., Professor of Biology in University College, Dundee. With a Preface by CHARLES DARWIN, F.R.S. With numerous Illustrations. Medium 8vo. 21s.

Oliver.—Works by DANIEL OLIVER, F.R.S., &c., Professor of Botany in University College, London, &c.
FIRST BOOK OF INDIAN BOTANY. With numerous Illustrations. Extra fcap. 8vo. 6s. 6d.
LESSONS IN ELEMENTARY BOTANY. With nearly 200 Illustrations. New Edition. Fcap. 8vo. 4s. 6d.

Parker.—A COURSE OF INSTRUCTION IN ZOOTOMY (VERTEBRATA). By T. JEFFREY PARKER, B.Sc. London, Professor of Biology in the University of Otago, New Zealand. With Illustrations. Crown 8vo. 8s. 6d.
LESSONS IN ELEMENTARY BIOLOGY. By the same Author. With Illustrations. 8vo. [*In the press.*

Parker and Bettany.—THE MORPHOLOGY OF THE SKULL. By Professor W. K. PARKER, F.R.S., and G. T. BETTANY. Illustrated. Crown 8vo. 10s. 6d.

Smith (W. G.)—DISEASES OF FIELD AND GARDEN CROPS, CHIEFLY SUCH AS ARE CAUSED BY FUNGI. By WORTHINGTON G. SMITH, F.L.S., M.A.I., Member of the Scientific Committee R.H.S. With 143 New Illustrations drawn and engraved from Nature by the Author. Fcap. 8vo. 4s. 6d.

Wiedersheim (Prof.).—ELEMENTS OF THE COMPARATIVE ANATOMY OF VERTEBRATES. Adapted from the German of ROBERT WIEDERSHEIM, Professor of Anatomy, and Director of the Institute of Human and Comparative Anatomy in the University of Freiburg-in-Baden, by W. NEWTON PARKER, Professor of Biology in the University College of South Wales and Monmouthshire. With Additions by the Author and Translator. With Two Hundred and Seventy Woodcuts. Medium 8vo. 12s. 6d.

MEDICINE.

Brunton.—Works by T. LAUDER BRUNTON, M.D., D.Sc., F.R.C.P., F.R.S., Assistant Physician and Lecturer on Materia Medica at St. Bartholomew's Hospital; Examiner in Materia Medica in the University of London, in the Victoria University, and in the Royal College of Physicians, London; late Examiner in the University of Edinburgh.

Brunton.—A TEXT-BOOK OF PHARMACOLOGY, THERAPEUTICS, AND MATERIA MEDICA. Adapted to the United States Pharmacopœia, by FRANCIS H. WILLIAMS, M.D., Boston, Mass. Third Edition. Adapted to the New British Pharmacopœia, 1885. Medium 8vo. 21s
    TABLES OF MATERIA MEDICA: A Companion to the Materia Medica Museum. With Illustrations. New Edition Enlarged. 8vo. 10s. 6d.
Hamilton.—A TEXT-BOOK OF PATHOLOGY. By D. J. HAMILTON, Professor of Pathological Anatomy University of Aberdeen. With Illustrations. 8vo. [*In the press.*
Klein.—MICRO-ORGANISMS AND DISEASE. An Introduction into the Study of Specific Micro-Organisms. By E. KLEIN, M.D., F.R.S., Lecturer on General Anatomy and Physiology in the Medical School of St. Bartholomew's Hospital, London. With 121 Illustrations. Third Edition, Revised. Crown 8vo 6s.
    THE BACTERIA IN ASIATIC CHOLERA. By the Same Author. Crown 8vo. [*In preparation.*
Ziegler-Macalister.—TEXT-BOOK OF PATHOLOGICAL ANATOMY AND PATHOGENESIS. By Professor ERNST ZIEGLER of Tübingen. Translated and Edited for English Students by DONALD MACALISTER, M.A., M.D., B.Sc., F.R.C.P., Fellow and Medical Lecturer of St. John's College, Cambridge, Physician to Addenbrooke's Hospital, and Teacher of Medicine in the University. With numerous Illustrations. Medium 8vo.
    Part I.—GENERAL PATHOLOGICAL ANATOMY. Second Edition.. 12s. 6d.
    Part II.—SPECIAL PATHOLOGICAL ANATOMY. Sections I.—VIII. Second Edition. 12s. 6d. Sections IX.—XII. 12s. 6d.

ANTHROPOLOGY.

Flower.—FASHION IN DEFORMITY, as Illustrated in the Customs of Barbarous and Civilised Races. By Professor FLOWER, F.R.S., F.R.C.S. With Illustrations. Crown 8vo. 2s. 6d. (*Nature Series.*)
Tylor.—ANTHROPOLOGY. An Introduction to the Study of Man and Civilisation. By E. B. TYLOR, D.C.L., F.R.S. With numerous Illustrations. Crown 8vo. 7s. 6d.

PHYSICAL GEOGRAPHY & GEOLOGY.

Blanford.—THE RUDIMENTS OF PHYSICAL GEOGRAPHY FOR THE USE OF INDIAN SCHOOLS; with a Glossary of Technical Terms employed. By H. F. BLANFORD, F.R.S. New Edition, with Illustrations. Globe 8vo. 2s. 6d.

SCIENCE.

Geikie.—Works by ARCHIBALD GEIKIE, LL.D., F.R.S., Director General of the Geological Survey of Great Britain and Ireland, and Director of the Museum of Practical Geology, London, formerly Murchison Professor of Geology and Mineralogy in the University of Edinburgh, &c.

PRIMER OF PHYSICAL GEOGRAPHY. With numerous Illustrations. New Edition. With Questions. 18mo. 1s. (*Science Primers.*)

ELEMENTARY LESSONS IN PHYSICAL GEOGRAPHY. With numerous Illustrations. New Edition. Fcap. 8vo. 4s. 6d. QUESTIONS ON THE SAME. 1s. 6d.

PRIMER OF GEOLOGY. With numerous Illustrations. New Edition. 18mo. 1s. (*Science Primers.*)

CLASS BOOK OF GEOLOGY. With upwards of 200 New Illustrations. Crown 8vo. 10s. 6d.

TEXT-BOOK OF GEOLOGY. With numerous Illustrations. Second Edition, Sixth Thousand, Revised and Enlarged. 8vo. 28s.

OUTLINES OF FIELD GEOLOGY. With Illustrations. New Edition. Extra fcap. 8vo. 3s. 6d.

THE SCENERY AND GEOLOGY OF SCOTLAND, VIEWED IN CONNEXION WITH ITS PHYSICAL GEOLOGY. With numerous Illustrations. Crown 8vo. 12s. 6d.

(See also under *History and Geography*.)

Huxley.—PHYSIOGRAPHY. An Introduction to the Study of Nature. By THOMAS HENRY HUXLEY, F.R.S. With numerous Illustrations, and Coloured Plates. New and Cheaper Edition. Crown 8vo. 6s.

Lockyer.—OUTLINES OF PHYSIOGRAPHY—THE MOVEMENTS OF THE EARTH. By J. NORMAN LOCKYER, F.R.S., Correspondent of the Institute of France, Foreign Member of the Academy of the Lyncei of Rome, &c., &c.; Professor of Astronomical Physics in the Normal School of Science, and Examiner in Physiography for the Science and Art Department. With Illustrations. Crown 8vo. Sewed, 1s. 6d.

Phillips.—A TREATISE ON ORE DEPOSITS. By J. ARTHUR PHILLIPS, F.R.S., V.P.G.S., F.C.S., M.Inst.C.E., Ancien Élève de l'École des Mines, Paris; Author of "A Manual of Metallurgy," "The Mining and Metallurgy of Gold and Silver," &c. With numerous Illustrations. 8vo. 25s.

AGRICULTURE.

Frankland.—AGRICULTURAL CHEMICAL ANALYSIS, A Handbook of. By PERCY FARADAY FRANKLAND, Ph.D., B.Sc., F.C.S., Associate of the Royal School of Mines, and Demonstrator of Practical and Agricultural Chemistry in the Normal School of Science and Royal School of Mines, South Kensington Museum. Founded upon *Leitfaden für die Agriculture Chemiche Analyse*, von Dr. F. KROCKER. Crown 8vo. 7s. 6d.

Smith (Worthington G.).—DISEASES OF FIELD AND GARDEN CROPS, CHIEFLY SUCH AS ARE CAUSED BY FUNGI. By WORTHINGTON G. SMITH, F.L.S., M.A.I., Member of the Scientific Committee of the R.H.S. With 143 Illustrations, drawn and engraved from Nature by the Author. Fcap. 8vo. 4s. 6d.

Tanner.—Works by HENRY TANNER, F.C.S., M.R.A.C., Examiner in the Principles of Agriculture under the Government Department of Science; Director of Education in the Institute of Agriculture, South Kensington, London; sometime Professor of Agricultural Science, University College, Aberystwith.
ELEMENTARY LESSONS IN THE SCIENCE OF AGRICULTURAL PRACTICE. Fcap. 8vo. 3s. 6d.
FIRST PRINCIPLES OF AGRICULTURE. 18mo. 1s.
THE PRINCIPLES OF AGRICULTURE. A Series of Reading Books for use in Elementary Schools. Prepared by HENRY TANNER, F.C.S., M.R.A.C. Extra fcap. 8vo.
    I. The Alphabet of the Principles of Agriculture. 6d.
    II. Further Steps in the Principles of Agriculture. 1s.
    III. Elementary School Readings on the Principles of Agriculture for the third stage. 1s.

POLITICAL ECONOMY.

Cossa.—GUIDE TO THE STUDY OF POLITICAL ECONOMY. By Dr. LUIGI COSSA, Professor in the University of Pavia. Translated from the Second Italian Edition. With a Preface by W. STANLEY JEVONS, F.R.S. Crown 8vo. 4s. 6d.

Fawcett (Mrs.).—Works by MILLICENT GARRETT FAWCETT:—
POLITICAL ECONOMY FOR BEGINNERS, WITH QUESTIONS. Fourth Edition. 18mo. 2s. 6d.
TALES IN POLITICAL ECONOMY. Crown 8vo. 3s.

Fawcett.—A MANUAL OF POLITICAL ECONOMY. By Right Hon. HENRY FAWCETT, F.R.S. Sixth Edition, revised, with a chapter on "State Socialism and the Nationalisation of the Land," and an Index. Crown 8vo. 12s.
AN EXPLANATORY DIGEST of the above. By CYRIL A. WATERS. Crown 8vo. [*In the press.*

MENTAL AND MORAL PHILOSOPHY.

Jevons.—PRIMER OF POLITICAL ECONOMY. By W. STANLEY JEVONS, LL.D., M.A., F.R.S. New Edition. 18mo. 1s. (*Science Primers.*)

Marshall.—THE ECONOMICS OF INDUSTRY. By A. MARSHALL, M.A., Professor of Political Economy in the University of Cambridge, and MARY P. MARSHALL, late Lecturer at Newnham Hall, Cambridge. Extra fcap. 8vo. 2s. 6d.

Marshall.—ECONOMICS. By ALFRED MARSHALL, M.A., Professor of Political Economy in the University of Cambridge. 2 vols 8vo. [*In the press.*

Sidgwick.—THE PRINCIPLES OF POLITICAL ECONOMY. By Professor HENRY SIDGWICK, M.A., LL.D., Knightbridge Professor of Moral Philosophy in the University of Cambridge, &c., Author of "The Methods of Ethics." Second Edition, revised. 8vo. 16s.

Walker.—Works by FRANCIS A. WALKER, M.A., Ph.D., Author of "Money," "Money in its Relation to Trade," &c.
POLITICAL ECONOMY. 8vo. 10s. 6d.
A BRIEF TEXT-BOOK OF POLITICAL ECONOMY. Crown 8vo. 6s. 6d.
THE WAGES QUESTION. 8vo. 14s.

MENTAL & MORAL PHILOSOPHY.

Boole.—THE MATHEMATICAL ANALYSIS OF LOGIC. Being an Essay towards a Calculus of Deductive Reasoning. By GEORGE BOOLE. 8vo. Sewed. 5s.

Calderwood.—HANDBOOK OF MORAL PHILOSOPHY. By the Rev. HENRY CALDERWOOD, LL.D., Professor of Moral Philosophy, University of Edinburgh. New Edition. Crown 8vo. 6s.

Clifford.—SEEING AND THINKING. By the late Professor W. K. CLIFFORD, F.R.S. With Diagrams. Crown 8vo. 3s. 6d. (*Nature Series.*)

Jardine.—THE ELEMENTS OF THE PSYCHOLOGY OF COGNITION. By the Rev. ROBERT JARDINE, B.D., D.Sc. (Edin.), Ex-Principal of the General Assembly's College, Calcutta. Third Edition, revised and improved. Crown 8vo. 6s. 6d.

Jevons.—Works by the late W. STANLEY JEVONS, LL.D., M.A., F.R.S.
PRIMER OF LOGIC. New Edition. 18mo. 1s. (*Science Primers.*)
ELEMENTARY LESSONS IN LOGIC; Deductive and Inductive, with copious Questions and Examples, and a Vocabulary of Logical Terms. New Edition. Fcap. 8vo. 3s. 6d.

Jevons.—Works by STANLEY W. JEVONS, *continued*—
   THE PRINCIPLES OF SCIENCE. A Treatise on Logic and Scientific Method. New and Revised Edition. Crown 8vo. 12s. 6d.
   STUDIES IN DEDUCTIVE LOGIC. Second Edition. Cr. 8vo. 6s.

Keynes.—FORMAL LOGIC, Studies and Exercises in. Including a Generalisation of Logical Processes in their application to Complex Inferences. By JOHN NEVILLE KEYNES, M.A., late Fellow of Pembroke College, Cambridge. Second Edition, Revised and Enlarged. Crown 8vo. 10s. 6d.

Kant—Max Muller.—CRITIQUE OF PURE REASON. By IMMANUEL KANT. In commemoration of the Centenary of its first Publication. Translated into English by F. MAX MÜLLER. With an Historical Introduction by LUDWIG NOIRÉ. 2 vols. Demy 8vo. 16s. each.
   Volume I. HISTORICAL INTRODUCTION, by LUDWIG NOIRÉ; &c., &c.
   Volume II. CRITIQUE OF PURE REASON, translated by F. MAX MÜLLER.
For the convenience of students these volumes are now sold separately.

McCosh.—PSYCHOLOGY. By JAMES McCOSH, D.D., LL.D., Litt.D., President of Princeton College, Author of "Intuitions of the Mind," "Laws of Discursive Thought," &c. Crown 8vo.
   I. THE COGNITIVE POWERS. 6s. 6d.
   II. THE MOTIVE POWERS. Crown 8vo. 6s. 6d.

Ray.—A TEXT-BOOK OF DEDUCTIVE LOGIC FOR THE USE OF STUDENTS. By P. K. RAY, D.Sc. (Lon. and Edin.), Professor of Logic and Philosophy, Presidency College Calcutta. Third Edition. Globe 8vo. 4s. 6d.
   The SCHOOLMASTER says:—"This work . . . is deservedly taking a place among the recognised text-books on Logic."

Sidgwick.—Works by HENRY SIDGWICK, M.A., LL.D., Knightbridge Professor of Moral Philosophy in the University of Cambridge.
   THE METHODS OF ETHICS. Third Edition. 8vo. 14s. A Supplement to the Second Edition, containing all the important Additions and Alterations in the Third Edition. Demy 8vo. 6s.
   OUTLINES OF THE HISTORY OF ETHICS, for English Readers. Crown 8vo. 3s. 6d.

Venn.—THE LOGIC OF CHANCE. An Essay on the Foundations and Province of the Theory of Probability, with special Reference to its Logical Bearings and its Application to Moral and Social Science. By JOHN VENN, M.A., Fellow and Lecturer in Moral Sciences in Gonville and Caius College, Cambridge, Examiner in Moral Philosophy in the University of London. Second Edition, rewritten and greatly enlarged. Crown 8vo. 10s. 6d.
   SYMBOLIC LOGIC. By the same Author. Crown 8vo. 10s. 6d.

HISTORY AND GEOGRAPHY.

Arnold (T.).—THE SECOND PUNIC WAR. Being Chapters from THE HISTORY OF ROME. By THOMAS ARNOLD, D.D. Edited, with Notes, by W. T. ARNOLD, M.A. With 8 Maps. Crown 8vo. 8s. 6d.

Arnold (W. T.).—THE ROMAN SYSTEM OF PROVINCIAL ADMINISTRATION TO THE ACCESSION OF CONSTANTINE THE GREAT. By W. T. ARNOLD, M.A. Crown 8vo. 6s.
"Ought to prove a valuable handbook to the student of Roman history."—GUARDIAN.

Beesly.—STORIES FROM THE HISTORY OF ROME. By Mrs. BEESLY. Fcap. 8vo. 2s. 6d.

Bryce.—THE HOLY ROMAN EMPIRE. By JAMES BRYCE, D.C.L., Fellow of Oriel College, and Regius Professor of Civil Law in the University of Oxford. Eighth Edition. Crown 8vo. 7s. 6d.

Buckland.—OUR NATIONAL INSTITUTIONS. A Short Sketch for Schools. By ANNA BUCKLAND. With Glossary. 18mo. 1s.

Buckley.—A HISTORY OF ENGLAND FOR BEGINNERS. By ARABELLA B. BUCKLEY. Author of "A Short History of Natural Science," &c. With Coloured Maps, Chronological and Genealogical Tables. Globe 8vo. 3s.

Clarke.—CLASS-BOOK OF GEOGRAPHY. By C. B. CLARKE, M.A., F.L.S., F.G.S., F.R.S. New Edition, with Eighteen Coloured Maps. Fcap. 8vo. 3s.

Dicey.—LECTURES INTRODUCTORY TO THE STUDY OF THE LAW OF THE CONSTITUTION. By A. V. DICEY, B.C.L., of the Inner Temple, Barrister-at-Law; Vinerian Professor of English Law; Fellow of All Souls College, Oxford; Hon. LL.D. Glasgow. Second Edition. Demy 8vo. 12s. 6d.

Dickens's DICTIONARY OF THE UNIVERSITY OF OXFORD, 1886-7. 18mo, sewed. 1s.
DICTIONARY OF THE UNIVERSITY OF CAMBRIDGE, 1886-7. 18mo, sewed. 1s.
Both books (Oxford and Cambridge) bound together in one volume. Cloth. 2s. 6d.

Freeman.—Works by EDWARD A. FREEMAN, D.C.L., LL.D., Regius Professor of Modern History in the University of Oxford, &c.
OLD ENGLISH HISTORY. With Five Coloured Maps. New Edition. Extra fcap. 8vo. 6s.
A SCHOOL HISTORY OF ROME. Crown 8vo. [*In preparation.*
METHODS OF HISTORICAL STUDY. A Course of Lectures. 8vo. 10s. 6d.

Freeman.—Works by EDWARD A. FREEMAN, D.C.L., LL.D., &c., *continued*—

THE CHIEF PERIODS OF EUROPEAN HISTORY. Six Lectures read in the University of Oxford in Trinity Term, 1885. With an Essay on Greek Cities under Roman Rule. 8vo. 10s. 6d.

HISTORICAL ESSAYS. First Series. Fourth Edition. 8vo. 10s. 6d.
Contents:—The Mythical and Romantic Elements in Early English History—The Continuity of English History—The Relations between the Crown of England and Scotland—St. Thomas of Canterbury and his Biographers, &c.

HISTORICAL ESSAYS. Second Series. Second Edition, with additional Essays. 8vo. 10s. 6d.
Contents:—Ancient Greece and Mediæval Italy—Mr. Gladstone's Homer and the Homeric Ages—The Historians of Athens—The Athenian Democracy—Alexander the Great—Greece during the Macedonian Period—Mommsen's History of Rome—Lucius Cornelius Sulla—The Flavian Cæsars, &c., &c.

HISTORICAL ESSAYS. Third Series. 8vo. 12s.
Contents:—First Impressions of Rome—The Illyrian Emperors and their Land—Augusta Treverorum—The Goths at Ravenna—Race and Language—The Byzantine Empire—First Impressions of Athens—Mediæval and Modern Greece—The Southern Slaves—Sicilian Cycles—The Normans at Palermo.

THE GROWTH OF THE ENGLISH CONSTITUTION FROM THE EARLIEST TIMES. Fourth Edition. Crown 8vo. 5s.

GENERAL SKETCH OF EUROPEAN HISTORY. New Edition. Enlarged, with Maps, &c. 18mo. 3s. 6d. (Vol. I. of Historical Course for Schools.)

EUROPE. 18mo. 1s. (*History Primers.*)

Fyffe.—A SCHOOL HISTORY OF GREECE. By C. A. FYFFE, M.A. Crown 8vo. [*In preparation.*

Geikie.—THE TEACHING OF GEOGRAPHY. A Practical Handbook for the use of Teachers. By ARCHIBALD GEIKIE, F.R.S., Director-General of the Geological Survey of the United Kingdom, and Director of the Museum of Practical Geology, Jermyn Street, London; formerly Murchison Professor of Geology and Mineralogy in the University of Edinburgh. Crown 8vo. 2s. Being Volume I. of a New Geographical Series Edited by ARCHIBALD GEIKIE, F.R.S.

* The aim of this volume is to advocate the claims of geography as an educational discipline of a high order, and to show how these claims may be practically recognised by teachers. This introductory volume is intended to be followed by a short Geography of the British Islands, and then by other volumes as announced on p. 79.

Green.—Works by JOHN RICHARD GREEN, M.A., LL.D., late Honorary Fellow of Jesus College, Oxford.

A SHORT HISTORY OF THE ENGLISH PEOPLE. With Coloured Maps, Genealogical Tables, and Chronological Annals. Crown 8vo. 8s. 6d. 126th Thousand.

HISTORY AND GEOGRAPHY.

Green.—Works by JOHN RICHARD GREEN, M.A., LL.D. &c. (*continued*)—
ANALYSIS OF ENGLISH HISTORY, based on Green's "Short History of the English People." By C. W. A. TAIT, M.A., Assistant-Master, Clifton College. Crown 8vo. 3s. 6d.
READINGS FROM ENGLISH HISTORY. Selected and Edited by JOHN RICHARD GREEN. Three Parts. Globe 8vo. 1s. 6d. each. I. Hengist to Cressy. II. Cressy to Cromwell. III. Cromwell to Balaklava.

Green.— A SHORT GEOGRAPHY OF THE BRITISH ISLANDS. By JOHN RICHARD GREEN and ALICE STOPFORD GREEN. With Maps. Fcap. 8vo. 3s. 6d.

Grove.—A PRIMER OF GEOGRAPHY. By Sir GEORGE GROVE, D.C.L. With Illustrations. 18mo. 1s. (*Science Primers.*)

Guest.—LECTURES ON THE HISTORY OF ENGLAND By M. J. GUEST. With Maps. Crown 8vo. 6s.

Historical Course for Schools—Edited by EDWARD A. FREEMAN, D.C.L., LL.D., late Fellow of Trinity College, Oxford, Regius Professor of Modern History in the University of Oxford.
I.—GENERAL SKETCH OF EUROPEAN HISTORY. By EDWARD A. FREEMAN, D.C.L. New Edition, revised and enlarged, with Chronological Table, Maps, and Index. 18mo. 3s. 6d.
II.—HISTORY OF ENGLAND. By EDITH THOMPSON. New Ed., revised and enlarged, with Coloured Maps. 18mo. 2s. 6d.
III.—HISTORY OF SCOTLAND. By MARGARET MACARTHUR. New Edition. 18mo. 2s.
IV.—HISTORY OF ITALY. By the Rev. W. HUNT, M.A. New Edition, with Coloured Maps. 18mo. 3s. 6d.
V.—HISTORY OF GERMANY. By J. SIME, M.A. New Edition Revised. 18mo. 3s.
VI.—HISTORY OF AMERICA. By JOHN A. DOYLE. With Maps. 18mo. 4s. 6d.
VII.—EUROPEAN COLONIES. By E. J. PAYNE, M.A. With Maps. 18mo. 4s. 6d.
VIII.—FRANCE. By CHARLOTTE M. YONGE. With Maps. 18mo. 3s. 6d.
GREECE. By EDWARD A. FREEMAN, D.C.L. [*In preparation*.
ROME. By EDWARD A. FREEMAN, D.C.L. [*In preparation*.

History Primers—Edited by JOHN RICHARD GREEN, M.A., LL.D., Author of "A Short History of the English People."
ROME. By the Rev. M. CREIGHTON, M.A., Dixie Professor of Ecclesiastical History in the University of Cambridge. With Eleven Maps. 18mo. 1s.

History Primers.—Edited by JOHN RICHARD GREEN, M.A., LL.D. (*continued*)—

GREECE. By C. A. FYFFE, M.A., Fellow and late Tutor of University College, Oxford. With Five Maps. 18mo. 1s.

EUROPEAN HISTORY. By E. A. FREEMAN, D.C.L., LL.D. With Maps. 18mo. 1s.

GREEK ANTIQUITIES. By the Rev. J. P. MAHAFFY, M.A. Illustrated. 18mo. 1s.

CLASSICAL GEOGRAPHY. By H. F. TOZER, M.A. 18mo. 1s.

GEOGRAPHY. By Sir G. GROVE, D.C.L. Maps. 18mo. 1s.

ROMAN ANTIQUITIES. By Professor WILKINS. Illustrated. 18mo. 1s.

FRANCE. By CHARLOTTE M. YONGE. 18mo. 1s.

Hole.—A GENEALOGICAL STEMMA OF THE KINGS OF ENGLAND AND FRANCE. By the Rev. C. HOLE. On Sheet. 1s.

Jennings—CHRONOLOGICAL TABLES. Compiled by Rev. A. C. JENNINGS. [*In the press.*

Kiepert.—A MANUAL OF ANCIENT GEOGRAPHY. From the German of Dr. H. KIEPERT. Crown 8vo. 5s.

Labberton.—NEW HISTORICAL ATLAS AND GENERAL HISTORY. By R. H. LABBERTON, Litt.Hum.D. 4to. New Edition Revised and Enlarged. 15s.

Lethbridge.—A SHORT MANUAL OF THE HISTORY OF INDIA. With an Account of INDIA AS IT IS. The Soil, Climate, and Productions; the People, their Races, Religions, Public Works, and Industries; the Civil Services, and System of Administration. By Sir ROPER LETHBRIDGE, M.A., C.I.E., late Scholar of Exeter College, Oxford, formerly Principal of Kishnaghur College, Bengal, Fellow and sometime Examiner of the Calcutta University. With Maps. Crown 8vo. 5s.

Michelet.—A SUMMARY OF MODERN HISTORY. Translated from the French of M. MICHELET, and continued to the Present Time, by M. C. M. SIMPSON. Globe 8vo. 4s. 6d.

Norgate.—ENGLAND UNDER THE ANGEVIN KINGS. By KATE NORGATE. With Maps and Plans. 2 vols. 8vo. 32s.

Otté.—SCANDINAVIAN HISTORY. By E. C. OTTÉ. With Maps. Globe 8vo. 6s.

Ramsay.—A SCHOOL HISTORY OF ROME. By G. G. RAMSAY, M.A., Professor of Humanity in the University of Glasgow. With Maps. Crown 8vo. [*In preparation.*

Seeley—Works by J. R. SEELEY, M.A., Regius Professor of Modern History in the University of Cambridge.
THE EXPANSION OF ENGLAND. Crown 8vo. 4s. 6d.
OUR COLONIAL EXPANSION. Extracts from the above. Crown 8vo. Sewed. 1s.

Tait.—ANALYSIS OF ENGLISH HISTORY, based on Green's "Short History of the English People." By C. W. A. TAIT, M.A., Assistant-Master, Clifton College. Crown 8vo. 3s. 6d.

Wheeler.—A SHORT HISTORY OF INDIA AND OF THE FRONTIER STATES OF AFGHANISTAN, NEPAUL, AND BURMA. By J. TALBOYS WHEELER. With Maps. Crown 8vo. 12s.
A COLLEGE HISTORY OF INDIA. By the same. With Maps. Crown 8vo. [*In the press.*

Yonge (Charlotte M.).—CAMEOS FROM ENGLISH HISTORY. By CHARLOTTE M. YONGE, Author of "The Heir of Redclyffe," Extra fcap. 8vo. New Edition. 5s. each. (1) FROM ROLLO TO EDWARD II. (2) THE WARS IN FRANCE. (3) THE WARS OF THE ROSES. (4) REFORMATION TIMES. (5) ENGLAND AND SPAIN. (6) FORTY YEARS OF STUART RULE (1603—1643).
EUROPEAN HISTORY. Narrated in a Series of Historical Selections from the Best Authorities. Edited and arranged by E. M. SEWELL and C. M. YONGE. First Series, 1003—1154. New Edition. Crown 8vo. 6s. Second Series, 1088—1228. New Edition. Crown 8vo. 6s.
THE VICTORIAN HALF CENTURY—A JUBILEE BOOK. With a New Portrait of the Queen. Crown 8vo., paper covers, 1s. Cloth, 1s. 6d.

MODERN LANGUAGES AND LITERATURE.

(1) **English**, (2) **French**, (3) **German**, (4) **Modern Greek**, (5) **Italian**, (6) **Spanish**.

ENGLISH.

Abbott.—A SHAKESPEARIAN GRAMMAR. An attempt to illustrate some of the Differences between Elizabethan and Modern English. By the Rev. E. A. ABBOTT, D.D., Head Master of the City of London School. New Edition. Extra fcap. 8vo. 6s.

Brooke.—PRIMER OF ENGLISH LITERATURE. By the Rev. STOPFORD A. BROOKE, M.A. 18mo. 1s. (*Literature Primers.*)

Butler.—HUDIBRAS. Edited, with Introduction and Notes, by ALFRED MILNES, M.A. Lon., late Student of Lincoln College, Oxford. Extra fcap 8vo. Part I. 3s. 6d. Parts II. and III. 4s. 6d.

Cowper's TASK: AN EPISTLE TO JOSEPH HILL, ESQ.; TIROCINIUM, or a Review of the Schools; and THE HISTORY OF JOHN GILPIN. Edited, with Notes, by WILLIAM BENHAM, B.D. Globe 8vo. 1s. (*Globe Readings from Standard Authors.*)

Dowden.—SHAKESPEARE. By Professor DOWDEN. 18mo. 1s. (*Literature Primers.*)

Dryden.—SELECT PROSE WORKS. Edited, with Introduction and Notes, by Professor C. D. YONGE. Fcap. 8vo. 2s. 6d.

Gladstone.—SPELLING REFORM FROM AN EDUCATIONAL POINT OF VIEW. By J. H. GLADSTONE, Ph.D., F.R.S., Member of the School Board for London. New Edition. Crown 8vo. 1s. 6d.

Globe Readers. For Standards I.–VI. Edited by A. F. MURISON. Sometime English Master at the Aberdeen Grammar School. With Illustrations. Globe 8vo.

Primer I. (48 pp.) 3d.	Book III. (232 pp.) 1s. 3d.
Primer II. (48 pp.) 3d.	Book IV. (328 pp.) 1s. 9d.
Book I. (96 pp.) 6d.	Book V. (416 pp.) 2s.
Book II. (136 pp.) 9d.	Book VI. (448 pp.) 2s. 6d.

"Among the numerous sets of readers before the public the present series is honourably distinguished by the marked superiority of its materials and the careful ability with which they have been adapted to the growing capacity of the pupils. The plan of the two primers is excellent for facilitating the child's first attempts to read. In the first three following books there is abundance of entertaining reading. . . . Better food for young minds could hardly be found."—THE ATHENÆUM.

*The Shorter Globe Readers.—With Illustrations. Globe 8vo.

Primer I. (48 pp.) 3d.	Standard III. (178 pp.) 1s.
Primer II. (48 pp.) 3d.	Standard IV. (182 pp.) 1s.
Standard I. (92 pp.) 6d.	Standard V. (216 pp.) 1s. 3d.
Standard II. (124 pp.) 9d.	Standard VI. (228 pp.) 1s. 6d.

* This Series has been abridged from "The Globe Readers" to meet the demand for smaller reading books.

GLOBE READINGS FROM STANDARD AUTHORS.

Cowper's TASK: AN EPISTLE TO JOSEPH HILL, ESQ.; TIROCINIUM, or a Review of the Schools; and THE HISTORY OF JOHN GILPIN. Edited, with Notes, by WILLIAM BENHAM, B.D. Globe 8vo. 1s.

Goldsmith's VICAR OF WAKEFIELD. With a Memoir of Goldsmith by Professor MASSON. Globe 8vo. 1s.

Lamb's (Charles) TALES FROM SHAKESPEARE. Edited, with Preface, by the Rev. CANON AINGER, M.A. Globe 8vo. 2s.

Scott's (Sir Walter) LAY OF THE LAST MINSTREL; and THE LADY OF THE LAKE. Edited, with Introductions and Notes, by FRANCIS TURNER PALGRAVE. Globe 8vo. 1s.

MARMION; and the LORD OF THE ISLES. By the same Editor. Globe 8vo. 1s.

The Children's Garland from the Best Poets.—Selected and arranged by COVENTRY PATMORE. Globe 8vo. 2s.

Yonge (Charlotte M.).—A BOOK OF GOLDEN DEEDS OF ALL TIMES AND ALL COUNTRIES. Gathered and narrated anew by CHARLOTTE M. YONGE, the Author of "The Heir of Redclyffe." Globe 8vo. 2s.

Goldsmith.—THE TRAVELLER, or a Prospect of Society; and THE DESERTED VILLAGE. By OLIVER GOLDSMITH. With Notes, Philological and Explanatory, by J. W. HALES, M.A. Crown 8vo. 6d.

THE VICAR OF WAKEFIELD. With a Memoir of Goldsmith by Professor MASSON. Globe 8vo. 1s. (*Globe Readings from Standard Authors.*)

SELECT ESSAYS. Edited, with Introduction and Notes, by Professor C. D. YONGE. Fcap. 8vo. 2s. 6d.

THE DESERTED VILLAGE AND TRAVELLER. Edited, with Introduction and Notes, by ARTHUR BARRETT, B.A., Professor of English Literature in the Elphinstone College, Bombay. Globe 8vo. [*In the press.*

Hales.—LONGER ENGLISH POEMS, with Notes, Philological and Explanatory, and an Introduction on the Teaching of English, Chiefly for Use in Schools. Edited by J. W. HALES, M.A., Professor of English Literature at King's College, London. New Edition. Extra fcap. 8vo. 4s. 6d.

Johnson's LIVES OF THE POETS. The Six Chief Lives (Milton, Dryden, Swift, Addison, Pope, Gray), with Macaulay's "Life of Johnson." Edited with Preface and Notes by MATTHEW ARNOLD. New and cheaper edition. Crown 8vo. 4s. 6d.

Lamb (Charles).—TALES FROM SHAKESPEARE. Edited, with Preface, by the Rev. CANON AINGER, M.A. Globe 8vo. 2s. (*Globe Readings from Standard Authors.*)

Literature Primers—Edited by JOHN RICHARD GREEN, M.A., LL.D., Author of "A Short History of the English People."
ENGLISH COMPOSITION. By Professor NICHOL. 18mo. 1s.
ENGLISH GRAMMAR. By the Rev. R. MORRIS, LL.D., sometime President of the Philological Society. 18mo. 1s.
ENGLISH GRAMMAR EXERCISES. By R. MORRIS, LL.D., and H. C. BOWEN, M.A. 18mo. 1s.
EXERCISES ON MORRIS'S PRIMER OF ENGLISH GRAMMAR. By JOHN WETHERELL, of the Middle School, Liverpool College. 18mo. 1s.
ENGLISH LITERATURE. By STOPFORD BROOKE, M.A. New Edition. 18mo. 1s.
SHAKSPERE. By Professor DOWDEN. 18mo. 1s.
THE CHILDREN'S TREASURY OF LYRICAL POETRY. Selected and arranged with Notes by FRANCIS TURNER PALGRAVE. In Two Parts. 18mo. 1s. each.
PHILOLOGY. By J. PEILE, M.A. 18mo. 1s.

A History of English Literature in Four Volumes. Crown 8vo.
EARLY ENGLISH LITERATURE. By STOPFORD BROOKE, M.A. [*In preparation.*
ELIZABETHAN LITERATURE. By GEORGE SAINTSBURY. 7s. 6d.
THE AGE OF QUEEN ANNE. By EDMUND GOSSE. [*In prep.*
THE MODERN PERIOD. By Professor E. DOWDEN. [*In prep.*

Macmillan's Reading Books.—Adapted to the English and Scotch Codes. Bound in Cloth.

PRIMER. 18mo. (48 pp.) 2d.
BOOK I. for Standard I. 18mo. (96 pp.) 4d.
BOOK II. for Standard II. 18mo. (144 pp.) 5d.
BOOK V. for Standard V. 18mo. (380 pp.) 1s.
BOOK III. for Standard III. 18mo. (160 pp.) 6d.
BOOK IV. for Standard IV. 18mo. (176 pp.) 8d.
BOOK VI. for Standard VI. Cr. 8vo. (430 pp.) 2s.

Book VI. is fitted for higher Classes, and as an Introduction to English Literature.

Macmillan's Copy-Books—
Published in two sizes, viz. :—
1. Large Post 4to. Price 4d. each.
2. Post Oblong. Price 2d. each.

1. INITIATORY EXERCISES AND SHORT LETTERS.
2. WORDS CONSISTING OF SHORT LETTERS
*3. LONG LETTERS. With Words containing Long Letters—Figures.
*4. WORDS CONTAINING LONG LETTERS.

MODERN LANGUAGES AND LITERATURE. 63

Macmillan's Copy Books (*continued*)—
- 4a. PRACTISING AND REVISING COPY-BOOK. For Nos. 1 to 4.
- *5. CAPITALS AND SHORT HALF-TEXT. Words beginning with a Capital.
- *6. HALF-TEXT WORDS beginning with Capitals—Figures.
- *7. SMALL-HAND AND HALF-TEXT. With Capitals and Figures.
- *8. SMALL-HAND AND HALF-TEXT. With Capitals and Figures.
- 8a. PRACTISING AND REVISING COPY-BOOK. For Nos. 5 to 8.
- *9. SMALL-HAND SINGLE HEADLINES—Figures.
- 10. SMALL-HAND SINGLE HEADLINES—Figures.
- 11. SMALL-HAND DOUBLE HEADLINES—Figures.
- 12. COMMERCIAL AND ARITHMETICAL EXAMPLES, &c.
- 12a. PRACTISING AND REVISING COPY-BOOK. For Nos. 8 to 12.

  * *These numbers may be had with Goodman's Patent Sliding Copies.* Large Post 4to. Price 6d. each.

Martin.—THE POET'S HOUR: Poetry selected and arranged for Children. By FRANCES MARTIN. New Edition. 18mo. 2s. 6d.

  SPRING-TIME WITH THE POETS: Poetry selected by FRANCES MARTIN. New Edition. 18mo. 3s. 6d.

Milton.—By STOPFORD BROOKE, M.A. Fcap. 8vo. 1s. 6d (*Classical Writers Series*.)

Milton.—PARADISE LOST. Books I. and II. Edited, with Introduction and Notes, by M. MACMILLAN, B.A. Oxon, Professor of Logic and Moral Philosophy, Elphinstone College, Bombay. Globe 8vo. 2s. 6d.

Morley.—ON THE STUDY OF LITERATURE. The Annual Address to the Students of the London Society for the Extension of University Teaching. Delivered at the Mansion House, February 26, 1887. By JOHN MORLEY. Globe 8vo. Cloth. 1s. 6d.

* *Also a Popular Edition in Pamphlet form for Distribution, price* 2d.

Morris.—Works by the Rev. R. MORRIS, LL.D.
  HISTORICAL OUTLINES OF ENGLISH ACCIDENCE, comprising Chapters on the History and Development of the Language, and on Word-formation. New Edition. Extra fcap. 8vo. 6s.
  ELEMENTARY LESSONS IN HISTORICAL ENGLISH GRAMMAR, containing Accidence and Word-formation. New Edition. 18mo. 2s. 6d.
  PRIMER OF ENGLISH GRAMMAR. 18mo. 1s. (See also *Literature Primers*.)

Oliphant.—THE OLD AND MIDDLE ENGLISH. A New Edition of "THE SOURCES OF STANDARD ENGLISH," revised and greatly enlarged. By T. L. KINGTON OLIPHANT. Extra fcap. 8vo. 9s.

  THE NEW ENGLISH. By the same Author. 2 vols. Cr. 8vo. 21s.

Palgrave.—THE CHILDREN'S TREASURY OF LYRICAL POETRY. Selected and arranged, with Notes, by FRANCIS TURNER PALGRAVE. 18mo. 2s. 6d. Also in Two Parts. 1s. each.

Patmore.—THE CHILDREN'S GARLAND FROM THE BEST POETS. Selected and arranged by COVENTRY PATMORE. Globe 8vo. 2s. (*Globe Readings from Standard Authors.*)

Plutarch.—Being a Selection from the Lives which Illustrate Shakespeare. North's Translation. Edited, with Introductions, Notes, Index of Names, and Glossarial Index, by the Rev. W. W. SKEAT, M.A. Crown 8vo. 6s.

Saintsbury.—A HISTORY OF ELIZABETHAN LITERATURE. By GEORGE SAINTSBURY. (Being Vol. II. of "A History of English Literature" in Four Volumes. Cr. 8vo. 7s. 6d.

Scott's (Sir Walter) LAY OF THE LAST MINSTREL, and THE LADY OF THE LAKE. Edited, with Introduction and Notes, by FRANCIS TURNER PALGRAVE. Globe 8vo. 1s. (*Globe Readings from Standard Authors.*)

MARMION; and THE LORD OF THE ISLES. By the same Editor. Globe 8vo. 1s. (*Globe Readings from Standard Authors.*)

MARMION. Edited, with Introduction and Notes, by M. MACMILLAN, B.A. Oxon, Professor of Logic and Moral Philosophy, Elphinstone College, Bombay. Globe 8vo. 3s. 6d.

Shakespeare.—A SHAKESPEARIAN GRAMMAR. By Rev. E. A. ABBOTT, D.D., Head Master of the City of London School. Globe 8vo. 6s.

A SHAKESPEARE MANUAL. By F. G. FLEAY, M.A., late Head Master of Skipton Grammar School. Second Edition. Extra fcap. 8vo. 4s. 6d.

PRIMER OF SHAKESPEARE. By Professor DOWDEN. 18mo. 1s. (*Literature Primers.*)

Sonnenschein and Meiklejohn.—THE ENGLISH METHOD OF TEACHING TO READ. By A. SONNENSCHEIN and J. M. D. MEIKLEJOHN, M.A. Fcap. 8vo.

COMPRISING:

THE NURSERY BOOK, containing all the Two-Letter Words in the Language. 1d. (Also in Large Type on Sheets for School Walls. 5s.)

THE FIRST COURSE, consisting of Short Vowels with Single Consonants. 6d.

THE SECOND COURSE, with Combinations and Bridges, consisting of Short Vowels with Double Consonants. 6d.

THE THIRD AND FOURTH COURSES, consisting of Long Vowels, and all the Double Vowels in the Language. 6d.

"These are admirable books, because they are constructed on a principle, and that the simplest principle on which it is possible to learn to read English."—SPECTATOR.

Taylor.—WORDS AND PLACES; or, Etymological Illustrations of History, Ethnology, and Geography. By the Rev. ISAAC TAYLOR, M.A., Litt. D., Hon. LL.D., Canon of York. Third and Cheaper Edition, revised and compressed. With Maps. Globe 8vo. 6s.

Tennyson.—The COLLECTED WORKS of LORD TENNYSON, Poet Laureate. An Edition for Schools. In Four Parts. Crown 8vo. 2s. 6d. each.

SELECTIONS FROM LORD TENNYSON'S POEMS. Edited with Notes for the Use of Schools. By the Rev. CANON AINGER, M.A., LL.D. [*In preparation.*

Thring.—THE ELEMENTS OF GRAMMAR TAUGHT IN ENGLISH. By EDWARD THRING, M.A., late Head Master of Uppingham. With Questions. Fourth Edition. 18mo. 2s.

Vaughan (C.M.).—WORDS FROM THE POETS. By C. M. VAUGHAN. New Edition. 18mo, cloth. 1s.

Ward.—THE ENGLISH POETS. Selections, with Critical Introductions by various Writers and a General Introduction by MATTHEW ARNOLD. Edited by T. H. WARD, M.A. 4 Vols. Vol. I. CHAUCER TO DONNE.—Vol. II. BEN JONSON TO DRYDEN.—Vol. III. ADDISON TO BLAKE.—Vol. IV. WORDSWORTH TO ROSSETTI. Crown 8vo. Each 7s. 6d.

Wetherell.—EXERCISES ON MORRIS'S PRIMER OF ENGLISH GRAMMAR. By JOHN WETHERELL, M.A. 18mo. 1s. (*Literature Primers.*)

Woods.—A FIRST SCHOOL POETRY BOOK. Compiled by M. A. WOODS, Head Mistress of the Clifton High School for Girls. Fcap. 8vo. 2s. 6d.

A SECOND SCHOOL POETRY BOOK. By the same Author. Fcap. 8vo. 4s. 6d.

Yonge (Charlotte M.).—THE ABRIDGED BOOK OF GOLDEN DEEDS. A Reading Book for Schools and general readers. By the Author of "The Heir of Redclyffe." 18mo. cloth. 1s.

GLOBE READINGS EDITION. Globe 8vo. 2s. (See p. 61.)

FRENCH.

Beaumarchais.—LE BARBIER DE SEVILLE. Edited, with Introduction and Notes, by L. P. BLOUET, Assistant Master in St. Paul's School. Fcap. 8vo. 3s. 6d.

Bowen.—FIRST LESSONS IN FRENCH. By H. COURTHOPE BOWEN, M.A., Principal of the Finsbury Training College for Higher and Middle Schools. Extra fcap. 8vo. 1s.

f

Breymann.—Works by HERMANN BREYMANN, Ph.D., Professor of Philology in the University of Munich.
A FRENCH GRAMMAR BASED ON PHILOLOGICAL PRINCIPLES. Second Edition. Extra fcap. 8vo. 4s. 6d.
FIRST FRENCH EXERCISE BOOK. Extra fcap. 8vo. 4s. 6d.
SECOND FRENCH EXERCISE BOOK. Extra fcap. 8vo. 2s. 6d.

Fasnacht.—Works by G. EUGÈNE FASNACHT, Author of "Macmillan's Progressive French Course," Editor of "Macmillan's Foreign School Classics," &c.
THE ORGANIC METHOD OF STUDYING LANGUAGES. Extra fcap. 8vo. I. French. 3s. 6d.
A SYNTHETIC FRENCH GRAMMAR FOR SCHOOLS. Crown 8vo. 3s. 6d.
GRAMMAR AND GLOSSARY OF THE FRENCH LANGUAGE OF THE SEVENTEENTH CENTURY. Crown 8vo. *[In preparation.*

Macmillan's Primary Series of French and German Reading Books.—Edited by G. EUGÈNE FASNACHT, Assistant-Master in Westminster School. With Illustrations. Globe 8vo.
DE MAISTRE—LA JEUNE SIBÉRIENNE ET LE LÉPREUX DE LA CITÉ D'AOSTE. Edited, with Introduction, Notes, and Vocabulary. By STEPHANE BARLET, B.Sc. Univ. Gall. and London; Assistant-Master at the Mercers' School, Examiner to the College of Preceptors, the Royal Naval College, &c. 1s. 6d.
FLORIAN—SELECT FABLES. Edited, with Notes, Vocabulary, and Exercises, by CHARLES YELD, M.A., Head Master of University School, Nottingham. Illustrated. *[In the press.*
GRIMM—KINDER UND HAUSMÄRCHEN. Selected and Edited, with Notes, and Vocabulary, by G. E. FASNACHT. 2s.
HAUFF.—DIE KARAVANE. Edited, with Notes and Vocabulary, by HERMAN HAGER, Ph.D. Lecturer in the Owens College, Manchester. 2s. 6d.
LA FONTAINE—A SELECTION OF FABLES. Edited, with Introduction, Notes, and Vocabulary, by L. M. MORIARTY, B.A., Professor of French in King's College, London. 2s.
PERRAULT—CONTES DE FÉES. Edited, with Introduction, Notes, and Vocabulary, by G. E. FASNACHT. 1s.
G. SCHWAB—ODYSSEUS. With Introduction, Notes, and Vocabulary, by the same Editor. *[In preparation.*

Macmillan's Progressive French Course.—By G. EUGÈNE FASNACHT, Assistant-Master in Westminster School.
I.—FIRST YEAR, containing Easy Lessons on the Regular Accidence. New and thoroughly revised Edition. Extra fcap. 8vo. 1s.

MODERN LANGUAGES AND LITERATURE.

Macmillan's Progressive French Course (*continued*)
II.—SECOND YEAR, containing an Elementary Grammar with copious Exercises, Notes, and Vocabularies. A new Edition, enlarged and thoroughly revised. Extra fcap. 8vo. 2s.
III.—THIRD YEAR, containing a Systematic Syntax, and Lessons in Composition. Extra fcap. 8vo. 2s. 6d.
THE TEACHER'S COMPANION TO MACMILLAN'S PROGRESSIVE FRENCH COURSE. With Copious Notes, Hints for Different Renderings, Synonyms, Philological Remarks, &c. By G. E. FASNACHT. Globe 8vo. *Second Year* 4s. 6d. *Third Year* 4s. 6d.

Macmillan's Progressive French Readers. By G. EUGÈNE FASNACHT.
I.—FIRST YEAR, containing Fables, Historical Extracts, Letters, Dialogues, Ballads, Nursery Songs, &c., with Two Vocabularies: (1) in the order of subjects; (2) in alphabetical order. Extra fcap. 8vo. 2s. 6d.
II.—SECOND YEAR, containing Fiction in Prose and Verse, Historical and Descriptive Extracts, Essays, Letters, Dialogues, &c. Extra fcap. 8vo. 2s. 6d.

Macmillan's Foreign School Classics. Edited by G. EUGÈNE FASNACHT. 18mo.

FRENCH.

CORNEILLE—LE CID. Edited by G. E. FASNACHT. 1s.
DUMAS—LES DEMOISELLES DE ST. CYR. Edited by VICTOR OGER, Lecturer in University College, Liverpool. 1s. 6d.
LA FONTAINE'S FABLES. Books I.—VI. Edited by L. M. MORIARTY, B.A., Professor of French in King's College, London.
[*In preparation.*]
MOLIÈRE—L'AVARE. By the same Editor. 1s.
MOLIÈRE—LE BOURGEOIS GENTILHOMME. By the same Editor. 1s. 6d.
MOLIÈRE—LES FEMMES SAVANTES. By G. E. FASNACHT. 1s.
MOLIÈRE—LE MISANTHROPE. By the same Editor. 1s.
MOLIÈRE—LE MÉDECIN MALGRE LUI. By the same Editor. 1s.
RACINE—BRITANNICUS. Edited by EUGÈNE PELLISSIER, Assistant-Master in Clifton College, and Lecturer in University College, Bristol. 2s.
FRENCH READINGS FROM ROMAN HISTORY. Selected from Various Authors and Edited by C. COLBECK, M.A., late Fellow of Trinity College, Cambridge; Assistant-Master at Harrow. 4s. 6d.

Macmillan's Foreign School Classics (*continued*)—

SAND, GEORGE—LA MARE AU DIABLE. Edited by W. E. RUSSELL, M.A., Assistant-Master in Haileybury College. 1s.

SANDEAU, JULES—MADEMOISELLE DE LA SEIGLIERE. Edited by H. C. STEEL, Assistant-Master in Winchester College. 1s. 6d.

THIERS'S HISTORY OF THE EGYPTIAN EXPEDITION. Edited by Rev. H. A. BULL, M.A. Assistant-Master in Wellington College. [*In preparation.*

VOLTAIRE—CHARLES XII. Edited by G. E. FASNACHT. 3s. 6d.

⁎ *Other volumes to follow*.

(See also *German Authors*, page 69.)

Masson (Gustave).—A COMPENDIOUS DICTIONARY OF THE FRENCH LANGUAGE (French-English and English-French). Adapted from the Dictionaries of Professor ALFRED ELWALL. Followed by a List of the Principal Diverging Derivations, and preceded by Chronological and Historical Tables. By GUSTAVE MASSON, Assistant-Master and Librarian, Harrow School. New Edition. Crown 8vo. 6s.

Molière.—LE MALADE IMAGINAIRE. Edited, with Introduction and Notes, by FRANCIS TARVER, M.A., Assistant-Master at Eton. Fcap. 8vo. 2s. 6d.

(See also *Macmillan's Foreign School Classics*.)

Pellissier.—FRENCH ROOTS AND THEIR FAMILIES. A Synthetic Vocabulary, based upon Derivations, for Schools and Candidates for Public Examinations. By EUGÈNE PELLISSIER, M.A., B.Sc., LL.B., Assistant-Master at Clifton College, Lecturer at University College, Bristol. Globe 8vo. 6s.

GERMAN.

Huss.—A SYSTEM OF ORAL INSTRUCTION IN GERMAN, by means of Progressive Illustrations and Applications of the leading Rules of Grammar. By HERMANN C. O. HUSS, Ph.D. Crown 8vo. 5s.

Macmillan's Progressive German Course. By G. EUGÈNE FASNACHT.

PART I.—FIRST YEAR. Easy Lessons and Rules on the Regular Accidence. Extra fcap. 8vo. 1s. 6d.

Part II.—SECOND YEAR. Conversational Lessons in Systematic Accidence and Elementary Syntax. With Philological Illustrations and Etymological Vocabulary. New Edition, enlarged and thoroughly recast. Extra fcap. 8vo. 3s. 6d.

Part III.—THIRD YEAR. [*In preparation.*

Macmillan's Progressive German Course (*continued*)

TEACHER'S COMPANION TO MACMILLAN'S PROGRESSIVE GERMAN COURSE. With copious Notes, Hints for Different Renderings, Synonyms, Philological Remarks, &c. By G. E. FASNACHT. Extra Fcap. 8vo. FIRST YEAR. 4s. 6d. SECOND YEAR. 4s. 6d.

Macmillan's Progressive German Readers. By G. E. FASNACHT.

I.—FIRST YEAR, containing an Introduction to the German order of Words, with Copious Examples, extracts from German Authors in Prose and Poetry; Notes, and Vocabularies. Extra Fcap. 8vo., 2s. 6d.

Macmillan's Primary German Reading Books.
(See page 66.)

Macmillan's Foreign School Classics. Edited by G. EUGÈNE FASNACHT, 18mo.

GERMAN.

FREYTAG (G.).—DOKTOR LUTHER. Edited by FRANCIS STORR, M.A., Head Master of the Modern Side, Merchant Taylors' School. [*In preparation.*

GOETHE—GÖTZ VON BERLICHINGEN. Edited by H. A. BULL, M.A., Assistant Master at Wellington College. 2s.

GOETHE—FAUST. PART I., followed by an Appendix on PART II. Edited by JANE LEE, Lecturer in German Literature at Newnham College, Cambridge. 4s. 6d.

HEINE—SELECTIONS FROM THE REISEBILDER AND OTHER PROSE WORKS. Edited by C. COLBECK, M.A., Assistant-Master at Harrow, late Fellow of Trinity College, Cambridge. 2s. 6d.

LESSING.—MINNA VON BARNHELM. Edited by JAMES SIME. [*In preparation.*

SCHILLER—SELECTIONS FROM SCHILLER'S LYRICAL POEMS. Edited, with Notes and a Memoir of Schiller, by E. J. TURNER, B.A., and E. D. A. MORSHEAD, M.A. Assistant-Masters in Winchester College. 2s. 6d.

SCHILLER—DIE JUNGFRAU VON ORLEANS. Edited by JOSEPH GOSTWICK. 2s. 6d.

SCHILLER—MARIA STUART. Edited by C. SHELDON, M.A., D.Lit., of the Royal Academical Institution, Belfast. 2s. 6d.

SCHILLER—WILHELM TELL. Edited by G. E. FASNACHT. 2s. 6d.

SCHILLER.—WALLENSTEIN. Part I. DAS LAGER. Edited by H. B. COTTERILL, M.A. 2s.

UHLAND—SELECT BALLADS. Adapted as a First Easy Reading Book for Beginners. With Vocabulary. Edited by G. E. FASNACHT. 1s.

*** *Other Volumes to follow.*
(See also *French Authors*, page 67.)

Pylodet.—NEW GUIDE TO GERMAN CONVERSATION; containing an Alphabetical List of nearly 800 Familiar Words; followed by Exercises; Vocabulary of Words in frequent use; Familiar Phrases and Dialogues; a Sketch of German Literature, Idiomatic Expressions, &c. By L. PYLODET. 18mo, cloth limp. 2s. 6d.

Whitney.—Works by W. D. WHITNEY, Professor of Sanskrit and Instructor in Modern Languages in Yale College.
A COMPENDIOUS GERMAN GRAMMAR. Crown 8vo. 4s. 6d.
A GERMAN READER IN PROSE AND VERSE. With Notes and Vocabulary. Crown 8vo. 5s.

Whitney and Edgren.—A COMPENDIOUS GERMAN AND ENGLISH DICTIONARY, with Notation of Correspondences and Brief Etymologies. By Professor W. D. WHITNEY, assisted by A. H. EDGREN. Crown 8vo. 7s. 6d.
THE GERMAN-ENGLISH PART, separately, 5s.

MODERN GREEK.

Vincent and Dickson. — HANDBOOK TO MODERN GREEK. By Sir EDGAR VINCENT, K.C.M.G. and T. G. DICKSON, M.A. Second Edition, revised and enlarged, with Appendix on the relation of Modern and Classical Greek by Professor JEBB. Crown 8vo. 6s.

ITALIAN.

Dante. — THE PURGATORY OF DANTE. Edited, with Translation and Notes, by A. J. BUTLER, M.A., late Fellow of Trinity College, Cambridge. Crown 8vo. 12s. 6d.
THE PARADISO OF DANTE. Edited, with Translation and Notes, by the same Author. Crown 8vo. 12s. 6d.

SPANISH.

Calderon.—FOUR PLAYS OF CALDERON. Edited, with Introduction and Notes, by NORMAN MACCOLL, M.A., Fellow of Downing College, Cambridge. Crown 8vo. [*In the press.*

DOMESTIC ECONOMY.

Barker.—FIRST LESSONS IN THE PRINCIPLES OF COOKING. By LADY BARKER. New Edition. 18mo. 1s.

Berners.—FIRST LESSONS ON HEALTH. By J. BERNERS. New Edition. 18mo. 1s.

Fawcett.—TALES IN POLITICAL ECONOMY. By MILLICENT GARRETT FAWCETT. Globe 8vo. 3s.

Frederick.—HINTS TO HOUSEWIVES ON SEVERAL POINTS, PARTICULARLY ON THE PREPARATION OF ECONOMICAL AND TASTEFUL DISHES. By Mrs. FREDERICK. Crown 8vo. 1s.

"This unpretending and useful little volume distinctly supplies a desideratum . . . . The author steadily keeps in view the simple aim of 'making every-day meals at home, particularly the dinner, attractive,' without adding to the ordinary household expenses."—SATURDAY REVIEW.

Grand'homme.— CUTTING-OUT AND DRESSMAKING. From the French of Mdlle. E. GRAND'HOMME. With Diagrams. 18mo. 1s.

Jex-Blake.—THE CARE OF INFANTS. A Manual for Mothers and Nurses. By SOPHIA JEX-BLAKE, M.D., Member of the Irish College of Physicians; Lecturer on Hygiene at the London School of Medicine for Women. 18mo. 1s.

Tegetmeier.—HOUSEHOLD MANAGEMENT AND COOKERY. With an Appendix of Recipes used by the Teachers of the National School of Cookery. By W. B. TEGETMEIER. Compiled at the request of the School Board for London. 18mo. 1s.

Thornton.—FIRST LESSONS IN BOOK-KEEPING. By J. THORNTON. New Edition. Crown 8vo. 2s. 6d.

The object of this volume is to make the theory of Book-keeping sufficiently plain for even children to understand it.

A KEY TO THE ABOVE FOR THE USE OF TEACHERS AND PRIVATE STUDENTS. Containing all the Exercises worked out, with brief Notes. By J. THORNTON. Oblong 4to. 10s. 6d.

Wright.—THE SCHOOL COOKERY-BOOK. Compiled and Edited by C. E. GUTHRIE WRIGHT, Hon Sec. to the Edinburgh School of Cookery. 18mo. 1s.

ART AND KINDRED SUBJECTS.

Anderson.—LINEAR PERSPECTIVE, AND MODEL DRAWING. A School and Art Class Manual, with Questions and Exercises for Examination, and Examples of Examination Papers. By LAURENCE ANDERSON. With Illustrations. Royal 8vo. 2s.

Collier.—A PRIMER OF ART. With Illustrations. By JOHN COLLIER. 18mo. 1s.

Delamotte.—A BEGINNER'S DRAWING BOOK. By P. H. DELAMOTTE, F.S.A. Progressively arranged. New Edition improved. Crown 8vo. 3s. 6d.

Ellis.—SKETCHING FROM NATURE. A Handbook for Students and Amateurs. By TRISTRAM J. ELLIS. With a Frontispiece and Ten Illustrations, by H. STACY MARKS, R.A., and Thirty Sketches by the Author. New Edition, revised and enlarged. Crown 8vo. 3s. 6d.

Hunt.—TALKS ABOUT ART. By WILLIAM HUNT. With a Letter from Sir J. E. MILLAIS, Bart., R.A. Crown 8vo. 3s. 6d.

Taylor.—A PRIMER OF PIANOFORTE PLAYING. By FRANKLIN TAYLOR. Edited by Sir GEORGE GROVE. 18mo. 1s.

WORKS ON TEACHING.

Blakiston—THE TEACHER. Hints on School Management. A Handbook for Managers, Teachers' Assistants, and Pupil Teachers. By J. R. BLAKISTON, M.A. Crown 8vo. 2s. 6d. (Recommended by the London, Birmingham, and Leicester School Boards.)

"Into a comparatively small book he has crowded a great deal of exceedingly useful and sound advice. It is a plain, common-sense book, full of hints to the teacher on the management of his school and his children."—SCHOOL BOARD CHRONICLE.

Calderwood.—ON TEACHING. By Professor HENRY CALDERWOOD. New Edition. Extra fcap. 8vo. 2s. 6d.

Carter.—EYESIGHT IN SCHOOLS. A Paper read before the Association of Medical Officers of Schools on April 15th, 1885. By R. BRUDENELL CARTER, F.R.C.S., Ophthalmic Surgeon to St. George's Hospital. Crown 8vo. Sewed. 1s.

Fearon.—SCHOOL INSPECTION. By D. R. FEARON, M.A., Assistant Commissioner of Endowed Schools. New Edition. Crown 8vo. 2s. 6d.

Gladstone.—OBJECT TEACHING. A Lecture delivered at the Pupil-Teacher Centre, William Street Board School, Hammersmith. By J. H. GLADSTONE, Ph.D., F.R.S., Member of the London School Board. With an Appendix. Crown 8vo. 3d.

"It is a short but interesting and instructive publication, and our younger teachers will do well to read it carefully and thoroughly. There is much in these few pages which they can learn and profit by."—THE SCHOOL GUARDIAN.

Hertel.—OVERPRESSURE IN HIGH SCHOOLS IN DENMARK. By Dr. HERTEL, Municipal Medical Officer, Copenhagen. Translated from the Danish by C. GODFREY SÖRENSEN. With Introduction by Sir J. CRICHTON-BROWNE, M.D. LL.D. F.R.S. Crown 8vo. 3s. 6d.

DIVINITY.

*** For other Works by these Authors, see THEOLOGICAL CATALOGUE.

Abbott (Rev. E. A.)—BIBLE LESSONS. By the Rev. E. A. ABBOTT, D.D., Head Master of the City of London School. New Edition. Crown 8vo. 4s. 6d.

"Wise, suggestive, and really profound initiation into religious thought."—GUARDIAN.

Abbott—Rushbrooke.—THE COMMON TRADITION OF THE SYNOPTIC GOSPELS, in the Text of the Revised Version. By EDWIN A. ABBOTT, D.D., formerly Fellow of St. John's College, Cambridge, and W. G. RUSHBROOKE, M.L., formerly Fellow of St. John's College, Cambridge. Cr. 8vo. 3s. 6d.

The Acts of the Apostles.— Being the Greek Text as revised by Professors WESTCOTT and HORT. With Explanatory Notes for the Use of Schools, by T. E. PAGE, M.A., late Fellow of St. John's College, Cambridge; Assistant Master at the Charterhouse. Fcap. 8vo. 4s. 6d.

Arnold.—A BIBLE-READING FOR SCHOOLS.—THE GREAT PROPHECY OF ISRAEL'S RESTORATION (Isaiah, Chapters xl.—lxvi.). Arranged and Edited for Young Learners. By MATTHEW ARNOLD, D.C.L., formerly Professor of Poetry in the University of Oxford, and Fellow of Oriel. New Edition. 18mo, cloth. 1s.

Arnold.—ISAIAH XL.—LXVI. With the Shorter Prophecies allied to it. Arranged and Edited, with Notes, by MATTHEW ARNOLD. Crown 8vo. 5s.

ISAIAH OF JERUSALEM, IN THE AUTHORISED ENGLISH VERSION. With Introduction, Corrections, and Notes. By MATTHEW ARNOLD. Crown 8vo. 4s. 6d.

Benham.—A COMPANION TO THE LECTIONARY. Being a Commentary on the Proper Lessons for Sundays and Holy Days. By Rev. W. BENHAM, B.D., Rector of S. Edmund with S. Nicholas Acons, &c. New Edition. Crown 8vo. 4s. 6d.

Calvert.—GREEK TESTAMENT, School Readings in the. A Course of thirty-six Lessons mainly following upon the Narrative of St. Mark. Edited and Arranged with Introduction, Notes and Vocabulary, by the Rev. A. CALVERT, M.A., late Fellow of St. John's College, Cambridge. Fcap. 8vo.

Cassel.—MANUAL OF JEWISH HISTORY AND LITERATURE; preceded by a BRIEF SUMMARY OF BIBLE HISTORY. By DR. D. CASSEL. Translated by Mrs. HENRY LUCAS. Fcap. 8vo. 2s. 6d.

Cheetham.—A CHURCH HISTORY OF THE FIRST SIX CENTURIES. By the Ven. ARCHDEACON CHEETHAM. Crown 8vo. [*In the press.*

Cross.—BIBLE READINGS SELECTED FROM THE PENTATEUCH AND THE BOOK OF JOSHUA. By the Rev. JOHN A. CROSS. Second Edition enlarged, with Notes. Globe 8vo. 2s. 6d.

Curteis.—MANUAL OF THE THIRTY-NINE ARTICLES. By G. H. CURTEIS, M.A., Principal of the Lichfield Theological College. [*In preparation*

Davies.—THE EPISTLES OF ST. PAUL TO THE EPHESIANS, THE COLOSSIANS, AND PHILEMON; with Introductions and Notes, and an Essay on the Traces of Foreign Elements in the Theology of these Epistles. By the Rev. J. LLEWELYN DAVIES, M.A., Rector of Christ Church, St. Marylebone; late Fellow of Trinity College, Cambridge. Second Edition. Demy 8vo. 7s. 6d.

Drummond.—THE STUDY OF THEOLOGY, INTRODUCTION TO. By JAMES DRUMMOND, LL.D., Professor of Theology in Manchester New College, London. Crown 8vo. 5s.

Gaskoin.—THE CHILDREN'S TREASURY OF BIBLE STORIES. By Mrs. HERMAN GASKOIN. Edited with Preface by Rev. G. F. MACLEAR, D.D. PART I.—OLD TESTAMENT HISTORY. 18mo. 1s. PART II.—NEW TESTAMENT. 18mo. 1s. PART III.—THE APOSTLES: ST. JAMES THE GREAT, ST. PAUL, AND ST JOHN THE DIVINE. 18mo. 1s.

Golden Treasury Psalter.—Students' Edition. Being an Edition of "The Psalms Chronologically arranged, by Four Friends," with briefer Notes. 18mo. 3s. 6d.

Greek Testament.—Edited, with Introduction and Appendices, by CANON WESTCOTT and Dr. F. J. A. HORT. Two Vols. Crown 8vo. 10s. 6d. each.
Vol. I. The Text.
Vol. II. Introduction and Appendix.

Greek Testament.—Edited by Canon WESTCOTT and Dr. HORT. School Edition of Text. 12mo. cloth. 4s. 6d. 18mo. roan, red edges. 5s. 6d.
GREEK TESTAMENT, SCHOOL READINGS IN THE. Being the outline of the life of our Lord, as given by St. Mark, with additions from the Text of the other Evangelists. Arranged and Edited, with Notes and Vocabulary, by the Rev. A. CALVERT, M.A., late Fellow of St. John's College, Cambridge. Fcap. 8vo. 4s. 6d.
THE ACTS OF THE APOSTLES. Being the Greek Text as revised by Drs. WESTCOTT and HORT. With Explanatory Notes by T. E. PAGE, M.A. Assistant Master at the Charterhouse. Fcap. 8vo. 4s. 6d.

THE GOSPEL ACCORDING TO ST. MARK. Being the Greek Text as revised by Drs. WESTCOTT and HORT. With Explanatory Notes by Rev. J. O. F. MURRAY, M.A., Lecturer in Emmanuel College, Cambridge. Fcap. 8vo. [*In preparation.*

Hardwick.—Works by Archdeacon HARDWICK:—
A HISTORY OF THE CHRISTIAN CHURCH. Middle Age. From Gregory the Great to the Excommunication of Luther. Edited by WILLIAM STUBBS, M.A., Regius Professor of Modern History in the University of Oxford. With Four Maps. New Edition. Crown 8vo. 10s. 6d.
A HISTORY OF THE CHRISTIAN CHURCH DURING THE REFORMATION. Eighth Edition. Edited by Professor STUBBS. Crown 8vo. 10s. 6d.

Jennings and Lowe.—THE PSALMS, WITH INTRODUCTIONS AND CRITICAL NOTES. By A. C. JENNINGS, M.A.; assisted in parts by W. H. LOWE, M.A. In 2 vols. Second Edition Revised. Crown 8vo. 10s. 6d. each.

Kay.—ST. PAUL'S TWO EPISTLES TO THE CORINTHIANS, A COMMENTARY ON. By the late Rev. W. KAY, D.D., Rector of Great Leghs, Essex, and Hon. Canon of St. Albans; formerly Principal of Bishop's College, Calcutta; and Fellow and Tutor of Lincoln College. Demy 8vo. 9s.

Kuenen.—PENTATEUCH AND BOOK OF JOSHUA: an Historico-Critical Inquiry into the Origin and Composition of the Hexateuch. By A. KUENEN, Professor of Theology at Leiden. Translated from the Dutch, with the assistance of the Author, by PHILLIP H. WICKSTEED, M.A. 8vo. 14s.

The OXFORD MAGAZINE says:—"The work is absolutely indispensable to all special students of the Old Testament."

Lightfoot.—Works by the Right Rev. J. B. LIGHTFOOT, D.D., D.C.L., LL.D., Lord Bishop of Durham.
ST. PAUL'S EPISTLE TO THE GALATIANS. A Revised Text, with Introduction, Notes, and Dissertations. Ninth Edition, revised. 8vo. 12s.
ST. PAUL'S EPISTLE TO THE PHILIPPIANS. A Revised Text, with Introduction, Notes, and Dissertations. Ninth Edition, revised. 8vo. 12s.
ST. CLEMENT OF ROME—THE TWO EPISTLES TO THE CORINTHIANS. A Revised Text, with Introduction and Notes. 8vo. 8s. 6d.
ST. PAUL'S EPISTLES TO THE COLOSSIANS AND TO PHILEMON. A Revised Text, with Introductions, Notes, and Dissertations. Eighth Edition, revised. 8vo. 12s.

Lightfoot.—Works by the Right Rev. J. B. LIGHTFOOT, D.D., D.C.L., LL.D., &c. (*continued*)—

THE APOSTOLIC FATHERS. Part II. S. IGNATIUS—S. POLYCARP. Revised Texts, with Introductions, Notes, Dissertations, and Translations. 2 volumes in 3. Demy 8vo. 48*s*.

Maclear.—Works by the Rev. G. F. MACLEAR, D.D., Canon of Canterbury, Warden of St. Augustine's College, Canterbury, and late Head-Master of King's College School, London :—

A CLASS-BOOK OF OLD TESTAMENT HISTORY. New Edition, with Four Maps. 18mo. 4*s*. 6*d*.

A CLASS-BOOK OF NEW TESTAMENT HISTORY, including the Connection of the Old and New Testaments. With Four Maps. New Edition. 18mo. 5*s*. 6*d*.

A SHILLING BOOK OF OLD TESTAMENT HISTORY, for National and Elementary Schools. With Map. 18mo, cloth. New Edition.

A SHILLING BOOK OF NEW TESTAMENT HISTORY, for National and Elementary Schools. With Map. 18mo, cloth. New Edition.

These works have been carefully abridged from the Author's large manuals.

CLASS-BOOK OF THE CATECHISM OF THE CHURCH OF ENGLAND. New Edition. 18mo. 1*s*. 6*d*.

A FIRST CLASS-BOOK OF THE CATECHISM OF THE CHURCH OF ENGLAND. With Scripture Proofs, for Junior Classes and Schools. New Edition. 18mo. 6*d*.

A MANUAL OF INSTRUCTION FOR CONFIRMATION AND FIRST COMMUNION. WITH PRAYERS AND DEVOTIONS. 32mo, cloth extra, red edges. 2*s*.

Maurice.—THE LORD'S PRAYER, THE CREED, AND THE COMMANDMENTS. A Manual for Parents and Schoolmasters. To which is added the Order of the Scriptures. By the Rev. F. DENISON MAURICE, M.A. 18mo, cloth, limp. 1*s*.

Pentateuch and Book of Joshua: an Historico-Critical Inquiry into the Origin and Composition of the Hexateuch. By A. KUENEN, Professor of Theology at Leiden. Translated from the Dutch, with the assistance of the Author, by PHILIP H. WICKSTEED, M.A. 8vo. 14*s*.

Procter.—A HISTORY OF THE BOOK OF COMMON PRAYER, with a Rationale of its Offices. By Rev. F. PROCTER. M.A. 17th Edition, revised and enlarged. Crown 8vo. 10*s*. 6*d*.

Procter and Maclear.—AN ELEMENTARY INTRODUCTION TO THE BOOK OF COMMON PRAYER. Rearranged and supplemented by an Explanation of the Morning and Evening Prayer and the Litany. By the Rev. F. PROCTER and the Rev. Dr. MACLEAR. New and Enlarged Edition, containing the Communion Service and the Confirmation and Baptismal Offices. 18mo. 2s. 6d.

The Psalms, with Introductions and Critical Notes.—By A. C. JENNINGS, M.A., Jesus College, Cambridge, Tyrwhitt Scholar, Crosse Scholar, Hebrew University Prizeman, and Fry Scholar of St. John's College, Carus and Scholefield Prizeman, Vicar of Whittlesford, Cambs.; assisted in Parts by W. H. LOWE, M.A., Hebrew Lecturer and late Scholar of Christ's College, Cambridge, and Tyrwhitt Scholar. In 2 vols. Second Edition Revised. Crown 8vo. 10s. 6d. each.

Ramsay.—THE CATECHISER'S MANUAL; or, the Church Catechism Illustrated and Explained, for the Use of Clergymen, Schoolmasters, and Teachers. By the Rev. ARTHUR RAMSAY, M.A. New Edition. 18mo. 1s. 6d.

Ryle.—AN INTRODUCTION TO THE CANON OF THE OLD TESTAMENT. By Rev. H. E. RYLE, M.A., Fellow of King's College, Cambridge, and Principal of St. David's College, Lampeter. Crown 8vo. [*In preparation.*

St. John's Epistles.—The Greek Text with Notes and Essays, by BROOKE FOSS WESTCOTT, D.D., Regius Professor of Divinity and Fellow of King's College, Cambridge, Canon of Westminster, &c. Second Edition Revised. 8vo. 12s. 6d.

St. Paul's Epistles.—Greek Text, with Introduction and Notes.
THE EPISTLE TO THE GALATIANS. Edited by the Right Rev. J. B. LIGHTFOOT, D.D., Bishop of Durham. Ninth Edition. 8vo. 12s.
THE EPISTLE TO THE PHILIPPIANS. By the same Editor. Ninth Edition. 8vo. 12s.
THE EPISTLE TO THE COLOSSIANS AND TO PHILEMON. By the same Editor. Eighth Edition. 8vo. 12s.
THE EPISTLE TO THE ROMANS. Edited by the Very Rev. C. J. VAUGHAN, D.D., Dean of Llandaff, and Master of the Temple. Fifth Edition. Crown 8vo. 7s. 6d.
THE EPISTLE TO THE PHILIPPIANS, with Translation, Paraphrase, and Notes for English Readers. By the same Editor. Crown 8vo. 5s.
THE EPISTLE TO THE THESSALONIANS, COMMENTARY ON THE GREEK TEXT. By JOHN EADIE, D.D., LL.D. Edited by the Rev. W. YOUNG, M.A., with Preface by Professor CAIRNS. 8vo. 12s.

St. Paul's Epistles, *continued*—
THE EPISTLES TO THE EPHESIANS, THE COLOSSIANS, AND PHILEMON; with Introductions and Notes, and an Essay on the Traces of Foreign Elements in the Theology of these Epistles. By the Rev. J. LLEWELYN DAVIES, M.A., Rector of Christ Church, St. Marylebone; late Fellow of Trinity College, Cambridge. Second Edition, revised. Demy 8vo. 7s. 6d.

THE TWO EPISTLES TO THE CORINTHIANS, A COMMENTARY ON. By the late Rev. W. KAY, D.D., Rector of Great Leghs, Essex, and Hon. Canon of St. Albans; formerly Principal of Bishop's College, Calcutta; and Fellow and Tutor of Lincoln College. Demy 8vo. 9s.

The Epistle to the Hebrews. In Greek and English. With Critical and Explanatory Notes. Edited by Rev. FREDERIC RENDALL, M.A., formerly Fellow of Trinity College, Cambridge, and Assistant-Master at Harrow School. Crown 8vo. 6s.

The Epistle to the Hebrews. The Greek Text with Notes and Essays by B. F. WESTCOTT, D.D. 8vo. [*In the press.*

Westcott.—Works by BROOKE FOSS WESTCOTT, D.D., Canon of Westminster, Regius Professor of Divinity, and Fellow of King's College, Cambridge.
A GENERAL SURVEY OF THE HISTORY OF THE CANON OF THE NEW TESTAMENT DURING THE FIRST FOUR CENTURIES. Sixth Edition. With Preface on "Supernatural Religion." Crown 8vo. 10s. 6d.
INTRODUCTION TO THE STUDY OF THE FOUR GOSPELS. Sixth Edition. Crown 8vo. 10s. 6d.
THE BIBLE IN THE CHURCH. A Popular Account of the Collection and Reception of the Holy Scriptures in the Christian Churches. New Edition. 18mo, cloth. 4s. 6d.
THE EPISTLES OF ST. JOHN. The Greek Text, with Notes and Essays. Second Edition Revised. 8vo. 12s. 6d.
THE EPISTLE TO THE HEBREWS. The Greek Text Revised, with Notes and Essays. 8vo. [*In the press.*
SOME THOUGHTS FROM THE ORDINAL. Cr. 8vo. 1s. 6d.

Westcott and Hort.—THE NEW TESTAMENT IN THE ORIGINAL GREEK. The Text Revised by B. F. WESTCOTT, D.D., Regius Professor of Divinity, Canon of Westminster, and F. J. A. HORT, D.D., Lady Margaret Professor of Divinity; Fellow of Emmanuel College, Cambridge: late Fellows of Trinity College, Cambridge. 2 vols. Crown 8vo. 10s. 6d. each.
Vol. I. Text.
Vol. II. Introduction and Appendix.

Westcott and Hort.—THE NEW TESTAMENT IN THE ORIGINAL GREEK, FOR SCHOOLS. The Text Revised by BROOKE FOSS WESTCOTT, D.D., and FENTON JOHN ANTHONY HORT, D.D. 12mo. cloth. 4s. 6d. 18mo. roan, red edges. 5s. 6d.

Wilson.—THE BIBLE STUDENT'S GUIDE to the more Correct Understanding of the English Translation of the Old Testament, by reference to the original Hebrew. By WILLIAM WILSON, D.D., Canon of Winchester, late Fellow of Queen's College, Oxford. Second Edition, carefully revised. 4to. cloth. 25s.

Wright.—THE BIBLE WORD-BOOK : A Glossary of Archaic Words and Phrases in the Authorised Version of the Bible and the Book of Common Prayer. By W. ALDIS WRIGHT, M.A., Fellow and Bursar of Trinity College, Cambridge. Second Edition, Revised and Enlarged. Crown 8vo. 7s. 6d.

Yonge (Charlotte M.).—SCRIPTURE READINGS FOR SCHOOLS AND FAMILIES. By CHARLOTTE M. YONGE. Author of "The Heir of Redclyffe." In Five Vols.
FIRST SERIES. GENESIS TO DEUTERONOMY. Extra fcap. 8vo. 1s. 6d. With Comments, 3s. 6d.
SECOND SERIES. From JOSHUA to SOLOMON. Extra fcap. 8vo. 1s. 6d. With Comments, 3s. 6d.
THIRD SERIES. The KINGS and the PROPHETS. Extra fcap. 8vo. 1s. 6d. With Comments, 3s. 6d.
FOURTH SERIES. The GOSPEL TIMES. 1s. 6d. With Comments. Extra fcap. 8vo, 3s. 6d.
FIFTH SERIES. APOSTOLIC TIMES. Extra fcap. 8vo. 1s. 6d. With Comments, 3s. 6d.

Zechariah—Lowe.—THE HEBREW STUDENT'S COMMENTARY ON ZECHARIAH, HEBREW AND LXX. With Excursus on Syllable-dividing, Metheg, Initial Dagesh, and Siman Rapheh. By W. H. LOWE, M.A., Hebrew Lecturer at Christ's College, Cambridge. Demy 8vo. 10s. 6d.

A NEW GEOGRAPHICAL SERIES.

Messrs. MACMILLAN & Co. propose to issue a series of geographical class-books prepared with this aim. They have placed the editorship of the series in the hands of Mr. ARCHIBALD GEIKIE, F.R.S., Director-General of the Geological Survey of the United Kingdom, and the following gentlemen have already expressed their interest in the undertaking, and their willingness to assist either as writers or advisers.

H. W. BATES, F.R.S., Assistant-Secretary of the Royal Geographical Society; Author of "The Naturalist on the River Amazons."

A. BUCHAN, M.A., F.R.S.E., Meteorological Secretary of the Scottish Meteorological Society.

A NEW GEOGRAPHICAL SERIES—*Continued.*

JOHN SCOTT KELTIE, Librarian and Inspector of Geographical Education to the Royal Geographical Society; Editor of "The Statesman's Year-Book."

J. NORMAN LOCKYER, F.R.S., Correspondent of the Institute of France; Author of "Solar Physics," "Elementary Lessons in Astronomy," &c.

CLEMENTS R. MARKHAM, C.B., F.R.S., Secretary of the Royal Geographical Society.

JOHN MURRAY, Ph.D., F.R.S.E., Director of the *Challenger* Expedition Commission.

Rev. H. F. TOZER, M.A., Fellow of Exeter College, Oxford; Author of "The Geography of Greece," "Highlands of Turkey," &c.

E. B. TYLOR, D.C.L., F.R.S., Keeper of the University Museum, Oxford; Author of "Primitive Culture," &c.

A. R. WALLACE, LL.D., F.R.G.S., Author of "The Malay Archipelago," "The Geographical Distribution of Animals," &c., &c.

Rev. EDMOND WARRE, D.D., Head Master of Eton.

Rev. J. E. C. WELLDON, M.A., Head Master of Harrow.

The following List of Volumes is contemplated; and it is hoped that one or more will be ready very soon:—

1. THE TEACHING OF GEOGRAPHY. A Practical Handbook for the use of Teachers. By ARCHIBALD GEIKIE, F.R.S., Director-General of the Geological Survey of the United Kingdom, and Director of the Museum of Practical Geology, Jermyn Street, London; formerly Murchison Professor of Geology and Mineralogy in the University of Edinburgh. Crown 8vo. 2s. [*Ready.*

*** The aim of this volume is to advocate the claims of geography as an educational discipline of a high order, and to show how these claims may be practically recognised by teachers.

2. A GEOGRAPHY OF THE BRITISH ISLES.
3. AN ELEMENTARY GENERAL GEOGRAPHY.
4. A GEOGRAPHY OF THE BRITISH COLONIES.
5. A GEOGRAPHY OF EUROPE.
6. A GEOGRAPHY OF AMERICA.
7. A GEOGRAPHY OF ASIA.
8. A GEOGRAPHY OF AFRICA.
9. A GEOGRAPHY OF THE OCEANS AND OCEANIC ISLANDS.
10. ADVANCED CLASS-BOOK OF THE GEOGRAPHY OF BRITAIN.
11. GEOGRAPHY OF AUSTRALIA AND NEW ZEALAND.
12. GEOGRAPHY OF BRITISH NORTH AMERICA.
13. GEOGRAPHY OF INDIA.
14. GEOGRAPHY OF THE UNITED STATES.
15. ADVANCED CLASS-BOOK OF THE GEOGRAPHY OF EUROPE.

LONDON: RICHARD CLAY AND SONS, PRINTERS.

www.ingramcontent.com/pod-product-compliance
Lightning Source LLC
Chambersburg PA
CBHW021811230426
43669CB00008B/709